GOD'S WILL
IS NOT ELUSIVE

GOD'S WILL
IS NOT
ELUSIVE

A Comprehensive,
In-Depth Study *on*
Discovering God's Will
and Experiencing
Divine Guidance

GORDON
HARESIGN

XULON PRESS

Xulon Press
2301 Lucien Way #415
Maitland, FL 32751
407.339.4217
www.xulonpress.com

Unless otherwise indicated, Scripture quotations taken from the Holy Bible, New International Version (NIV). Copyright © 1973, 1978, 1984, 2011 by Biblica, Inc.™. Used by permission. All rights reserved.

Scripture quotations taken from the Amplified Bible (AMP). Copyright © 1954, 1958, 1962, 1964, 1965, 1987 by The Lockman Foundation. Used by permission. All rights reserved.

Printed in the United States of America.

LCCN: 2019911551

ISBN-13: 978-1-5456-7452-9

Endorsements

This book, *God's Will Is Not Elusive,* explores a topic that will transform your Christian walk. I've known and respected the author, Gordon Haresign, as a gifted Bible teacher and solid Christian leader for more than forty years. This book is biblically focused and enormously practical in an area where most believers still struggle -knowing, understanding, and doing the will of God. I highly recommend this compelling book.

—**Terry Wilson,** Executive Director Emmaus International

I just started reading *God's Will Is Not Elusive* and was afraid I would not be able to put it down. My friend Gordon Haresign's insight and knowledge of the Scriptures is phenomenal. He is a wonderful preacher and teacher, and his latest book is a must-read.

—**Tunch Ilkin,** Pastor of Men's Ministry at
The Bible Chapel in McMurray Pennsylvania.

Ilkin played in the NFL for fourteen years, thirteen for the Pittsburgh Steelers, and appeared in two Pro Bowls. He has served as a Steelers broadcaster and analyst for the past twenty years and is host of the long-running *In the Locker Room* radio show with former teammate Craig Wolfley on ESPN 970.

Gordon Haresign's commitment to Kingdom building is made manifest in *God's Will Is Not Elusive*. All who have pondered and prayed for enlightenment about what God wants of them will be blessed by Gordon's message. The body of Gordon's work is seen not only in this book, but in every step he has trod in his own Christian journey across the world.

—**D. Chris Miller,** former chair of Scripture Union USA, retired banking executive, and management consultant in the financial service industry.

I finished reading your manuscript. What a wonderful guideline for following hard after our Lord, filled with wisdom and solid Scripture. And I very much enjoyed the anecdotes and background story of your own journey. They made the quest for learning God's will much more realistic. Placing responsibility on us, the readers, brings about a partnership with Him, highlighting that it is a relationship we must seek.

—**Cindy Nicastro,** retired physical therapist

"Gordon Haresign has been at the forefront of directing organizations, individuals and institutions in life-changing Bible study for over sixty years. The one question he has repeatedly received is, "How can I know God's will for my life?" While Gordon has answered this from a biblical standpoint countless times, he has now made the answer to this question available in what will likely become the preeminent work on the subject in his new book, "*God's Will is Not Elusive*." This excellent illuminating work should be required reading for every person who is serious about their faith."

—**Fred Scheeren,** Distinguished Financial Planner ® and Managing Director-Investments for a major international investment firm. Ranked as one of the top financial advisors in the United States by *Forbes Magazine*. He is the author of the Dynamic Bible Study Series.

―――

Gordon Haresign is highly qualified to lead us on a journey to discover God's will. Using his experiences as a successful businessman, visionary pastor, and Bible scholar, Gordon helps us cut through feelings, emotions, and self-doubt to uncover the foundational truths of God's Word. This book is chalked full of engaging stories, biblical illustrations, and personal examples that will help you find the life that God made you to live.

—**Ron Moore**, Senior Pastor at The Bible Chapel in McMurray, Pennsylvania

―――

Packed with real life experience and brimming with scripture-based insight, Gordon Haresign's book *God's Will Is Not Elusive*, is a must read for everyone seeking to know and follow God's will for their lives. Whether you are at the start of this journey or entering its last stages, you can be certain that God does indeed have a plan for your life, and that His plan can be known and acted upon. My friend, Gordon Haresign, is well equipped to guide you on life's journey, and his book may well prove to be the most important counsel you will receive on pursuing, and living out, God's unique plan for you!

—**David Jones**, Managing Director, Cedarstone

―――

While I never recommend opening an argument with a negative statement, Gordon Haresign brings us to the reality that not only is God's will not elusive, it is as clear as the evidence for God himself. As a businessman, I am bound to envision and establish plans, chart goals within measurable time, and execute them to the best of my ability. God works with us much differently. We discover God's vision for our uniquely created existence by learning and practicing His will for our lives one step at a time. Life is a moving target. We grow, study, learn, and develop throughout the span of years God gives us to prepare for an eternity only He can imagine. Gordon Haresign's engaging style lays out Biblical in-depth facts via scores of scriptures related to compelling anecdotes. He guides the reader to a progressive understanding of why God's Will Is Not Elusive. Gordon makes the case that the successful plans of men are informed and impacted by God's will for each thought, decision, and action of our life story. Gordon Haresign guides us to read and ponder God's Word to realize that God's Will Is Not Elusive.

—**Fred Baker,** Founder of Baker Installations, Inc.,
a $30 Million tele-communications service provider
solving installation problems in the
'First 100 Feet' of broadband technology.
Baker Installations' technicians service
over 20,000 homes and businesses every week.

Acknowledgments

First of all, I acknowledge all those who have listened to me preach and teach over the years on the subject of discovering God's will and experiencing God's guidance. Many have given me valuable feedback by adding their own testimonies, insights, and encouragement. More recently, friends in small group Bible studies have journeyed with me as I worked through my first drafts. I am grateful for the help and encouragement my good friends, Cheryl Hanson and Rhonda Kifer-Moore, provided in critiquing my first few chapters.

I dedicate this book to those who encouraged me to seek God's will for my life, first as a child and then as a teenager. They include my parents, Roland and Catherine. Then there were businessmen like Doug Fuzzy and Charlie Lee-Spratt; Alec Anderson, a high school teacher; and Bill Watson, a government hydraulic engineer. All encouraged me to think in terms of eternity.

I am indebted to friends like Tom Wilson and Dennis Payne who were seniors in high school when I was a freshman. Their commitment to Jesus Christ certainly impacted me.

I am further indebted to all those who have ministered to me over the years through their preaching and teaching, friendship, example, and writings. I have served with many fantastic people who have enriched my life and encouraged me to cross the finish line running.

I am also grateful to family and friends, such as Brian Atmore, Fred Baker, Fred Scheeren, Cindy Nicastro, and Lou Motter, who critiqued my "final" manuscript and offered helpful suggestions.

Finally, I want to thank my dear wife, Nancy, who has constantly encouraged me to seek God's will and who has never blocked that pursuit.

Contents

Foreword

Knowing the will of God is an aspect of the Christian life many believers feel is most important but about which they feel the least confident. They wonder, "How can I know what God wants me to do when I can't even see or hear Him?" For them, discovering God's will is confusing, uncertain—and elusive.

That's exactly why my friend, Gordon Haresign, wrote this book. He wants to convince you that God's will is not out of reach for average, everyday Christians. That's encouraging. But what gives Gordon's writing such power is that he bases it on a lifetime of reading, studying, and living God's Word. That's reassuring.

Another strength of Gordon's work is that even though he's clear that God's will is not elusive, he's not willing to offer superficial approaches to finding it. As he says, "The challenge is knowing, understanding, and doing God's will."

If you are a student of God's Word, you have probably come across one of the classic books on this subject, like *Can I Know God's Will?* by R. C. Sproul, or *God's Will: Finding Guidance for Everyday Decisions* by J. I. Packer, or even *Found: God's Will* by John MacArthur. I pray that, when you finish reading *God's Will Is Not Elusive* by Gordon Haresign, you'll have a new favorite to add to your library of books on divine guidance.

May God bless you as you begin this journey into discovering God's will and to experiencing His loving guidance in your life every day!

—Whitney T. Kuniholm

Senior Vice President of Advancement Ministries at American Bible Society, President at Essential Bible Ministries, President Emeritus, Scripture Union USA, Former Executive Vice President at Prison Fellowship International

Preface

Why do so many Christians struggle to know God's will? Some are apprehensive or ambivalent. Others find it confusing, conflicting, and challenging. In this book, *God's Will Is Not Elusive,* I take you on what I trust will be a life-changing journey. I'll explain why there is no greater achievement than to know the will of God and to do it.

While much has already been written on the subject, most believers still find God's will elusive. I'll show why it isn't. In the process, I'll direct you to the only place where God's will is clearly revealed. I'll engage you in a comprehensive, in-depth study that facilitates your personal discovery of God's will. You will also learn how to experience God's guidance and direction regarding both big and small decisions. *God's Will Is Not Elusive* is designed to inform and inspire you to seek the very best God has planned for you.

Speaking from a lifetime of experience, I unequivocally declare God has a divine purpose for you and that satisfaction will only be experienced as you do God's will. But first, you need to know God's will. You should find the book convicting as you are constantly challenged to apply what you learn. Hopefully, it will drive you to your knees in prayer.

God's Will Is Not Elusive will be a compelling read for those who really want to know, understand, and do God's will. It helps answer the common questions regarding the nature, relevance, and extent of God's purpose for your life. Personal stories and illustrations corroborate biblical teaching. I encourage every follower of Christ—young and old, whether new believers or seasoned veterans of the faith—to grapple with the necessity to know God's will and to do it.

While you may choose to read through the book quickly to get the overall message, as you would a novel, I urge you to take time to reflect on each chapter. You may wish to read and pray through some chapters several times. Allow yourself time to meditate and pray on the lessons God may be teaching you. You will find your life transformed in the process.

While this book can never replace the Bible, I pray it will be a book you won't put down for a long while...one you will constantly refer to as you grapple with knowing God's will for your life. Hopefully, it will lead you to a personal study of God's Word on a regular basis. This is how you will develop an intimate personal encounter with the Triune God; a God existing in three persons, Father, Son, and Holy Spirit.

We are starting a journey together. Begin what could be the second greatest journey you will ever take. The first takes you to the Cross. If you have never taken that journey, I trust this book will help lead you to Calvary.

During our journey we will learn the greatest thing in life is to do the will of God. For that to occur, we need to develop a deep desire for God's will. Then we need to discover God's will, to know it, to understand it, and finally, to do it.

We will consider the big picture, those things God sovereignly planned in advance for our good and for His glory. We will ponder the assertion that 98 percent of God's will has already been revealed in His Word, and all we need do is read the Bible to discover every aspect of His revealed will. We will also discover God's will is found in the divine imperatives located in the Holy Scriptures. His Word is true. We will learn that obedience to God's revealed will is essential if we really want to bring Him praise and glory.

We will discover how to experience God's guidance and direction in our lives on a daily basis. We will contemplate how God has uniquely made us, and how we can become His masterpiece. We will meditate on the fact that God created us with a divine purpose in view. We will learn how God can direct our lives as a shepherd guides his sheep. We will identify guiding principles for discovering circumstantial aspects of God's will not specifically mentioned in Scripture. We will reflect on examples of how we can pray for God's specific guidance and direction. We will learn what to do when we miss God's will through ignorance, defiance, or disobedience. We will also learn that God is loving, gracious, merciful, and kind and readily gives us second chances when we mess up. We will consider the difference between God's perfect and permissive will. Finally, we will try answering the question why unpleasant and undesirable things happen to us and to the world around us.

I will do my best to explain and illustrate God's will. I can only pray God's will be done in your life...and mine, that seeking it will become our top priority and consuming passion. God's overarching will is that everything we do be for His praise and glory and, in the process, we be conformed into the image of Christ...to be more like Him each day.

That pretty much sums it up. We live at a time when Christians tend to love their sports teams, movies, jobs, houses, and lands more than God. We know sports and social trivia better than we know Bible trivia. We are better acquainted with movie stars than we are with Bible characters, and we love the world's heroes more than we do God's heroes. Little wonder we miss out on God's will and direction for our lives.

It is time to thank you for joining me on what I trust will be a memorable journey. I pray God's blessing each step of the way. Don't turn back. Don't quit. The writer to the Hebrews expressed it succinctly. "You need to persevere so that when you have done the will of God, you will receive what he has promised" (Hebrews 10:36).

Part One

Contemplating the Journey

Helping You Make up your Mind to Seek God's Will

Chapter One

Do I Really want to do God's Will?

You may be thinking, *Oh no, not another book on discovering God's will.* There are already hundreds of books and thousands of sermons on the subject. Do we really need another book?"

Despite these reactions, people constantly ask, "How can I know God's will for my life? What is God's will for my life? How do I know if this is what God wants me to do?" Others comment, "I have important decisions to make and need God's guidance and direction right now." Others lament, "I thought it was God's will, but it went terribly wrong."

The frequent response when something bad happens, when a severe illness strikes, when a loved one or friend is accidentally killed, or when they lose their job is, "That must have been God's will." Some think God is out to zap them.

Why don't the sceptics and critics research and read the books already in print or available on Kindle? Maybe they are not eager enough to do so or desperate enough to know God's will. Many people are confident of success without any "outside" interference and believe life has panned out exactly as they planned without God's help.

I recently received an unsolicited "inspirational thought" on my iPhone attributed to Christopher Morley (1890–1957). Morley was a novelist, essayist, theater producer, and poet. The quote read, "There is only one success—to be able to spend your life in your own way." It was probably that thinking that gave rise to the "Me" generation.

The "Me" generation (also known as the baby-boomers in the United States) refers to the generation born between 1946 and 1964. The soldiers' homecoming following World War II led to a baby boom. This generation was dubbed the "Me" generation or baby-boomers because of its preoccupation with self. It represented a rising culture of narcissism when "self-realization" and "self-fulfillment" became higher aspirations than social responsibility.

That thinking has caused many Christians to conclude God's will is so elusive it's not worth the effort to continue searching. Nothing has worked, so they give up trying. They do their own thing, rely on their own judgment, and hope for the best. Many believers mistakenly think God's will is limited to only important decisions, such as selecting a college, researching job opportunities, considering relocations, who and when to date or marry, joining a church, and making major investments. While these decisions are important, the issue of God's will is far broader and deeper than that. God's will should impact your entire life.

The purpose of this book is to convince you that God's will is not elusive. It is possible to discover God's will. The challenge is *knowing, understanding,* and *doing* it. Knowing and understanding God's will impacts our decisions. Doing God's will is the ultimate Christian experience. It is the most rewarding thing a follower of the Lord Jesus Christ can do. More than that, it is possible to experience God's guidance and direction daily. But this is predicated by one thing—obedience.

Obedience lies at the heart of doing God's will. When we find ourselves in a compromising situation that violates God's Word, we must resolutely refuse to yield to the temptation to entertain that impure thought, say that unkind word, do that shady deal, fudge the truth, or cross the forbidden line.

God's will calls for sacrifice. This can be tough and even dangerous. The martyrdom of five missionaries on the banks of the Curaray River in Ecuador's Amazon jungle in January 1956 was because they responded to God's call to reach the Auca Indians with the Gospel. You might say, "I am not willing to go that far." While martyrdom is the exception, you may not be really serious about doing God's will if you are hesitant to sacrifice everything for the sake of Christ. After all, He made the ultimate sacrifice for you.

With the exception of Judas, the Lord Jesus completely changed the lives of the men He chose as His disciples. They had no idea what lay ahead. He taught them and trained them. The Holy Spirit empowered them. They became witnesses. Their critics marveled that relatively uneducated men could have such a powerful impact for God and turn the world upside-down. God can use you to impact the world around you.

Reflect on how far the Lord Jesus went to do His Father's will. He went all the way to Calvary's cross for you and for me. Jesus told His followers that whoever wanted to be His disciple had to deny themselves and take up their cross and follow Him, and that whoever wanted to save their life would lose it, but whoever loses their life for Him and for the gospel will save it. He concluded His comments by telling His disciples that gaining the whole world and losing their soul in the process was sheer folly (Mark 8:34–36).

This led Jim Elliott, one of the five missionaries slain on the banks of the Curaray River, to write in his journal: "He is no fool who gives what he cannot keep to gain what he cannot lose."

Fred Baker, a good friend, shared that while on his last trip to Israel, the tour guide challenged the group to relocate to Gaza and live among the Palestinians and Hamas terrorists in order to befriend them and tell them about Jesus. Fred seriously questioned his willingness to do that. So would I, unless I believed God was unequivocally calling me to do so. I am confident God would make it known if that's what He wanted me to do. Then I would have no alternative but to obey.

Men and women are motivated to scale the highest mountains, explore the deepest caves, walk the most rugged terrain, and go to unimaginable lengths to satisfy their dreams. Thrill-seekers participate in extreme sports, drive at tremendous speeds, ski down terrifying slopes, and plumb the deepest oceans. They surf gigantic waves and jump from the highest bridges in attempts to satisfy their adventurous cravings. They are regarded as heroes. But the world would call them fools if they were to take those same risks for the sake of Christ. The reality is that only what's done for Jesus will last.

Your response might be, "There's no way I'm giving up what I have worked so hard to attain." Well, your attainments could vanish like the morning mist, fade like a rainbow, or slip through your fingers like mercury, as employees and investors in the Enron Corporation discovered to their horror. The Enron scandals resulted in the bankruptcy of a multi-billion dollar company in 2007 as well as the dissolution of Arthur Andersen LLP, one of the largest auditing and accounting firms in the world.

In my youth, I heard testimonies from those who sincerely wanted to do God's will. Some told how they bargained with God saying, "Lord, I'll do anything you want, but I won't be a missionary." Then the struggle began, and the dialogue went something like this:

"I want you to be a missionary."

"No, Lord!"

"Yes, I want you to be a missionary!"

"OK, Lord, but I won't go to China or India."

"I want you to be a missionary to China!"

"No, Lord!"

6

"Yes!"

"All right, Lord. I'll be a missionary to China."

"No, I don't really want to send you to China. I wanted to ensure that you were willing to go whenever I called you and wherever I sent you and that you were willing to be willing to do my will. I have other plans for you!"

While you may not think God is calling you to serve in a foreign land, you could well visit another country for purposes of education, military, business, or tourism. Those factors alone make you a "foreign missionary" because God expects you to be His witness and ambassador wherever you are.

A good example involves the building of Argentinian railroads during the second half of the nineteenth century. This was largely the work of British engineers, many of whom were committed Christians. These workers witnessed to the local people and were instrumental in establishing evangelical churches in the towns and villages along the railroads. This resulted in the strong evangelical presence in the country today. Those engineers regarded themselves as self-supporting missionaries.

God wants you to represent Him where you are, in whatever job you are doing, in whatever profession you are pursuing, and in whatever neighborhood you are living. Be faithful where you are, and trust God to lead you where He wants you. He will make that plain.

William Carey (1761–1834) was often called the "Founder of Modern Missions." Before going to India as a missionary, he was a minister, school teacher, and cobbler; shoe-making was his trade and livelihood. On one occasion, a friend accused him of neglecting his business and not doing enough to provide more for his family. He replied, "My real business is to preach the gospel and win lost souls. I cobble shoes to pay expenses." We all need Carey's attitude. Our job is never an end in itself. Our goal should always be to exalt the Lord Jesus, extend God's kingdom, and bring Him praise and glory in the process. That's God's will.

You may be in a better position now to echo the comment my good friend Richard Moore made one time: "It's often only when you look in your rearview mirror that you can discern how God was leading you." Someone else might retort, "That illness completely changed my focus in life." Another person might reflect, "I see now, that during all those times when I prayed so earnestly and was willing to trust God, He was actually guiding me and cutting out a path for me, even though I never realized it at the time." The poem, "*Footprints in the Sand*" illustrates this truth.

One night I dreamed a dream. As I was walking along the beach with my Lord, across the dark sky flashed scenes from my life. For each scene, I noticed two sets of footprints in the sand, one belonging to me and one to my Lord.

After the last scene of my life flashed before me, I looked back at the footprints in the sand. I noticed that at many times along the path of my life, especially at the very lowest and saddest times, there was only one set of footprints.

This really troubled me, so I asked the Lord about it "Lord, you said once I decided to follow you, you'd walk with me all the way. But I noticed that during the saddest and most troublesome times of my life, there was only one set of footprints. I don't understand why, when I needed you the most, you would leave me." He whispered, "My precious child, I love you and will never leave you. Never ever. During your trials and testing, when you saw only one set of footprints, it was then that I carried you." (Authorship uncertain)

Will you accompany me on a journey as we together look into the only Book that reveals God's will and guides us down the path God has planned for us? God has a divine purpose for you. Will you follow the signs God has posted to enable you to experience His guidance and direction?

I want to help you discover God's will for your life. Only one thing really matters in life, and that is that you *know* the will of God and *do* it. It boils down to being in the center of God's will each day, ensuring you are making the decisions that will prepare you for tomorrow.

You are probably thinking of the immediate decisions you need to make. Many of those decisions will become clearer when your priorities are right, when you delve into God's Word, and earnestly seek His face through prayer.

The sad thing is most Christians seldom read God's Word. In partnership with The American Bible Society, Barna Research Group regularly conducts a survey of Bible readership. In their *State of the Bible 2018: Seven Top Findings*, they reported on the behaviors and beliefs about the Bible among U.S. adults. Their top finding revealed 48% of Americans use the Bible outside of a church service. Bible engagement is defined as reading, listening to, watching, or praying it on one's own. Only 14% use the Bible daily, 13% use it several times a week, 8% do so once a week, 6% about once a month, while some 8% use it three or four times a year. Bible illiteracy won't help anyone discover God's will.

Many professing Christians disobey biblical commands and yet expect God to guide and bless them in life decisions. It doesn't matter whether that disobedience is inadvertent, intentional, or blatant. Disobedience is disobedience. Most followers of Christ don't have a Bible reading program. No wonder they struggle to personally discover God's will and find it elusive.

Throughout our journey together, I will repeatedly emphasize the need to read God's Word. The Bible is the road map, or in today's language, the GPS we need to listen to and follow; the textbook or blueprint we need to study; the love letter we need to pour over; the polar star we need to look at; and the plumb line to keep us straight. It is essential that we allow God's Word to transform us for the simple reason it is the only Book to do so. God has clearly revealed His will. All we need to do is to read His Word with an open mind to discover it. God's will is not elusive.

I pray this book will help you become the person God intends you to be. It calls for a serious commitment on your part. I also pray your interest in discovering God's will is sufficiently piqued by now that you will continue reading. I trust this first chapter whets your appetite to start on our journey. Getting this far means you have taken one small step, but in the end it could turn out to be a gigantic step. As an ancient Chinese proverb says, "The longest journey begins with the first step." Take that step and prayerfully continue reading. Let your motto be, *no turning back.*

My Prayer

Dear God. I really don't know what I'm getting into.

I find the prospect of discovering Your will for my life both intriguing and daunting. I am somewhat apprehensive about Your expectations of me. I want to make right decisions, but I am afraid where You might take me. I certainly don't want to live in a mud hut in some jungle. However, I admit my life has turned around since I trusted Jesus Christ, so I can only ask that You lead me down the road I am embarking on. I desperately want to know You more. I know very little of Your Word, so I desire to become familiar with it. I realize Your Word is important, so I commit to spending a little time each day reading it to help me discover Your will.

I pray this in the name of the Lord Jesus. Amen!

Application

1. How serious are you about knowing God's will for your life? Are you willing to make it your top priority?
2. Reading this book could be a life-changing journey for you. Are you ready to take the journey?
3. Will you commit to reading through this entire book, even if you have to wrestle with many issues?
4. Are you willing to make the Bible your textbook?
5. Are you willing to have an open mind and ask God to guide you along the journey we are undertaking together?

Chapter Two

I Am Still Making Up My Mind

It is fantastic that you are resonating with the concept of knowing God's will and purpose for your life. That purpose is extensive. It includes receiving Jesus Christ as your Lord and Savior and experiencing forgiveness, reconciliation, redemption, eternal life, and a lot more as a result. It includes receiving the Holy Spirit to enlighten, empower, enable, and equip you to live for Him and to serve Him.

You may have been a Christian for many years without ever seriously endeavoring to know God's will. You tried, but God's will was so elusive that you quit trying. You even stopped praying. You became perplexed and bewildered, always believing there was something better.

You may consider yourself a mature follower of Jesus Christ and claim to know God's will for your life, and you think this study is somewhat irrelevant. You consider yourself to have already been tested in the crucible and have come out refined, like silver or gold. That's great. But maybe, just maybe, you can learn something to pass on to someone who hasn't yet been molded into the vessel

God intends, someone who is really struggling to find and experience God's will.

Countless people ask the basic questions of life: Where did I come from? Why am I here? Where am I going? Only the Bible provides the answer to those soul-searching questions. Without the Scriptures, people are left in the dark and confused, and for most individuals, life is futile and purposeless. Their motto is pretty much that of the rich farmer the Lord Jesus spoke about in Luke 12:16–21.

Jesus told the parable of that farmer who had an abundant harvest, but his barns were too small to store the bumper crop. He decided to tear his barns down and build bigger ones. He then dreamed of taking life easy—eating, drinking, and being merry. For him, there was nothing more to live for. God called him a fool for thinking like that. But that is exactly how most people live. They believe wealth generation is all that matters. Jesus said that while that farmer was rich in this world's goods, he was actually bankrupt in his soul.

It is good to use your God-given talents and follow your passions even though you may deny God's existence and impact on your life. God exists, whether you believe it or not. God nevertheless has a purpose for your life, but it will only be fully realized when you place your faith and trust in His only Son, the Lord Jesus Christ, for salvation. Even when you do that, you will still need to *discover, understand,* and *do* God's will. Only Christ can satisfy your deepest longings.

You may be successfully following your passions with the talents God built into you at birth and the skills you subsequently developed, but still feel unfulfilled—even though you have reached the top in your company, profession, or sport. You achieved that with your own determination and the help of others. A different dynamic operates once you commit your life to Christ and experience His saving grace and regenerating power. As a follower of

Jesus Christ, I recommend you echo the prayer Paul prayed on the Damascus road, "Lord, what do you want me to do?" (Acts 9:3–19; 22:10) That should be a daily prayer. It is that important.

There's nothing wrong with money or wealth. It's the love of money and wealth that is the problem. People idolize their jobs and possessions. Some actually realize their dreams in the corporate and professional worlds. Others live out their dreams in the academic, entertainment, medical, military, legal, literary, scholastic, sports, or technical fields. Some people do make a distinct impact on their community, and even the world, because of their inventions, philanthropy, or service. But all the while, they have an emptiness and a cosmic loneliness within them that nothing can fill. They are like the caterpillar slowly climbing a stick, only to find when it reaches the top, there's nowhere else to go but down.

If that's where you are right now, I want to point you to Jesus Christ, the only One who can save you and give you a genuine purpose in living—something that far exceeds your present expectations. More than that, He gives you the power and enabling to live out His grander purpose for you. If you have never trusted in Christ alone to save you, I urge you do it now.

Maybe you have been a Christian for many years, but never really sought God's will for your life. Your intent was to rely on your own natural talents, learned skills, and personal judgments. Some three thousand years ago, King Solomon wrote, "The fear of the Lord is the beginning of knowledge, but fools despise wisdom and instruction" (Proverbs 1:7).

I suspect the burning question on your mind right now is, "OK, I am really serious, so cut to the chase and show me how I can discover God's will for my life; I am tired of looking for the proverbial "pot of gold at the end of the rainbow."

I can assure you there is no pot of gold at the end of the rainbow. I looked for it one time but could not find it. On one of my visits to the Cape Peninsular in South Africa, I was driving along the coastal road between Muizenburg and Fish Hoek when I saw the most magnificent rainbow, one you could only imagine seeing. It extended over the entire bay and literally touched the ocean about one hundred yards from the rocky shoreline. I had my swim shorts on, so I decided to swim to the point where the rainbow and the turquois-green ocean met. I swam around the end of that rainbow. I dove into the surrounding waters. There was no pot of gold to be found. The only "pot of gold" at the end of a rainbow is the covenant God made to Noah that he would never again destroy the earth with a flood (Genesis 9:8–17).

Many Christians are looking in the wrong place for God's will and find it elusive. In reality, God's will it is not elusive if you only know where to look for it and how to find it.

There's some groundwork to cover first. Let me begin by sharing three Scriptures with you.

The first Scripture is Colossians 1:9–11. In that passage, the apostle Paul informed the Christians in Colossae that, since the day he and his fellow missionaries heard about them, they hadn't stopped praying for them. They prayed God would fill them with the knowledge of His will through the wisdom and understanding the Holy Spirit provides.

The reason they prayed that prayer was *so that* the Colossian Christians would live a life worthy of the Lord and please Him in every way, *so that* they would be fruitful in every good work and grow in the knowledge of God, *so that* they would be strengthened with all power according to God's glorious might, *so that* they would have great endurance and patience. You say, "That's what I want!" Great! But it all begins with discovering God's will and being filled with the knowledge of it. That's really the starting point.

The second Scripture is Colossians 4:12. Epaphras, who probably founded the church in Colossae, sent his greetings to the believers in that city through the apostle Paul. Paul informed the church that Epaphras constantly wrestled in prayer for them, *so that* they would stand firm in all the will of God, mature and fully assured. You say, "That's what I desire; I want to stand firm in God's will—like a solid rock. I don't want to be blown about by every wind of doctrine that abounds today. I want to know what I believe."

The third Scripture is 1 John 2:17. There the apostle John told his readers the world was passing away—but the one who does the will of God abides forever. Living for God and following hard after Him has eternal benefits!

These verses teach us three things. First, we are to *know* the will of God. Second, we are to *understand* the will of God. Finally, we are to *do* the will of God. There is no greater thing in life than to know the will of God and do it.

You need to take your cue from the Lord Jesus Christ. Doing the will of God was the supreme purpose of His life. This is clearly evident from the following four verses. "My food is to do the will of him who sent me and to accomplish his work" (John 4:34). "In the volume of the book it is written of me, I delight to do your will, O my God" (Psalm 40:7–8; Hebrews 10:7, 9). "I have glorified you on the earth, having accomplished the work you gave me to do" (John 17:4). "My Father, if it be possible, let this cup pass from me, nevertheless not my will but yours be done" (Matthew 26:39; Luke 22:42).

It is essential that we *know, understand, and do* the will of God, if only for the fact the Lord Jesus taught His disciples to pray, "Your will be done on earth as it is in heaven" (Matthew 6:10). While God acts in accordance with His own sovereign will, He also is at work in believers, accomplishing His good pleasure in and through them (Philippians 2:13).

Romans 12:1–2 informs us part of the process of *discovering, understanding,* and *doing* God's will comes through presenting our bodies worshipfully as living and holy sacrifices to God. There is a commitment not to be conformed to the standards of this world or age. The commitment comes through the constant renewing of our minds. Then and only then will we be able to prove, or approve, what the good, acceptable, and perfect will of God is. Did you notice that before you can *prove* the will of God, you need to *present* yourself as a living sacrifice to God? There is a direct correlation.

From the outset, as we prepare for our journey together, I urge you to offer yourself to God as a living sacrifice. You can pray a prayer like this: "Lord Jesus, You unconditionally gave Yourself for me at Calvary's cross; I now unconditionally give myself to You. I am yours, Lord. I am ready to do whatever Your will is." You may also want to pray Samuel's prayer in the Old Testament: "Speak Lord, Your servant is listening" (1 Samuel 3:10).

Early in His ministry, the Lord Jesus told the multitude gathered around Him that those who did the will of God enjoyed a close filial relationship with Him, such as brother, sister, and mother (Mark 3:35). Do you long for that kind of bond with the Lord Jesus? It can be realized by doing the will of God.

Reading this book will help answer questions, such as:

- Does God have a divine purpose for my life?
- How can I discover God's will for my life?
- Is it actually possible to do God's will?
- How can I experience God's guidance and direction in my life?
- How will I know if I am out of the will of God?
- Can I miss God's will for my life?
- What if I mess up, can I get back into the will of God?
- Can I know God's will for the rest of my life?
- Does God have my life mapped out for me in advance?
- How do I make major decisions with the assurance they are right?

- Is God really interested in the little things of my life?
- Does God really want the best for me?

We will consider six aspects of God's will as we help you discover His will for your life. *First* is what I call the sovereign or decretive will of God—what God in His sovereignty has planned and determined to take place in accordance with His eternal counsels. *Second* is the revealed will of God—what God has already revealed about His will. *Third* is the unrevealed will of God—the issues we are most concerned about on a daily basis. *Fourth* is the perfect will of God. He does have a perfect plan for our lives. *Fifth* is the permissive will of God—why does God permit certain things to happen? *Sixth* is the moral will of God.

This book is the result of a life-long discipline seeking to know God's will for my life. Regretfully, there have been many, many occasions, times without number, when I have failed to implement God's will, when I have deliberately and knowingly disobeyed God's will, and when I proceeded without seeking God's will. There have been times when I have second-guessed my decisions and continue to do so. I wish I could do many things over again. So, I plan to share with you what I have learned over the years as well as the experiences of others.

The thoughts expressed in this book represent some of my life's experiences, as well as my teaching and preaching on the subject over six decades. As a young man, I probably read all available books on the subject of discovering God's will. There are many more available today, but I have deliberately avoided reading them for research purposes as my desire is to let this book reflect my own personal studies, thoughts, insights, experiences, and convictions. As a result, in the words of the psalmist in Psalm 19:14, I sincerely trust the words of my mouth and the meditations of my heart are acceptable in God's sight and be a blessing to those who read this book.

I invite you to stay with me throughout the journey we are embarking on because it's over the course of this journey that you will be equipped to *discover, know,* and *understand* God's will for your life. I want you to imagine being part of a small group as we travel together. You will enter into discussions, ask questions, and even conclude some things are impossible to implement at times. That's good because I want your interaction.

I have intentionally quoted and referenced a lot of Scripture, for two reasons. First, I want to authenticate my insights and comments from the Bible. Second, my hope is you will read all the Scriptures referenced and quoted. Having your Bible open beside you will help you do that. I encourage you to also read the passages quoted in the translation you normally use—I have used the New International Version. My intent is to facilitate your interaction with Scripture. This is far more important than anything I might write. My purpose is to coach you along the way.

My Prayer

Dear God, I really want to know Your will. Please help me to discover it and then understand it, so I can actually do Your will. I am beginning to realize this is important. I have already learned a little about Your will by getting this far in the book. I don't want Your will to be elusive like the morning fog that quickly disappears. I truly want to discover it.

I believe You do have a purpose for my life, and I want to know what that is. Please help me as I prepare for the journey I am undertaking. I am trusting You to reveal both Yourself and Your will to me. I want to know You better. My desire is to know You personally and intimately. I am frustrated at finding Your will so elusive. I know it's because I have never really tried to discover it. So please help me, God.

I am asking all this in Jesus's name. Amen!

Application

Stephen R. Covey, author of *7 Habits of Highly Successful People—The Art of Thinking Smart,* made the following quote, "The key is not to prioritize your schedule, but to schedule your priorities." What do you think about that statement?

Determine to make the discovery of God's will your top priority. Then schedule the time to seek it. Reading this book may just be the start. Pray God will create the desire within you to truly seek His will.

Chapter Three

Every Journey Begins with a Desire

very journey begins with a desire to travel. The desire leads to decision, which in turn generates action, preparation, and finally departure.

We are beginning the first stage of our journey, the desiring stage. The fact you have started reading this book at least indicates an inquisitiveness concerning the subject of God's will. Hopefully your curiosity develops into a sincere desire to *discover, know, understand, and do* God's will. On the other hand, you may be so frustrated at finding God's will elusive that you have reservations about continuing the journey. If you are hesitant about proceeding, I trust the inquisitiveness prompting you to get this far will turn into a wholehearted commitment to take the next step.

I often pose a conundrum to those in a quandary about making a decision. There were three frogs sitting on a lily pad in a pond. One decided to jump into the water. How many frogs were left on the lily pad? The answer is three because the frog only decided to jump—he never jumped.

Your decision to discover God's will needs to be followed by action. This involves a step of faith. Take that step with me. More importantly, trust God to lead you in the process as we consider Psalm 143, a psalm of David that contains fifteen prayer requests. I will primarily focus on one.

Psalm 143 is one of seven psalms the early church called penitential psalms. It is also included in the list of imprecatory psalms because David prayed his enemies be silenced and his foes destroyed. In reality, the psalm provides an insight into David's inward desires as he pours out his heart and soul to God, something we are all encouraged to do. David's heartfelt desire is found within the first twelve verses of the psalm. Read and reflect on them before continuing further. I want you to personally glean from the passage lessons God wants you to learn. These verses may possibly summarize your feelings right now:

Lord, hear my prayer, listen to my cry for mercy; in your faithfulness and righteousness come to my relief. Do not bring your servant into judgment, for no one living is righteous before you. The enemy pursues me, he crushes me to the ground; he makes me dwell in the darkness like those long dead. So my spirit grows faint within me; my heart within me is dismayed. I remember the days of long ago; I meditate on all your works and consider what your hands have done. I spread out my hands to you; I thirst for you like a parched land. Answer me quickly, Lord; my spirit fails. Do not hide your face from me or I will be like those who go down to the pit. Let the morning bring me word of your unfailing love, for I have put my trust in you. Show me the way I should go, for to you I entrust my life. Rescue me from my enemies, Lord, for I hide myself in you. Teach me to do your will, for you are my God; may your good Spirit lead me on level ground. For your name's sake, Lord, preserve my life; in your righteousness, bring me out of trouble. In your unfailing love, silence my enemies; destroy all my foes, for I am your servant. (Psalm 143:1–12)

Does the psalm resonate with you? What struck you?

David was in dire distress. He wrote the psalm in the midst of his troubles, probably while fleeing from his son Absalom. While the psalm contains his prayer for mercy, deliverance, and divine enablement, it also reveals the extent of his trust in God as he meditated on God's wondrous deeds—probably in creation. He was at his wit's end. His spirit was weak, his soul was parched, and his arms were outstretched to God. He needed assurance of God's unfailing love. He desperately needed God's intervention.

Central to the passage is David's heart cry for divine guidance. He prayed first of all in verse eight that God would show or teach him the way he should go. Then he prayed in verse ten: *"Teach me to do your will."* The prayer reveals how desperately David wanted to do God's will. Often, it is only when we are broken, confused, and desperate, as David was, that we utter a similar prayer. I have often wondered what troubles could be avoided if only we sought God's will in the first place—and did it.

Life offers different scenarios. You may be a brand-new Christian and excited at the dramatic change in your life. You found yourself praying, "Lord, what's next?" or "Lord, what is Your purpose in saving me?" Maybe, without even knowing the source, you prayed "Lord, show me or teach me Your will." With God's help, you determined to do great things for Him.

You may have trusted Christ as a child, but, for the first time in your teenage or young adulthood years, you feel God tugging at your heart for a total commitment to do His will, to being "all-out" for Him, to being a devout follower of the Lord Jesus.

You may possibly feel you are walking in David's sandals. You placed your trust in the Lord Jesus several years ago but something is missing. Over those years, you enjoyed periodic times in

God's Word. You conversed with God as one friend to another. You endeavored to live as you believed a Christian should. Outwardly, you showed all the signs of being a devout believer, but now you are frustrated by your complacency and indifference. You exclaim, "What happened? Where is the joy I once had?"

While life has frequently been challenging, it has been good. You achieved straight A's in college, found a good job, worked your way through several promotions, and even reached what you consider the pinnacle of your career. You married, had kids, and live in a desirable neighborhood. Your dreams have been realized. You may have played on a championship team, won an Olympic gold medal, and starred in some show, all the while realizing there was something more to life than fame and fortune.

Whatever your situation, I want to walk you through some important lessons that need to be learned. Respond as a serious student would. Aim high. Don't be satisfied with mediocrity.

In this preparatory stage of our journey, I want to focus on verse ten, probably the most important of all David's fifteen petitions in the psalm because everything else hinged on it. David asked God to teach him His will. Everything hinges on *discovering, knowing, understanding,* and *doing* God's will. While many are self-taught, it is preferable to let God teach you. The Holy Spirit is the divine instructor and illuminator. My job as an author is to merely help you in the process, to help make things a little plainer.

We observe two things from this verse.

- A teachable spirit is essential to discovering God's will. Not everyone is teachable; some are incorrigible.
- Prayer is imperative because it puts us in touch with an omnipotent God and reflects our dependence on Him and our need for the Holy Spirit to lead us. We need divine intervention and divine illumination. The Holy Spirit knows the

mind and will of God and intercedes for us appropriately (Romans 8:26–27). We can't go it alone. Those who do find God's will elusive.

God reveals wonderful truths in His Word if we only ask Him to show us. In another psalm, David prayed, "Open my eyes that I may see wonderful things in your law" (Psalm 119:18). Pray that prayer right now. The Holy Spirit will readily provide the insights you need.

It is essential we *discover, understand,* and *do* God's will. It doesn't just happen. It takes commitment, time, and trust. Do you have David's desire for God to teach you His will? Be like the psalmist who wrote, *"As the deer pants for streams of water, so my soul pants for you, my God"* (Psalm 42:1). Are you panting and thirsting for God?

We note at least five things from David's six-word prayer, *"Teach me to do your will."* We learn what should be the first heart cry of every follower of Christ. Then we learn God has a plan for every believer and He is ready and willing to reveal His will. David's prayer also indicates certain conditions must be met if we are to know and do God's will. All this leads to the question, "How can I know God's will?"

David's prayer states what should be the heart cry of every Christian.

David was distressed when he uttered this prayer. Unfortunately, many wait until they are at their wit's end before echoing David's heart cry. It is amazing how adversity, distress, and calamity drive us to God. They are wake-up calls.

Ideally, praying that God teach us His will should be one of the first prayers we offer as a follower of Christ. However, to my amazement, I discovered in one group of mature believers that no one had actually prayed that prayer. They just grew in their desire to be all God wanted them to be.

The apostle Paul is a classic example, a model we could follow, even though his confrontation with the risen Lord on the road to Damascus was unique as to the set of circumstances relating to his conversion to Christ. He was "fighting" God as he witnessed the stoning of Stephen, the first Christian martyr (Acts 7:58). He continued fighting until he personally met Christ.

At the time of his conversion, Saul, as he was known then, was a member of the Jewish Sanhedrin, a strong antagonist of the church, and he was threatening to kill followers of the Lord Jesus. Armed with letters from the high priest in Jerusalem, he was traveling to Damascus, seeking to arrest the believers there and bring them bound to Jerusalem for certain imprisonment and probable execution.

Luke vividly tells the story of Saul's conversion in Acts 9:3–19:

As he neared Damascus on his journey, suddenly a light from heaven flashed around him. He fell to the ground and heard a voice say to him, "Saul, Saul, why do you persecute me?"

"Who are you, Lord?" Saul asked.

"I am Jesus, whom you are persecuting," he replied. "Now get up and go into the city, and you will be told what you must do."

The men traveling with Saul stood there speechless; they heard the sound but did not see anyone. Saul got up from the ground, but when he opened his eyes, he could see nothing. So they led him by the hand into Damascus. For three days he was blind and did not eat or drink anything.

In Damascus there was a man named Ananias. The Lord called to him in a vision, "Ananias!"

"Yes, Lord," he answered.

The Lord told him, "Go to the house of Judas on Straight Street and ask for a man from Tarsus named Saul, for he is praying. In a vision he has seen a man named Ananias come and place his hands on him to restore his sight."

"Lord," Ananias answered, "I have heard many reports about this man and all the harm he has done to your holy people in Jerusalem. And he has come here with authority from the chief priests to arrest all who call on your name."

But the Lord said to Ananias, "Go! This man is my chosen instrument to proclaim my name to the Gentiles and their kings and to the people of Israel. I will show him how much he must suffer for my name."

Then Ananias went to the house and entered it. Placing his hands on Saul, he said, "Brother Saul, the Lord—Jesus, who appeared to you on the road as you were coming here—has sent me so that you may see again and be filled with the Holy Spirit." Immediately, something like scales fell from Saul's eyes, and he could see again. He got up and was baptized, and after taking some food, he regained his strength.

Turn a few pages in your Bible and read from Acts 21:40 to 22:21. Paul had been arrested and was giving his defense before the people. In his address, he specifically stated it was after his dramatic confrontation with the risen Christ on the Damascus road that he asked the question, "What shall I do, Lord?" Underline Acts 22:10 in your Bible.

As a teenager, I was taught to pray that prayer from the King James Version that reads, "Lord, what do you want me to do?" I have asked that question a "zillion" times over the years and believe every follower of Christ needs to ask it—the sooner the better. It is an essential question. We should pray that prayer every day, "Lord, what do you want me to do today?

Solomon declared our natural tendencies are to take charge and plan our own lives (Proverbs 16:9) because the plans in a person's heart are many (Proverbs 19:21).

Jeremiah states it more emphatically in his indictment of the people of Judah who stated, "It's no use. We will continue with our own plans; we will all follow the stubbornness of our evil hearts" (Jeremiah 18:12).

Isaiah declared "we all, like sheep, have gone astray, each of us has turned to our own way" (Isaiah 53:6).

The apostle James taught us to prayerfully seek God's will in regard to every plan we make, whether it involves a business decision or something related to daily living for the simple reason life is just a vapor, or moment in time, to prepare us for eternity (James 4:13–17).

Before we received the Lord Jesus as our personal Savior, our selfish nature contributed to doing our own will—just as a child will stubbornly and resolutely disobey its parents. I urge you to take a timeout to pray, "Lord Jesus, what do You want me to do. What is Your will for my life? I know You have a divine purpose for me. What is it, Lord? Teach me Your will!"

You may be hesitant because you feel the need for more information before sincerely and genuinely uttering that prayer. I sense your heart is open to discovering God's will; otherwise, you would not have committed to this journey. The preparatory stage of any journey is important, so I again urge you to pray that God teach you His will. It may be difficult to do so. You may feel you will lose control of your life. Take another time out and pray "Teach me to do your will!" Make that your heart cry right now.

David's prayer declares the fact that God has a plan for every believer.

The truth that God has a plan for every Christian is found throughout the pages of Scripture. Read the stories of Joseph, Daniel, Jonah, and Nehemiah in the Old Testament and the stories of Peter, Paul, James, and John in the New Testament. I throw these names out so you can study them on your own.

God had a plan for men like George Mueller, Hudson Taylor, Billy Graham, Francis Schaeffer, and Chuck Colson. He also had a plan for women like Gladys Aylward, Corrie ten Boom, Isobel Kuhn, Mary Slessor, Elizabeth Elliott, and Helen Roseveare. Their biographies inspired me in my youth. You possibly have your own heroes of the faith.

It's not just missionaries and preachers God has in mind. God has a divine plan for all who place their faith in Jesus Christ. Many in their professional lives and in the marketplace have made tremendous impacts for God. He has a plan for you which will unfold as we continue our journey. For now, accept the fact that "You are God's handiwork, created in Christ Jesus to do good works, which he prepared in advance for you to do" (Ephesians 2:10). Become the masterpiece God intends you to be. He is the potter; you are the clay (Isaiah 45:9; 64:8; Jeremiah 18:1–4). Let God mold you into the vessel He wants you to be.

We have already referenced Paul's classic prayer for the Colossian Christians in the previous chapter. It is worth repeating. Paul constantly asked God to fill them with the knowledge of His will in all spiritual wisdom and understanding. He prayed this prayer so they would live worthy of the Lord and please Him in every way, that they would bear fruit in every good work, and grow in the knowledge of God" (Colossians 1:9–10). Note the progression as each result, like building blocks, is contingent on the previous ones.

We won't grow in the knowledge of God unless we are first filled with the knowledge of His will and do it. We all need the experiential, intimate knowledge of God. The closer we are to God, the plainer His will becomes. There is a starting point.

Paul then assured the Colossians each step was achievable because of God's power and might. The end result was they would experience endurance and patience (Colossians 1:11). Living a God-glorifying life is never easy. It is only through the enabling and equipping power of the Holy Spirit that we can endure the inevitable adversities of life.

Epaphras was an evangelist and probably planted the church in Colossae. Paul informed the believers there that Epaphras not only sent greetings, but more importantly constantly wrestled in prayer for them, so they would stand firm in all the will of God, mature and fully assured (Colossians 4:12). Before believers can stand firm in God's will, they have to know God's will. It is *knowing, understanding,* and *doing* God's will that makes followers of Christ strong, mature, and confident in their faith.

God's plan for our lives is infinitely better than any plan we could conceive, for several reasons.

First, God fully understands us.

God created us with unique talents and skills. He knew us intimately while we were still in our mother's womb. The psalmist made that clear when he wrote, "You have searched me, Lord, and you know me. You know when I sit and when I rise; you perceive my thoughts from afar. You discern my going out and my lying down; you are familiar with all my ways" (Psalm 139:1–3).

The psalmist went on to proclaim

> For you created my inmost being; you knit me together in my mother's womb. I praise you because I am fearfully and wonderfully made; your works are wonderful, I know that full well. My frame was not hidden from you when I was made in the secret place, when I was woven together in the depths of the earth. Your eyes saw my unformed body; all the days ordained for me were written in your book before one of them came to be. (Psalm 139:11–16)

We have a God who is in tune with who we are. He understands us. "He knows how we are formed, he remembers that we are dust" (Psalm 103:14). He knows all about our frailties. He knows our every weakness. He knows when we are sad, glad, and mad.

Second, God alone sees things in true perspective.

Because God is infinite, He sees the end from the beginning in a way we never could. Our perspective is marred by a sinful nature, a warped world, and a selfish desire. David acknowledged his trust in a God who is all-knowing, all-wise, all-powerful, and all-loving. He is a God full of compassion, grace, and mercy; a God who will not allow us to be tempted beyond what we can endure (1 Corinthians 10:13).

Third, God has the power to complete His plan for our lives.

In his letter to the Philippians, Paul assured them that He who began a good work in them would carry it on to completion until the day of Christ Jesus (Philippians 1:6). God never abandons His projects. He sees each one through to completion. We are all a work in progress. One day we will be perfect. What a day that will be when we see Jesus.

Fourth, God's approach is productive because He desires the very best for us and wants us to be successful and fruitful in light of eternity.

The adage is true: "God gives the very best to those who leave the choice to Him." It is only as we know the plan God has for us that we can respond appropriately. That plan, as we shall learn, is clearly revealed in His Word.

The premise that successful businesses are brilliant on the essentials and core values is also true for Christian living. Discovering the revealed will of God is foundational to experiencing divine guidance and direction. We will address that dynamic as we proceed on our journey. For now, it is essential we demonstrate a teachable spirit.

David's prayer affirms that God is ready and willing to reveal His will.

God really does want us to know His will. He doesn't want it to be His best-kept secret. This begs the question: "Then why is God's will so elusive?" It is elusive because we make it elusive. We do so for several reasons.

- We are not sufficiently serious about knowing God's will. We haven't made the commitment to do what God desires. We need to make God's will the top priority in our lives.
- We don't give sufficient time and effort to discovering God's will. We expect everything to fall into place despite the fact that things don't just happen. There's God's part

and our part. We need to schedule the priority to do God's will in our lives.

- We are not sure what we are looking for. Most of the time we seek confirmation of our own decisions and actions. We merely ask God to bless our plans, which are often worldly, selfish, and contrary to His Word.

- We don't look in the right place to discover it. We won't find the answer in worldly textbooks or late-night comedy shows. Psychologists, professors, and even pastors won't help us unless they are deeply committed Christians and have themselves committed to discovering God's will for their lives.

You may be frustrated and thinking, "Get to the point. Tell me God's will." We are, however, still in the preparatory stage of our journey, building the desire to know His will. How committed are you to knowing God's will? How desirous are you of continuing this journey?

God's will is clearly revealed in His Word. All we have to do is study the Scriptures to discover it. It's those domestic, recreational, and vocational decisions that are often difficult to make. Those decisions are easier than we think when we have done the necessary groundwork.

I contend God has already revealed ninety-eight percent of His will in His Word. So all we have to do is to read the Bible, find the divine imperatives, and obey them. It's that simple.

It is harder to contend with what I call the intuitive will of God. This covers decisions not clearly addressed in the Bible—decisions such as the college to attend, the career to follow, the person to marry, the suburb to reside in, the house to buy, and the number of children to have. There is no direct instruction in the Bible concerning those issues, only guiding principles. The Bible is clear, for instance, that followers of Christ should only marry another believer. The question is which one?

We have already noted that only 14 percent of Americans read the Bible on a daily basis, despite the availability of scores of Bible-reading programs.

No wonder professing followers of Christ find God's will elusive. It's elusive because they choose, intentionally or by default, to make it elusive. God's will is there for discovering. The problem is that most Christians only spend two percent of their time and effort trying to discover the 98 percent of God's revealed will, and 98 percent of their time concerned about the intuitive or unrevealed aspect of God's will. Things couldn't be more backward.

God wants us to *know* His will. We need to constantly affirm that God does not make His will elusive. We do.

God is more willing to guide us than we are to be guided. We make our own plans, believing we know best. We readily ignore God and fail to realize He has given us all the tools we need. In reality, we only need to read, study, and digest the instructions and follow the guideposts God has already provided in order to discover His highest purposes for us.

We should regularly consult the Operator's manual. Our highest priority should be to *know, understand, and do* God's will, a message that will be stressed throughout our journey.

David's prayer indicates the conditions that must be met if we are to know and do God's will.

God's will is not revealed in a vacuum, through lightning flashes or writing in the sky. It is learned through meeting three simple conditions.

First, there must be a teachable spirit.

David prayed, "Teach me!" Not everyone is teachable. Some people are incorrigible.

Jeremiah succinctly wrote:

> Do not learn the ways of the nations . . . For the practices
> of the peoples are worthless . . . Everyone is senseless and
> without knowledge . . . The shepherds are senseless and do
> not inquire of the Lord; so they do not prosper and all their
> flock is scattered . . . Lord, I know that people's lives are not
> their own; it is not for them to direct their steps." (Jeremiah
> 10:2–3, 14, 21, 23)

The issue is where we go for instruction. We certainly should
not look to this world for wisdom. The apostle James clearly tells
us why (James 3:15). David prayed to the Lord. He is the only
One we need turn to. The Holy Spirit will teach us as we echo the
psalmist's prayer, "Open my eyes that I may see wonderful things
in your law" (Psalm 119:18).

Possibly the greatest obstacle to discovering God's will is the
lack of a teachable spirit. Don't rely on your own understanding.
Read and study God's Word.

Second, there must be an intense desire to know God's will.

David's prayer was prompted by a desire borne out of desper-
ation. I pray God creates that desire within you. There are several
specific promises in Scripture that stimulate a desire for God to
teach us and direct us. I reference two.

- "Take delight in the Lord, and he will give you the desires of
  your heart. Commit your way to the Lord; trust in him and
  he will do this" (Psalm 37:4–5). We need to ensure though
  that our desires don't conflict with God's direction. When
  we delight ourselves in the Lord, we start thinking God's
  thoughts after Him and instinctively want to please Him.
- "Trust in the Lord with all your heart and lean not on your
  own understanding; in all your ways submit to him, and he

will make your paths straight" (Proverbs 3:5–6). We will consider this passage in greater detail in a later chapter. Meanwhile, there needs to be implicit trust in the Lord and a commitment not to resort to our own understanding but to submit our ways to Him. Then and only then will we experience His overruling providence in our lives.

Our greatest priority as a follower of the Lord Jesus Christ is to know God's will and to do it. It should be the top priority. This commitment is borne out of an intense longing. Do you have that longing? Are you crying out for God to teach you? James taught us that when we draw near to God, He will draw near to us (James 4:8). Again, the psalmist expressed it beautifully when he wrote, "As the deer pants for streams of water, so my soul pants for you, my God. My soul thirsts for God, for the living God" (Psalm 42:1–2). Have you ever wondered why God seems so distant at times? It is because we don't approach Him and sufficiently thirst for Him.

Pay attention to Romans 12:1–2. "Therefore, I urge you, brothers and sisters, in view of God's mercy, to offer your bodies as a living sacrifice, holy and pleasing to God—this is your true and proper worship. Do not conform to the pattern of this world, but be transformed by the renewing of your mind. Then you will be able to test and approve what God's will is—his good, pleasing and perfect will." We can only prove God's will after presenting ourselves as a living sacrifice to Him. Discovering God's will must be a serious pursuit.

Third, there must be a willingness to do God's will regardless of the involvement or consequences.

It is possible to know God's will and not do it. God's will involves obedience—obeying what God has revealed and taught. Doing God's will calls for unconditional surrender. It also calls for implicit trust. Many are afraid of seeking God's will, not knowing what He has in store for them. Others are even uncertain of their willingness to obey. They are afraid God's will might conflict with their own will, that God might want them to do something outside their comfort zones. Whenever we hesitate to obey, we need to pray one line of the Lord's Prayer—"Your will be done!" Sadly, we glibly recite that prayer without any intent of personal implementation. That prayer should be our ultimate daily proclamation.

David's prayer invokes the question: how does God teach us to do His will?

My aim right now is to lay a foundation for our ongoing deliberations. There's no point in continuing this journey if you are not serious about discovering God's will for your life and for finding the keys that enable you to experience God's guidance and direction.

Stay with me as we travel together along the road ahead. We are on a journey, and my purpose as we progress is to build on the foundation we are laying together. No one building a house starts with the roof. So be patient if right now you are looking for help in choosing a college. There are fundamental principles you need to learn if you are really serious about discovering God's will.

I close this chapter by quoting an old-time hymn, *Teach Me Thy Way* by B. Mansell Ramsay (1849–1943). Make this hymn your prayer before you proceed any further.

> Teach me Thy way, O Lord, Teach me Thy way!
> Thy gracious aid afford, teach me Thy way!
> Help me to walk aright; more by faith, less by sight;
> Lead me with heav'nly light, teach me Thy way!
> When I am sad at heart, teach me Thy way!
> When earthly joys depart, teach me Thy way!
> In hours of loneliness, in times of dire distress,
> In failure or success, teach me Thy way!
> When doubts and fears arise, teach me Thy way;

When storms o'erspread the skies, Teach me Thy way.
Shine through the cloud and rain, through sorrow, toil, and pain;
Make Thou my pathway plain, teach me Thy way.
Long as my life shall last, teach me Thy way;
Where'er my lot be cast teach me Thy way.
Until the race is run, until the journey's done,
Until the crown is won, teach me Thy way."
(Public Domain)

This completes our preparation for the journey. As we proceed to the next stages, expect the terrain to be often rugged and the road sometimes hilly and mountainous as we explore glorious truths and view some of the majestic scenery pertaining to God's will.

Application

Reflect on what you have read about desiring God's will. What is your action plan at this stage of the journey to help you discover God's will?

1.

2.

3.

4.

5.

Part Two

Discovering God's Will

Looking in the Only Place Where God's Will
Can Be Found

Chapter Four

The Big Picture

Growing up in South-Central Africa had some advantages. Among them were frequent visits to Victoria Falls, one of the seven natural wonders of the world. Its beauty is stunning. Its thunderous roar as the mile-wide Zambezi River plunges three hundred and sixty feet into the gorge below is forever etched in my memory.

Standing on the edge of Livingstone Island, accessed by canoe, and peering down to the gorge below was scary. Gazing at the majestic view from Devil's Point across the gorge was breathtaking. Descending the man-made steps leading to the bottom of the gorge and looking up at the torrent of cascading water as its spray billowed several hundred feet into the sky was awesome.

No wonder the locals call it "the smoke that thunders." I have spent countless hours looking at this amazing natural wonder. Its grandeur, however, can never be captured from an altitude of thirty thousand feet. I realized that while on a flight from Johannesburg to Brussels.

We miss the expanse of a forest by focusing on individual trees. We also lose sight of a city with its skyscrapers, factories, parks, and expressways when we focus solely on a single neighborhood. In the same way, we can become so engrossed in the intricacies of life and an in-depth study of the Bible that we miss the big picture.

Both perspectives are necessary. Seeing the big picture God has outlined is impactful.

The big picture has to do with God's sovereign will, also known as His decretive will. You are probably thinking "What on earth is that all about, and what has this to do with God's will for my life?" Everything! Discussion of this theological topic at this stage of our journey, while daunting, is necessary. I anticipate this will possibly be one of the hardest chapters to assimilate, but don't be deterred from continuing. Don your climbing shoes as we ascend to some of the mountain peaks of God's Word.

The decretive will of God is that aspect of His will contained in His decrees or purposes. It is also known as His eternal counsel. God is sovereign. That means He can choose to do anything He wants. This is possible because He possesses the attributes of *omnipotence, omnipresence,* and *omniscience.* Being omnipotent, or all-powerful, means He can perform anything He chooses to do. Being omnipresent means He is not limited by time or space. Being omniscient means He is all-knowing; He knows everything from the beginning to the end. Nothing in the past, present, or future is hidden from Him.

The first stage of our climb into God's Word takes us back to the seventeenth century in the British Isles. In 1646 and 1647, a synod of English and Scottish theologians and laymen, with the intent of bringing the Church of England and the Church of Scotland into greater conformity, wrote what is now known as the Westminster Shorter Catechism. In the catechism, the theologians both asked and answered a total of 107 questions related to God, doctrine, faith, and practice.

Question seven asks: "What are the decrees of God?"

The theologians wrote their response. "The decrees of God are His eternal purpose, according to the counsel of His will, whereby, for His own glory, He hath foreordained whatsoever comes to pass."

They based their answer on two passages of Scripture.

The first in Paul's letter to the Ephesians. "For he chose us in him (Jesus Christ) before the creation of the world to be holy and blameless in his sight . . . In him we were also chosen, having been predestined according to the plan of him who works out everything in conformity with the purpose of his will" (Ephesians 1:4, 11).

God's purpose from the beginning of time was that we be holy and blameless in His sight. Sin entered the world with catastrophic results. Sin separated man from His Creator. However, God had a plan. He purposed Jesus Christ would restore the paradise that was lost in the Garden of Eden. It is through Christ, then, that God's purpose for us to be holy and blameless is realized. He is the epicenter of redemption's story. God predetermined this in conformity with His eternal counsel and will.

The second Scripture is found in Paul's letter to the Romans. "What if God, although choosing to show his wrath and make his power known, bore with great patience the objects of his wrath— prepared for destruction? What if he did this to make the riches of his glory known to the objects of his mercy, whom he prepared in advance for glory" (Romans 9:22–23).

From this short response, we learn God demonstrated His wrath and revealed His power while still demonstrating His patience and forbearance. We also learn there is a hell to shun and a heaven to gain, a condemnation to avoid and a glory to experience. In addition, we learn at least eight characteristics of the decrees of God. These characteristics provide the big picture by which we can better appreciate the nature of God's divine and sovereign plan as it relates to believers.

The decrees of God consist of an eternal plan.

The verses referenced by the theologians reveal the depth and scope of God's eternal plan for believers. God's purpose from before creation was that those described as being "in Christ" were to be holy and blameless before Him. Redemption's plan included our sanctification—the process by which we are conformed into the image of His Son (Romans 8:29) as God also predestined or predetermined. He would sovereignly work out everything in accordance with His divine purpose. Like a golden thread, the overarching will of God weaves its way through Scripture, from Genesis through Revelation. It also cuts its path through the adversities and atrocities of history.

God has a plan that was conceived in the bygone ages of a past eternity. That plan included redemption's story. It includes you and me. However, something needs to happen before that plan takes effect in our lives. We need to be "in Christ." That occurs the moment we receive the Lord Jesus Christ as our personal Savior.

God's redemptive plan unfolds through Jesus Christ. The plan is exclusionary. That means there is absolutely no other way to God except through Jesus Christ. Jesus Himself declared that He is "the Way, the Truth, and the Life" (John 14:6). That makes Christianity offensive to the vast majority of people in the world and to every opposing religion. That unequivocal plan was conceived before the world existed. The apostle John referred to Jesus Christ as "the Lamb that was slain from the creation of the world" (Revelation 13:8). Christ's death was in the mind of God before His creative power ever became evident.

In his sermon on the day of Pentecost, the apostle Peter declared, "This man (Jesus) was handed over to you by God's deliberate plan and foreknowledge; and you, with the help of wicked men, put him to death by nailing him to the cross" (Acts 2:23).

God used the wickedness of man to accomplish His redemptive purpose, which included Christ's sacrificial death on a Roman cross. There were two plans in effect: the plan of God to offer His Son as atonement for our sins and the counter plan of wicked men to crucify Him. As we gaze at the cross, we see a gory mess on one hand and the glory of God in redemption's story on the other. We see extreme hatred in opposition to everlasting love. We see an injustice being committed in that an innocent man was crucified. On the other hand, we see God's justice displayed in that Jesus was bearing the judgment we deserve.

God did all this to make the riches of His glory known to the objects of His mercy who He is preparing for the glory to come. His purpose in saving us is to prepare us for eternity. That preparation begins the moment He saves us. God's predetermined plan is that we bring Him praise and glory not just in this life, but in the ages to come. One day the whole of creation will glorify Him. That's God's ultimate purpose, all part of His divine plan—a plan that relates to all those who respond to His call and place their faith and trust in the Lord Jesus Christ alone for salvation. That means God has a plan for your life. He has a purpose in calling you to Himself.

The plan is founded on the infinite wisdom of God.

God is all-wise. He never makes a mistake. In His wisdom, God chose Israel to be the channel through which the surrounding nations would come to know Him. Israel was not the largest nation; it was the smallest. So why did God choose them? He chose Israel to honor the oath made to Abraham (Genesis 12:1–3) because He loved them and chose to make them a special nation (Deuteronomy 7:6–11).

Israel constantly failed as a nation, was frequently judged, and finally set aside when it rejected His beloved Son. God turned to the Gentiles who were always in view.

The book of Acts records the transition from Israel as a nation to the incorporation of Jews and Gentiles into something entirely different. This occurred with the birth of the church at Pentecost, its rapid growth, and the inclusion of Gentile believers. Something new burst onto the scene and soon turned the world upside down. Its impact is still felt today. The apostle Paul was assigned to declare what happened.

The mystery of the church is revealed in the third chapter of Ephesians. It is only a mystery in the sense it was always in God's mind from the beginning but remained hidden throughout the Old Testament period. Paul was the one God chose to talk and write about the church and His intent for it. God's design was that the church comprise both Jews and Gentiles who jointly become members of the same body and sharers together in the promise in Christ Jesus. While this truth was also known to the prophets and apostles (Ephesians 3:5), God chose Paul to declare it.

The word *church* is from the Greek word *ekklésia* and means a group of people who are called to assemble. The church consists of people called out from the world to God and includes the universal body of believers in Christ since it was inaugurated after Christ's resurrection and ascension to heaven.

Paul revealed God had a broader plan and purpose for the church. His intent was that now, through the church, the manifold wisdom of God should be made known to the rulers and authorities in the heavenly realms, according to the eternal purpose He accomplished in Christ Jesus, our Lord. In Him and through faith in Him, we may approach God with freedom and confidence (Ephesians 3:11–12).

Not only is the church to be a witness to the nations of the earth, including every people group, it is to be a witness to the heavenly realm consisting of good and evil angels. Jesus taught there is joy in the presence of angels whenever a sinner repents (Luke 15:10). On the other hand, we can only imagine how mad the devil gets when one of his dupes is lost. The church is on display not only to the world, but also to the heavenly hosts, something our finite minds find difficult to comprehend.

God's purpose is that His Son, Jesus Christ, be the fulcrum upon which our relationship to Him exists and rests, and through whom we have direct access to a heavenly Father who sits upon a throne and who is in control of the world's final destiny.

The plan for the Church was formed for God's glory.

Two scriptures relate to this truth.

Paul wrote the first passage which has already been referenced. "In him we were also chosen, having been predestined according to the plan of him who works out everything in conformity with the purpose of his will, in order that we, who were the first to put our hope in Christ, might be for the praise of his glory" (Ephesians 1:11–12).

This passage clearly teaches God's plan and purpose for every believer chosen in Christ is for all to bring Him glory and praise. That's part of His eternal plan. He saved us so we would magnify Him and bring Him glory. That is God's big picture for you and me. If we are not doing that, we are missing His plan, will, and purpose for our lives.

The second passage was written by the apostle Peter to Jewish believers who would have been familiar with the reference to Exodus 19:5–6. "But you are a chosen people, a royal priesthood, a holy nation, God's special possession, that you may declare the praises of him who called you out of darkness into his wonderful light" (1 Peter 2:9). As those readers were also members of the one body, the church, that truth applies to us whether we are Jewish or Gentile believers. God's plan is every believer declare the praises of God to a world darkened by sin. We should all be testifying to the change God wrought in our lives the moment we trusted the Savior. This exalts Him and brings Him glory. What an incentive to give God our very best.

God's plan can never be thwarted.

God is sovereign and alone has the power to bring His plans to fruition. Look at His creative acts in bringing the universe into existence. God said, "Let there be light," and there was light. We should consider each creative act recorded in the first chapter of Genesis and marvel at His creative power, as did many throughout the Old Testament narrative.

Satan did everything he could to thwart God's plan. He rebelled against God with the result he was cast out of heaven together with one third of the angelic host (Isaiah 14:12–15; Ezekiel 28:11–19; Revelation 12:3–4). He tempted Adam and Eve, and through Adam's sin, disobedience and death entered the world. This resulted in increased disobedience, defiance, destruction, and decay.

Satan desperately tried to break the genealogical line from Adam to Jesus. He put it into the heart of King Herod to have every young boy in Israel killed. He tempted Jesus in Israel's wilderness. He took him to the pinnacle of the temple in Jerusalem and tempted Him to jump to the ground below, telling Him angels would dramatically come to His rescue. He tried his hardest to divert Jesus from the Cross. Finally, he stirred the hearts of religious bigots to have Him killed at Golgotha, thinking that was the end of the story.

But such is the mighty power of God that Jesus rose from the dead on the third day. Indisputable evidence of that exists—just read the books *Who Moved the Stone* by Frank Morrison and *The Case for Christ* by Lee Strobel. When the risen Christ ascended back to the throne of God, He had to pass through the heavens, limiting Satan's principalities and powers. Nothing could thwart the eternal plans and purposes of God. In the end, Satan was left a defeated foe, and is awaiting his final judgment to the pits of hell. God is still on the throne. God is still in control.

Nebuchadnezzar, the heathen and despotic king of Babylon, came to this realization after God utterly humiliated him—read Daniel chapter four. We pick up the story of his amazing proclamation in verse thirty-four:

> At the end of that time, I, Nebuchadnezzar, raised my eyes toward heaven, and my sanity was restored. Then I praised the Most High; I honored and glorified him who lives forever. His dominion is an eternal dominion; his kingdom endures from generation to generation. All the peoples of the earth are regarded as nothing. He does as he pleases with the powers of heaven and the peoples of the earth. No one can hold back his hand or say to him: "What have you done?"
>
> At the same time that my sanity was restored, my honor and splendor were returned to me for the glory of my kingdom. My advisers and nobles sought me out, and I was restored to my throne and became even greater than before. Now I, Nebuchadnezzar, praise and exalt and glorify the King of heaven, because everything he does is right and all his ways are just. And those who walk in pride he is able to humble. (Daniel 4:34–37)

The point of all this is to emphasis the acknowledgment of a heathen and despotic king who came to realize the God of heaven was indeed almighty and sovereign in the affairs of men as He sets up and takes down human leaders in accordance with His will and purposes.

This raises the question of why there is still so much evil in the world? Why isn't God doing something about it? He did. He sent His Son to be the Savior of the world. The struggle between good and evil will continue until God's ultimate purposes are achieved. Nothing will thwart that purpose. God is sovereign. Everything will ultimately work out according to His eternal purposes and plans.

We see His plan clearly in the fulfillment of Old Testament prophecies concerning the birth, life, death, resurrection, and ascension of Jesus Christ. Over three hundred and fifty Old Testament prophecies were fulfilled in and during the first advent of Jesus Christ. Applying the science of probability to these prophecies, the chance of each one being literally fulfilled is astronomical. The fact they were fulfilled proves the accuracy and veracity of the Old Testament Scriptures. It also proves that Jesus of Nazareth is the promised Messiah.

In addition, the fact that the Holy Spirit also inspired the writings of the New Testament ensures the accuracy of those Scriptures concerning the second advent of the Lord Jesus and end-time events. Over three hundred references and prophecies relate to Christ's second coming. If the prophecies relating to Christ's first coming were literally fulfilled, why won't the prophecies relating to His second coming not be literally fulfilled? Everything will consummate according to God's eternal plan.

Satan did everything he could to derail the first advent and ministry of the Lord Jesus. He failed. He will do everything he can to thwart the plans God has for the future. He will fail again. The devil is a defeated foe. He lost the battle at Calvary and at the garden tomb. The Bible makes that fact clear.

God's eternal decrees will never change because He is immutable and unchanging.

This truth is clearly proclaimed in multiple passages, such as the following: "Remember the former things, those of long ago; I am God, and there is no other; I am God, and there is none like me. I make known the end from the beginning, from ancient times, what is still to come. I say, 'My purpose will stand, and I will do all that I please" (Isaiah 46:9–10). "I the Lord do not change" (Malachi 3:6). "Every good and perfect gift is from above, coming down from the Father of the heavenly lights, who does not change like shifting shadows" (James 1:17).

Everything God has decreed will materialize. Nothing will thwart His divine purposes. His mind is set. The devastating course of human history will not frustrate God's plans. What He has decreed will take place.

Jesus said the conditions existing when He comes again will resemble those in the days of Noah when the earth was destroyed by a flood (Matthew 24:37–39). The frightening thing is the conditions in the world today closely resemble those during Noah's lifetime. This makes me wonder how much longer it will be before God's patience is exhausted and His predicted judgment takes place. God's clock keeps perfect time. Many Bible scholars believe it's just a few minutes to midnight before the clock strikes and Jesus comes again.

There is an all-inclusive idea in God's plan.

Not only has God decreed His sovereignty in the course of human history, He has foreordained His plan for the lives of those saved by grace through faith. Salvation is an undeserved and unmerited gift from God. It is not based on any works we have done (Ephesians 2:8).

Included in those plans are the means to achieve God's end. Joseph is a classic example. Joseph was hated by his brothers to the extent they plotted to kill him. They threw him into a pit intending him to die there but then sold him to Midianite traders who took him to Egypt where he was re-sold as a slave to Potiphar, Pharaoh's right-hand man. We won't go into the entire story other than to acknowledge God had a plan for Joseph, a plan he never fully understood while the events were unfolding. It was only when he eventually looked in his rearview mirror that Joseph realized God was sovereignly in charge and things had happened for a purpose. He only knew God was doing something in his life, and all he could do was to trust Him through every situation.

Listen to Joseph's testimony at the end of the book of Genesis when he finally met his brothers face to face, something they never expected. Looking in his rearview mirror, he proclaimed, "You intended to harm me, but God intended it for good to accomplish what is now being done, the saving of many lives" (Genesis 50:20).

We may not clearly discern how God is working and directing us through life while we genuinely seek His will. God uses the circumstances of life to direct us, to carve out the path He wants us to tread. He is at work in our lives without our ever realizing it. He is at work in the midst of our brokenness, confusion, strife, and grief to bring us to the place He wants us to be.

There is value in knowing the doctrine of God's decretive will.

As a starter, there is *security* in knowing we are in the center of God's eternal plan. Nothing can thwart that plan. God is in sovereign control. The universe is not running amok. To know God has included me in His divine plan is amazing. It's awesome. It gives me the sense of real security, knowing nothing can pluck me out of my Father's hand. As a believer in Christ, I am destined for glory.

Then there is *comfort* in knowing God has included us as believers in His eternal plan. We have the assurance our ultimate glorification depends on God's ability to keep us safe for that day when we shall see our Savior face to face.

Jude captured this assurance in his doxology when he wrote, "To him who is able to keep you from stumbling and to present you before his glorious presence without fault and with great joy—to the only God our Savior be glory, majesty, power and authority, through Jesus Christ our Lord, before all ages, now and forevermore" (Jude 24–25).

Finally, there is *hope* in knowing God will accomplish everything He has purposed. Being all-powerful, God will accomplish His overall plan, and He will do it irrespective of you or me. Knowing this gives us a basis for being eternal optimists. As we look at the mess, confusion, and insecurity in the world, we confidently rest on the hope and confident expectation God will bring His word to pass.

We need the right attitude to God's decretive will.

We need to cultivate *a solemn sense of responsibility* to pray like Daniel did when he became aware of the edict that resulted in his being thrown into a den of lions. When he learned of the decree, he went home to his upstairs room where the windows opened toward Jerusalem over 1,650 miles away. He did what he always did three times a day—he fell on his knees and prayed with thanksgiving to God (Daniel 6:10). His commitment was to obey the God of heaven and earth, not the king of Persia. He trusted in the overruling providence of God, even if it meant being torn apart and devoured by hungry lions. He had the confidence fate would not prevent his eternal destiny in heaven.

Then we need to display *a quiet resignation* to God's will. Don't fight it. Submit to it. Let your attitude be that of the Lord Jesus in the garden of Gethsemane: "Not my will, but your will be done" (Matthew 26:39). God, in His divine and sovereign will, has already decreed how things will end. The book of Revelation outlines the course of those climactic times. As believers, we are on the winning side.

All this was predicted in the Old Testament when Isaiah announced the first coming of the Savior, and then referred to His second advent and the time when Jesus Christ would reign on earth. He wrote:

> For to us a child is born, to us a son is given, and the government will be on his shoulders. And he will be called Wonderful Counselor, Mighty God, Everlasting Father, and Prince of Peace. Of the greatness of his government and peace there will be no end. He will reign on David's throne and over his kingdom, establishing and upholding it with justice and righteousness from that time on and forever. (Isaiah 9:6–7)

The angel Gabriel told the virgin Mary the same thing, "He will be great and will be called the Son of the Most High. The Lord God will give him the throne of his father David, and he will reign over Jacob's descendants forever; his kingdom will never end" (Luke 1:32–33).

Jesus will reign on the earth one day. Many Bible students believe that time is not too far distant.

The apostle Paul addressed the subsequent exaltation of Christ in his first letter to the Corinthian church when he referred to the culmination of Christ's millennial reign.

Then the end will come when he (Christ) hands over the kingdom to God the Father after he has destroyed all dominion, authority and power. For he must reign until he has put all his enemies under his feet. The last enemy to be destroyed is death. For he "has put everything under his feet." Now when it says that "everything" has been put under him, it is clear that this does not include God himself, who put everything under Christ. When he has done this, then the Son himself will be made subject to him who put everything under him, so that God may be all in all. (1 Corinthians 15:24–28)

Then, in the second chapter of his letter to the Philippian church, after describing the sevenfold humiliation of the Lord Jesus culminating in His excruciating death on the cross, Paul describes His sevenfold exaltation as follows:

Therefore God exalted him to the highest place and gave him the name that is above every name, that at the name of Jesus every knee should bow, in heaven and on earth and under the earth, and every tongue acknowledge that Jesus Christ is Lord, to the glory of God the Father. (Philippians 2:9–11)

As assuredly as day follows night, all this will happen. It's all part of God's eternal plan and decrees. God's clock keeps on ticking. The paradise that was lost in the Garden of Eden will be restored in heaven.

That's a lot to grasp. We will stop here while you catch your breath and take a timeout. Take time during this break to reflect on the magnitude of God's decretive will. Sleep on it. Pray that you will fully understand the implications of our reflections together. Rejoice that as someone who has placed their faith in Jesus Christ alone for salvation, you are included in that chain of events.

The next stage of our journey takes us into the Arabian Desert where we will consider a monumental event in Israel's history. It is an event that addresses God's standard for our lives. It is a standard unattainable by human effort but lies at the very heart of discovering and understanding God's "revealed will."

My Prayer

Father, I still don't understand everything, but I thank You that You have included me in Your big picture. I thank You for the security I enjoy through Christ that brings me both comfort and peace, knowing that nothing can destroy my position in Christ. I thank You, too, for the blessed hope and certainty of Christ's return one day. I look forward to the day when I shall see Jesus face to face and forever dwell in Your presence.

Father, I thank You for Your eternal plan and that You are in control of the universe. I thank You that one day, Satan will finally be cast into the pits of hell You created for him. I thank You that one day there will be no more tears, death, mourning, crying, or pain (Revelation 21:4). I thank You that one day I shall live with You throughout the countless ages of eternity—all because of my Lord and Savior Jesus Christ.

I thank and praise You in the precious name of the Lord Jesus. Amen!

Application

Reflect on what you have learned in this chapter. Then list your responses and how you will apply them to your life.

1.

2.

3.

4.

5.

Chapter Five

Lessons from the Arabian Desert

I have long ascertained God has already revealed 98 percent of His will. All we need do is to read the Bible to discover it. But there is a problem. Professing Christians are not reading the Bible. It's not much better with evangelical believers. The statistics are not good. No wonder followers of Christ find God's will elusive. It doesn't have to be.

We need to study the Bible as students study a textbook. We are to consult it as we do our global positioning system. That device tells us what road to take and when we have left the planned route. It even asks if we need new directions. It sometimes tells us to make a U-turn. The Bible does the same and is totally reliable and trustworthy.

As good as my OnStar system is, it has occasionally dumped me in the middle of nowhere, somewhere I never intended to be. It has even directed me down a road leading to a dead end. While the Bible may take you down a road you are reluctant to travel, it will never land you in trouble. The Scriptures are God's love letter to the world. Read them as you would a message from someone you love. Just as military personnel obey standing orders and commands, we need to implicitly obey God's instructions.

It's the 2 percent of God's will, what I call His "unrevealed" or "circumstantial" will that unfortunately absorbs 98 percent of our time. We get things backwards and wonder why we find God's will elusive. We are going to engage in some serious Bible study as we continue on the road to discovering God's will.

This stage of our journey takes us to a mountain in Saudi Arabia, formerly the land of Midian, where the children of Israel wandered for a period of forty years. Moses interchangeably referred to the mountain as Mount Sinai and Mount Horeb. Many biblical scholars believe they are one and the same. So, let's follow the route the children of Israel took from the Red Sea to the Sinai Peninsula.

God called Moses to join Him at the top of the mountain where he then spent forty days and forty nights. While there, the nation waited anxiously in the wilderness below, oblivious to what was transpiring on the mountain above. As the mountain quaked, all the people saw were lightning flashes and smoke enveloping its peak like a thick cloud. All they heard were thunderous roars and trumpet-like sounds. They had no idea what was happening. The people feared for their leader's safety. Moses himself was afraid and trembled throughout his interaction with Jehovah. We will climb that mountain together and shall endeavor to recapture that historic encounter with Almighty God.

But first, let's backtrack some twenty-five hundred years to the beginning, to the book of Genesis, to learn why God called Moses to meet Him on those rugged mountain heights.

The first two chapters of the book of Genesis describe God's creative acts. The first verse referencing time, energy, action, space, and substance emphatically states, "In the beginning God created the heavens and the earth" (Genesis 1:1). The chapters provide a mere glimpse of the majestic sweep of God's creativity, culminating in the creation of Adam and Eve.

It was a perfect world, a perfect environment, until Adam and Eve deliberately chose to disobey God's command and eat the forbidden fruit from the tree in the middle of the garden, the details of which are provided in the third chapter. The results were catastrophic. Not only were they banished from the garden, but through Adam's disobedience, sin entered the world and death by sin. This resulted in everyone born after Adam and Eve inheriting a sinful nature with the propensity to sin. Because of that fallen nature, everyone since Adam, apart from the Lord Jesus, are also sinners by practice. That simply means everyone has sinned. Paul made that clear in his letter to the Romans when he wrote, "All have sinned and fallen short of God's glory" (Romans 3:23), and "Sin entered the world through one man, and death through sin, and in this way death came to all people, because all sinned" (Romans 5:12).

Things grew worse through the centuries as the earth's population increased. Sin climaxed during the days of Noah and became so rampant God decided to destroy the world by means of an historic flood, the likes of which hasn't been seen since. Only Noah and his wife and their three sons and their wives escaped the catastrophic judgment. Read the account in the sixth chapter of Genesis.

By tabulating the genealogies from Adam to Noah found in the book of Genesis, biblical scholars estimate that the Genesis flood occurred about 1,650 years after man's creation.

Lest you are skeptical about the extent of this flood, examine the overwhelming evidence available today to support the biblical account of a universal flood. Tropical fauna has been discovered in the Arctic regions. Fish fossils have been found on some of the highest mountains. Frozen mammoths have been found buried standing on their feet in the Siberian ice, with grass still in their mouths. This could only have resulted from a catastrophic event. The arguments for creation science and a universal flood are overwhelming—just follow the experts in ministries, such as the

Institute of Creation Research, Creation Ministries International, and Answers in Genesis.

After the flood, Noah's family continued to procreate, and sin again proliferated. Then out of the earth's population, God chose one man, Abram, who was raised in Ur of the Chaldees in the southern part of Mesopotamia. He later migrated to the northern region of what is now Iraq. It wasn't a chance selection because Abram happens to be in the direct genealogical line from Adam to Christ. Read the genealogies in Matthew 1:1–16 and Luke 3:23–38. It was from northern Mesopotamia that God called Abram to become the father of a great nation. Read Genesis chapter 12. That nation was Israel. Why Israel?

The book of Deuteronomy provides the answer. Moses addressed the children of Israel and told them:

> The Lord did not set his affection on you and choose you because you were more numerous than other peoples, for you were the fewest of all peoples. But it was because the Lord loved you and kept the oath he swore to your ancestors that he brought you out with a mighty hand and redeemed you from the land of slavery, from the power of Pharaoh, king of Egypt. (Deuteronomy 7:7–8)

We learn from 1 Kings 6:1 that the exodus from Egypt occurred 480 years before Solomon began building the temple in Jerusalem. That occurred in the fourth year of his reign, about 965 BC, making the date of the Exodus around 1445 BC.

Two months after the children of Israel crossed the Red Sea on dry land, their journey brought them to Rephidim on the edge of the Sinai wilderness, now the Arabian Peninsula. The next leg of their journey through the wilderness brought them to the foot of Mount Sinai where they camped (Exodus 19:1–2). It was then God called Moses to join Him at the top of the mountain where He gave him commandments to deliver to the nation of Israel. Those commandments became the gold standard by which God held the nation accountable.

God had lofty intentions for the Israelites. His purpose was they follow Him and become a beacon of light to the known world at that time and that through them, He would be made known to every people group, no matter how distant they were from Him.

Through Moses, God challenged Israel to stay true to Him and keep His covenant with them through these words: "Now if you obey me fully and keep my covenant, then out of all nations you will be my treasured possession. Although the whole earth is mine, you will be for me a kingdom of priests and a holy nation" (Exodus 19:5–6).

King Solomon later captured God's intentions when, in his dedicatory prayer for the Temple, he envisioned it becoming a bridge and a beacon to the surrounding heathen nations. Sadly, the temple became a "tower" blocking the vision of God's majestic glory.

But let's turn back to what occurred in the Arabian Desert. Apart from God's voice in the stars (Psalm 19:1), the only verbal communications to live by were delivered from generation to generation. There was no written law the nation of Israel could follow. Only the moral law prevailed as it was ingrained into the human conscience and reinforced by godly men and women.

As sin proliferated after the flood, God wanted Israel to be different from the surrounding nations. He wanted them to have a moral standard by which they could be held accountable. So, about nine hundred years after the flood, amidst the terrifying sights and sounds, God gave commandments to Moses on Mount Sinai for the nation of Israel to follow.

The people quickly became impatient during Moses' absence and persuaded his brother, Aaron, the spiritual leader, to make a golden calf to worship in place of Jehovah God. When Moses eventually descended the mountain with two stone tablets inscribed with the commandments written by God himself, he was angered by what he saw. In his rage at seeing the nation worshipping the calf, he threw the tablets to the ground, breaking them. Literally, he was the first one to break the commandments. God had no option but to recall him to the mountain summit and start the process over. Moses captures those dramatic moments and events in the thirty-second chapter of Exodus.

For the second time, Moses descended Mount Sinai, this time with the stone tablets intact. Turn to the fifth and sixth chapters of the book of Deuteronomy, to the time Moses summoned the nation of Israel to hear him read the commandments he had received from the hand of God.

Listen to his passionate address, "Hear, Israel, the decrees and laws I declare in your hearing today. Learn them and be sure to follow them" (Deuteronomy 5:1).

There were ten specific commandments written on both sides of the two stone tablets Moses had carried up the mountain:

1. You shall have no other gods before me.
2. You shall not make for yourself an image in the form of anything in heaven above or on the earth beneath or in the waters below. You shall not bow down to them or worship them; for I, the Lord your God, am a jealous God, punishing the children for the sin of the parents to the third and fourth generation of those who hate me, but showing love to a thousand generations of those who love me and keep my commandments.
3. You shall not misuse the name of the Lord your God, for the Lord will not hold anyone guiltless who misuses his name.
4. Observe the Sabbath day by keeping it holy, as the Lord your God has commanded you. Six days you shall labor and do all your work, but the seventh day is a Sabbath to the Lord your God. On it you shall not do any work, neither

you, nor your son or daughter, nor your male or female servant, nor your ox, your donkey or any of your animals, nor any foreigner residing in your towns, so that your male and female servants may rest, as you do. Remember that you were slaves in Egypt and that the Lord your God brought you out of there with a mighty hand and an outstretched arm. Therefore the Lord your God has commanded you to observe the Sabbath day.

5. Honor your father and your mother, as the Lord your God has commanded you, so that you may live long and that it may go well with you in the land the Lord your God is giving you.
6. You shall not murder.
7. You shall not commit adultery.
8. You shall not steal.
9. You shall not give false testimony against your neighbor.
10. You shall not covet your neighbor's wife. You shall not set your desire on your neighbor's house or land, his male or female servant, his ox or donkey, or anything that belongs to your neighbor."

Moses concluded his message with these words: "These are the commandments the Lord proclaimed in a loud voice to your whole assembly there on the mountain from out of the fire, the cloud and the deep darkness; and he added nothing more. Then he wrote them on two stone tablets and gave them to me" (Deuteronomy 5:6–22). How God inscribed the commandments on the stone tablets will remain a mystery this side of eternity. Moses only testifies to the fact it was God who wrote them.

Drop down to the sixth chapter: "These are the commands, decrees and laws the Lord your God directed me to teach you to observe . . . so that you, your children and their children after them may fear the Lord your God as long as you live by keeping all his decrees and commands" (Deuteronomy 6:1–2). With one exception, those commandments are repeated in the New Testament. The single exception concerns the keeping of the Sabbath. The letter to the Hebrews explains why. It is because we now find our rest in Christ, a subject I won't expand on here.

In his gospel, Luke records the conversation the Lord Jesus had with a certain lawyer, an expert in the Mosaic Law, who asked what he should do to inherit eternal life. The Lord Jesus replied, "What is written in the law?" The lawyer responded, "Love the Lord your God with all your heart and with all your soul and with all your strength and with all your mind; and love your neighbor as yourself" (Luke 10:27).

The lawyer aced his response.

The apostle Paul later elaborated on what loving our neighbors is all about when he wrote:

> Let no debt remain outstanding, except the continuing debt to love one another, for whoever loves others has fulfilled the law. The commandments, "You shall not commit adultery," "You shall not murder," "You shall not steal," "You shall not covet," and whatever other command there may be, are summed up in this one command: "Love your neighbor as yourself." Love does no harm to a neighbor. Therefore love is the fulfillment of the law. (Romans 13:8–10)

The lawyer's response summed up the Ten Commandments God gave to Moses. The first four commandments cover our relationship to God. The remaining six address our relationship to others. The problem the lawyer faced was that he would never be able to keep those commandments and therefore could not inherit eternal life by attempting to do so. The only way to gain eternal life is through faith in Jesus Christ, not by the works of the Law.

Because of His covenant with them, God specifically honored Israel with being the nation to receive and treasure the commandments until they had been universally acknowledged. The commandments were to be the capstone for civilizations to follow ever since they were given to Moses on Mount Sinai. They did become the standard in many countries as the church and Christianity took the gospel around the world. As a result, millions of people have benefitted from these divine laws honoring God and the sanctity of human life.

The Bible makes it clear sin reigned from Adam to Moses (Romans 5:14) and it was because of man's abject failure to love God and their neighbors that He gave the commandments to Israel. The Commandments became known as the Law and were to be the benchmark by which the nation of Israel was to live and be judged.

With a written code to remind them and convict them when they sinned, they had no excuse. Unfortunately, by virtue of their disobedience and inability to keep the commandments, the Law became a millstone around the necks of the Jewish people. While they were intended to be the moral standard, God knew they were unattainable because of man's sinful nature. He nevertheless expected the Israelites to live obediently, even though they could not do that perfectly. It was only through faith that a person could ever be justified before God, as Abraham himself discovered (Genesis 15:6; Romans 4:3; Galatians 3:6; James 2:23).

Over the centuries, God judged the nation of Israel for their gross disobedience. He withheld the rain, delivered them into the hands of their enemies, and even had them exiled to a foreign land. In Galatians 3:23–24, Paul taught that the purpose of the Law was to make them long for a Savior, for Someone who could give them a righteous standing before a holy God and who would then help them live righteously.

I draw your attention to the Ten Commandments. God gave the commandments to the nation of Israel because He wanted them to love Him supremely and to love those around them. He desired the very best for them and for others.

I sense some of you beginning to sigh, groan, and cry out, "We are not under law; we are under grace. Let's not get legal. Let's not promote the Law that was intended for Israel to follow. It didn't do them much good." Well, would abandoning the Law give us the freedom to sin and break the very commandments God wants us to keep? That would make us lawless.

The critics are right in the sense that keeping the Law could never save us or give us a righteous standing before a holy God. We are not under law but under grace. Grace is undeserved kindness, unmerited favor. Under grace we are governed by the law of *love*—love for God and love for our neighbors.

God's laws are for universal application. We observe the law of gravity, for instance. Try jumping off a skyscraper without a parachute and see what happens. We had better observe laws. The law God gave to Moses was designed to be a tutor, a pedagogue, to lead the children of Israel to Christ and reinforce the fact they could never be saved by attempting to keep the law. The only way a person can be saved is by grace through faith in the finished work of Jesus Christ on the Cross (Ephesians 2:8). Nevertheless, these commandments are a standard for today, particularly if we heed the Jewish lawyer's response to Jesus and what Paul wrote in Galatians 5:14.

God is not a killjoy. He wants us to be joyful. But that only occurs as we live in a right relationship with Him, having first trusted in Christ as the only one who can save us. When he delivered the commandments to the Jewish people, Moses conveyed God's desire to them: "Oh, that their hearts would be inclined to fear me and keep all my commands always, so that it might go well with them and their children forever" (Deuteronomy 5:29).

Do you detect God's heart throb for His ancient people? In the same way, His heart yearns for your love and obedience that it might be well with you.

This begs the questions: What if the Ten Commandments were a standard by which you and I lived today? What if we only worshipped the Lord God instead of the countless things preventing that relationship from becoming intimate and experiential?

What if followers of Christ today devoted more time to God? What impact would that have on relationships and marriages? The Lord Jesus took the matter of adultery beyond our literal interpretation by saying that anyone who looks at a woman lustfully has already committed adultery with her in his heart (Matthew 5:27–28). Incidentally, the reverse is true of women. Men don't have exclusivity when it comes to lust. Women dress provocatively and can be extremely seductive. Both men and women engage in sexual fantasizing. What if we honored our parents; were free of murderous intent, theft, and covetousness; and from bearing false testimony? What if you and I truly loved God with all our heart, mind, soul, and strength, and our neighbor as ourselves? Imagine what a different home, community, and world it would be!

To reiterate, keeping the commandments will never save us. They do, however, reinforce how far short each one of us has fallen and that we need a Savior. The Law can and never will save us. Only Christ can do that. Further good news is the fact that followers of Christ have the enabling power of the Holy Spirit to help them please God by living lives for His praise and glory.

Today in the United States of America, there is increasing opposition to the Ten Commandments. They are generally prohibited from being displayed in federal, state, and community buildings and property. They are banned from being displayed or taught in public schools, despite the fact that many school districts permit the teaching of Islam and most promote the religion of evolution. No wonder America has become increasingly godless, permissive, and violent as more and more people live with almost total abandonment to decency and respect of others and their property.

The "law" God gave to Moses was a comprehensive set of guidelines, given to ensure the Israelites' behavior would reflect their status as God's chosen people. It encompassed moral behavior, their position as a godly example to other nations, and systematic procedures for acknowledging God's holiness and mankind's sinfulness.

An attempt to better understand the purpose of these laws led to the distinction between moral, ceremonial, and judicial laws — a topic beyond the purpose of this book, other than to state they were all included in Jewish practice and are variously described in the Old Testament. Many aspects of our judicial system today are derived from these laws and have become the basis of societal practice. For example, we have laws against murder and theft.

Theft, murder, and violence are becoming rampant in the USA, as well. The Declaration of Independence included the words "life, liberty, and pursuit of happiness" as inalienable rights.

The United States Constitution is one of the most influential legal documents in existence. Since its creation over two hundred years ago, more than one hundred countries around the world have used it as a model for their own constitutions. The Judeo-Christian value system has validity, even though it is being increasingly attacked. As the world worsens, its validity is reaffirmed as the vacuum without it leaves proof that alternative values are drastically deficient in improving individuals and deteriorating world conditions.

While many of the Old Testament laws applied specifically to Israel, some of the health and dietary laws included in the ceremonial laws encompass applicable principles for today. In their book, *None of These Diseases*, S. I. McMillen, MD, and David E. Stern, MD cover extraordinary medical benefits available to those who follow the Bible's teachings. The authors deal with a number of diseases and medical issues. With over one million copies sold, the book has become a classic. Recently revised and updated for a new generation, the book shows how to obtain extraordinary medical benefits simply by heeding God's instructions for healthy living. It covers vital information on issues facing the current generation such as AIDS, STDs, homosexuality, euthanasia, stress, anger, and depression. In an engaging style, peppered with anecdotes from both of their medical practices, Doctors McMillen and Stern take us back to the Bible and show us how to apply our Creator's guidelines to our modern lifestyles.

All I am trying to do is to get you to listen up and pay attention to God's Word. It is priceless and transforming.

As a boy I was encouraged to read, study, and memorize much of Psalm 119. I was taught to pray the eighteenth verse before opening my Bible: "Open my eyes that I may see wonderful things in your law."

As a teenager, I made verse nine one of my life verses: "How can a young person stay on the path of purity? By living according to your word." I still refer to my old King James Bible to read marginal comments I made as a young adult. This is a note I wrote next to Psalm 119:9: "The thought is not that of cleansing from contracted defilement as much as keeping clean in the presence of defilement." That followed a note I had written on the flyleaf of an earlier Bible: "This book keeps me from sin, and sin keeps me from this book."

It wasn't until Robert Constable—at the time the Executive Vice President of Moody Bible Institute in Chicago and long-time elder and Bible teacher at River Forest Bible Chapel in River Forest, Illinois—took me on a tour of the Institute that I learned D. L. Moody had written the same words on the fly-leaf of his Bible. Someone had obviously impressed me by quoting it.

The 105th verse in Psalm 119 stood out like a beacon for me, "Your word is a lamp for my feet, a light on my path." Imagine in those days traveling at night with hands full, maybe a staff in one hand and baggage in the other. You tied the oil lamp to your foot rather than to your head. This prevented you from stumbling and shed enough light on the pathway ahead. God's Word is like that.

I am struck by the many descriptions of God's Word in Psalm 119. For instance, mention is repeatedly made to His law, testimonies, ways, precepts, statutes, commandments, decrees, and judgments—some of the very words Moses used when he delivered the Decalogue to the children of Israel in the Sinai Peninsula.

Consider the first eight verses of the psalm, for example:

> Blessed are those whose ways are blameless, who walk according to the *law* of the Lord. Blessed are those who keep his *statutes* and seek him with all their heart—they do no wrong but follow his *ways*. You have laid down *precepts* that are to be fully obeyed. Oh, that my ways were steadfast in obeying your *decrees!* Then I would not be put to shame when I consider all your *commands*. I will praise you with an upright heart as I learn your righteous *laws*. I will obey your *decrees;* do not utterly forsake me. (Emphasis added)

Psalm 19 sums up the benefits of following these concepts, and is worth noting:

> The *law* of the Lord is perfect, refreshing the soul. The *statutes* of the Lord are trustworthy, making wise the simple. The *precepts* of the Lord are right, giving joy to the heart. The *commands* of the Lord are radiant, giving light to the eyes. The fear of the Lord is pure, enduring forever. The *decrees* of the Lord are firm, and all of them are righteous. They are more precious than gold, than much pure gold;

they are sweeter than honey, than honey from the honey-comb. By them your servant is warned; in keeping them there is great reward. (Psalm 19:7–11, emphasis added)

Imagine if you and I followed these concepts from day to day. Our lives would be very different. Not for one moment am I suggesting we attempt to follow all the laws God gave Israel for specific purposes at the time. The ceremonial laws and many of the dietary laws are not relevant today. We have our own sanitary laws, and food is generally better prepared and preserved.

I spent my very early childhood on a mission station in an equatorial African climate. Refrigeration was non-existent. That made eating meat, particularly pork, virtually taboo unless it was well salted and cooked soon after a pig was killed; otherwise, it would soon be riddled with parasitic worms. Tapeworms commonly grow up to twenty feet in human intestines and have been known even to exceed eighty feet. This is generally not a problem in first-world countries today. Even then, with our food supply being increasing genetically modified, there is an alarming increase in certain diseases. So it may behoove us to pay closer attention to God's dietary laws. This could be significant in third-world countries.

What I am suggesting is that we find principles in the Old Testament that conform to New Testament teaching. What God was looking for in Old Testament times, He is looking for today — hearts that are in tune with Him and each other.

We are on a journey to discover, understand, and do God's will. It all begins with loving the Lord God with everything we've got and loving our neighbors. It means we will not allow anything or anyone to take the place God deserves in our life. We will give Him our time, talents, and treasures. We will not misuse His name, commit murder or adultery, or engage in illicit affairs. We will not steal, give false testimony, or covet.

Wow, that's a lot to expect. Yes, but that is God's gold standard. It is His will for us. We readily acknowledge, however, that keeping them is unattainable in our own strength.

The children of Israel failed miserably, and so do we. While attempts to keep those commandments will never save us, obeying them will keep us from heaps of trouble and pain. The good news is God forgives us the micro-second we place our faith and trust in Jesus Christ for salvation. The blood of Jesus Christ cleanses us from all unrighteousness, and the slate is wiped clean. Once saved, God expects us to live righteously and obey the commands He gave Moses on Mount Sinai some thirty-five hundred years ago. While disobeying any one of those commands will not break our relationship with God through Christ, breaking them disrupts, disturbs, and destroys our fellowship with Him and our relationship with others. It places us outside the circumference of His will. However, there is a process whereby we can get back into the will of God which we will address in due course.

The good news is God has given the Holy Spirit to those who trust in Christ to strengthen them; to convict them when they stray or even think about it; and to enlighten, equip, and empower them to live according to His rules. Furthermore, the Lord Jesus is the only one to have lived a sinless life, and He resides in those who have placed their faith and trust in Him (Ephesians 3:17; Colossians 1:27). God gives us victory through our Lord Jesus Christ (1 Corinthians 15:57). There is no need to live defeated lives. In Christ, we are more than conquerors (Romans 8:37).

All this is a prelude to discovering those aspects of God's will that He has already specifically revealed. It takes time, effort, and diligence to discover them and commitment to understand and obey them. If we are not willing to take the time, we will find God's will elusive.

We are on a journey, a long way from our desired destination. There is still much territory to cover, much dialogue to ensue, and many issues to confront before you will feel confident about knowing and doing God's will.

Start by offering yourself completely to the One who loved you with an incredible love and demonstrated it by sending His only Son to die on the Cross for you. Respond to whatever light God gives you along the way.

Stay on course as we travel toward our next destination. Where you choose to do this is your decision. It could be your bedroom, living room, office, or patio. It could be your favorite picnic spot—beside a river, on a beach, overlooking a lake or ocean, or facing some other majestic scenery. It could be your own backyard, beside your outdoor grill. Ensure it is a quiet spot where you interact with God and His Word. In the meanwhile, take time to pray the truths learned in this chapter into your life.

My Prayer

Heavenly Father, I again approach You in the precious name of the Lord Jesus. I confess I have broken every one of Your commandments to one degree or another, and that I still fall far short of Your divine standard. I have a mammoth task ahead of me. But discovering Your will is something I really desire, so I commit myself to seeking it.

First of all, please help me to love You with my whole being—heart, soul, strength, and mind. Then help me to demonstrate that love to others—my spouse, children, parents, relatives, friends, associates, colleagues, and neighbors; in fact, everyone I come into contact with.

I realize trying to keep Your commandments could never on its own save me. That's why I placed my faith in Your Son,

Jesus Christ. I offer myself as a living sacrifice, just as Paul instructed the Roman believers to do. I want my life to be acceptable in Your sight and to bring You glory.

Father help me desire Your Word. Help me to study it daily, and to practice what I learn. Help me to obey Your Word. I desperately want Your will to be done.

Help me digest what I have learned this far into my journey. Then help me respond accordingly. I want my life to be monumental for You. For that to occur, I need the Holy Spirit's enabling. I pray there will be no obstacle in my life that prevents Him from empowering me to do Your will

I pray all this in Jesus's name. Amen!

Application

The children of Israel spent forty years wandering in the wilderness before entering the Promised Land. In fact, an entire generation died in the wilderness. Think of what might have been had they done a better job keeping God's commandments and been faithful to Him. Israel's entire history reflected their disobedience and reluctance to love God supremely. Even though God loved them, Israel suffered the consequences of their reluctance to follow Him. How does this relate to you today?

As you reflect on this chapter, list some practical things you need to do to demonstrate your love for God and for your neighbors, that is, those who cross your path. What confessions do you need to make? What attitudes do you need to change? What actions do you need to take?

1.

2.

3.

4.

5.

Chapter Six

Where on Earth Has God Revealed His Will?

G old has been prized and accumulated by both ancient and modern civilizations. It was used in the structure and furnishings of the tabernacle in the wilderness as well as the temple in Jerusalem. It has filled vaults, adorned palaces, and been molded into jewelry, ornaments, and vessels. Ships laden with gold have sunk to the ocean floor. Many have risked their lives to find it. Eight of the ten deepest gold mines are in South Africa where excavations extend over 10,000 feet, or two miles, below the earth's surface.

The California Gold Rush began on January 24, 1848, when gold was discovered by James W. Marshall at Sutter's Mill in Coloma. The discovery soon brought some three hundred thousand people to California. The sudden influx of gold into the money supply quickly reinvigorated the American economy.

The psalmist, however, declared that God's laws, testimonies, precepts, commandments, and judgments are more precious and more desirable than gold (Psalm 19:7–10).

In His letter to the Laodicean churchgoers at the end of the first century, the Lord Jesus accused them of trading for the wrong gold. More concerned with financial prosperity, Jesus invited them to buy "gold" from Him in order to accumulate spiritual riches (Revelation 3:17–18). Those professing Christians missed the mark, just like those today who find God's will elusive.

The fact that God has already revealed His will leaves people questioning: "If God has revealed His will, why has hasn't He revealed it to me?" "Why can't I find it?" "Where is it?" "How can I know it?" "Why is it so elusive?"

There are no shortcuts or magic formulas to discovering God's will. My aim is to direct you to the only authoritative place where God's will can be discovered. Get ready to do some digging as we delve into the Bible and discover a few of the golden nuggets relating to God's will.

Over fifty verses in the New Testament address God's will. Two different Greek words, *boule* and *thelema,* are used to describe it. Both words have been translated by the English words *will*, *wants*, or *desires*. This is more fully covered in the appendix where I list all the verses in which the Greek words *boule* and *thelema* appear.

God's desire (thelema) is that men and women be saved.

The apostle Paul wrote to Timothy informing him God desires all people to be saved and to come to a knowledge of the truth (1 Timothy 2:4). This passage has been variously interpreted because the King James translation conveys the impression that God has "willed," meaning predetermined or predestined, the salvation of all men and women, implying that all will be saved.

Only a few people accept Jesus Christ. Most neglect or reject Him. While some are sympathetic to the Gospel, most are apathetic. Atheists deny the existence of God. Agnostics claim nothing is known or can be known of God's existence or nature or of anything beyond material phenomena. They claim neither faith nor disbelief in God and remain neutral.

Despite volumes of extra-biblical evidence, some don't even believe Jesus Christ existed. God nevertheless desires everyone to come to faith in Him through His Son, Jesus Christ.

The Bible makes it clear God loved the world of lost sinners. While that clarion call is sounded, it doesn't mean everyone will respond. Despite the evidence of His miraculous powers, His sinless life, sacrificial death, and triumphant resurrection, most rejected Jesus Christ during His earthly sojourn. The Savior invited all those who were weak and burdened to come to Him (Matthew 11:28). Only a few responded. While on the cross His arms were extended wide. Only a few believed in Him and accepted Him then. It is the same today.

Translations such as the New King James version translates the Greek word *will* as *desires*. The New American Standard Version and the New International Version translate the word as *wants*. So the idea is God wants or desires all men and women to be saved, even the most violent criminal. Some find this offensive.

During the early 1990s I was leading a Bible study in the Gospel of John in the home of Rich and Carol Hamilton in Pittsburgh. At one point, the discussion centered on how a person is saved by grace through faith, not by works. One person mentioned Ted Bundy as an example.

Bundy, one of the most notorious criminals of the late twentieth century, confessed to thirty homicides in seven states between 1974 and 1978. The true victim count is unknown and could be much higher. He also confessed to trusting Christ and experiencing God's forgiveness during an interview with Focus on the Family Founder, Dr. James Dobson, on the day before his execution on January 23, 1989.

At the mention of Bundy's name, Ginny who was struggling to believe in Christ, went ballistic. She cried, "That's not fair," and stormed out of the room. Carol followed her, embraced her, and persuaded her to return to the group.

Ginny listened quietly as some twenty people tried reasoning with her. One quoted two lines from the hymn *To God Be the Glory,* "The vilest offender who truly believes, that moment from Jesus a pardon receives." Is that fair when others who have lived a decent life are never saved? No! It is a reminder, however, that a person is saved by God's grace, His unmerited or undeserved favor, and by His mercy when He withholds what we deserve.

Someone else mentioned the dying thief on the cross, one of two criminals crucified with Christ (Luke 23:39–43). This dying convict acknowledged his guilt, recognized Jesus as innocent, and proclaimed Him Messiah when he said, "Lord, remember me when you come into your kingdom." Jesus assured him he would be with Him in Paradise, not purgatory, that very day.

Death-row convicts teach us God's grace is truly amazing — so amazing it overwhelms human emotion, reason, and comprehension.

The following week, Ginny trusted Christ as her personal Savior and experienced the forgiveness and peace she had been seeking. The change in her life was immediate.

Jesus proclaimed He is the Way, the Truth, and the Life, and that no one comes to the Father except through Him (John 14:6). He also declared that no one could come to Him unless the Father who sent Him drew them to Him (John 6:44).

While God has made provision for people to be saved, the enemy of souls is actively at work, blinding people's eyes so they won't believe (2 Corinthians 4:4). Because all have sinned (Romans 3:23), the Bible teaches everyone is under condemnation until they put their faith and trust in Jesus Christ, and that those who reject Christ will spend eternity in hell.

Just as God constantly reached out to the nation of Israel in Old Testament times despite their open hostility, so He reaches out to people today. He reaches out in many ways, but hearts are hardened, eyes are blinded, and Satan is active. The clarion call of the Gospel goes out to the whole world, but in the end only a portion believes.

The apostle Peter informed Jewish believers scattered throughout the Roman Empire that the Lord does not want any to perish. He wants everyone to come to repentance (2 Peter 3:9). That concept is certainly consistent with God's character, and the words the Lord Jesus spoke in what has probably become the best-known, best-loved, and best-quoted verse in the entire Bible, "For God so loved the world that he gave his one and only Son, that whoever believes in him shall not perish but have eternal life" (John 3:16). That's pretty broad.

The apostle John wrote in his first letter that Jesus Christ is the atoning sacrifice for the sins of the whole world (1 John 2:1–2). That's surely embracive. This verse does not mean everyone will be saved. It does mean that whoever calls on the name of the Lord Jesus will be saved because there is no other name under heaven whereby we can be saved (Romans 10:13; Acts 4:12).

We approach the heart of God to hear as well as feel it beat and throb. We glimpse into the purpose and scope of God's redemptive plan as it unfolded in the first advent of His Son one Christmas night in the hills of Bethlehem some two thousand years ago. It unfolded further some thirty-three years later on a Roman cross on the outskirts of Jerusalem at a place called Calvary, or Golgotha.

God's redemptive plan looked beyond Calvary's cross to include an innumerable host of Christ's followers—all saved by grace and trusting in Him alone for salvation and bringing Him praise and glory. Christ came to redeem us. He did that by offering Himself as a perfect sacrifice on the Cross and shedding His precious blood as the price of our redemption (1 Peter 1:18–19).

Luke tells us Jesus Christ came to seek and to save those who were lost. That embrace includes Jews and Gentiles. Luke mentioned Zacchaeus who was hated by his fellow countrymen on account of extorting excessive taxes from them while working for the Roman government (Luke 19:9–10). He was the last one you would think Christ would seek and save, but He did. Christ can and does save the worst of sinners.

John Newton, a converted slave trader who wrote the hymn "Amazing Grace," probably the best-known and best-loved hymn of all time, is another example of God's great grace. There are countless others. Your own conversion to Christ is a powerful testimony to God's saving grace and power.

I was always impressed when Billy Graham invited those who wished to receive Christ to come forward and stand in front of the podium. They walked down the stadium aisles as the choir sang the hymn, "Just as I Am." It was a moving sight as hundreds responded to the invitation to receive Christ. In the end, people from all walks of life stood beneath the "cross" irrespective of gender, nationality, color, and status in life. A window cleaner could be standing next to a corporate executive. A homeless person could be standing next to a brilliant surgeon. A college dropout could be standing next to a college president. A felon could be standing next to a prosecutor. They were there for one purpose.

Christ attracts sinners to Himself. The Father draws or calls them to His Son. The Holy Spirit begins His convicting work in a human heart without the person necessarily knowing it at the time (John 16:8). The triune God speaks in many ways. God speaks through the spoken Word, through the transformed lives of others, through radio and television broadcasts, and through literature, movies, and song. He also speaks through circumstances and calamities. After hearing Paul and Silas singing praises to God, it took an earthquake for the Philippian jailor to realize he needed to be saved (Acts 16:30).

The Holy Spirit woos people to Christ as He convicts them of sin, righteousness, and judgment to come (John 16:8–11). Jesus compared the Holy Spirit's working to the wind, which normally blows as a gentle breeze. Other times it blows with hurricane and tornado force. Something prompts a person to listen to a Christian radio or television station, attend church, or read a pamphlet or book. They don't know why they are doing it, but they are. The Holy Spirit is at work.

Today, the good news that Jesus saves has gone around the world. Many have accepted the message. Sadly, the majority are indifferent and either neglect or reject it. Some are outright hostile to that message. Only a relatively few place their faith and trust in Jesus Christ.

The book of Revelation makes it clear not everyone will be saved. There will be a day of judgment, when all whose names are not recorded in the Lamb's Book of Life will be thrown into the lake of fire (Revelation 20:11–15).

If you have never received the Lord Jesus Christ as your own personal Savior, I urge you do it right now. There is no other way because salvation is in Jesus Christ alone. Christ came to save the lost. Everyone is lost without Christ as their personal Savior.

God's will (thelema) is that those who are saved be sanctified.

Sanctification is a process and is quite different from regeneration, which has to do with our spiritual birth and entrance into God's kingdom and family. When we trust Christ and are born-again, our lives turn around, and we find ourselves desiring things we never desired before. These include a desire for God Himself. A desire to get to know Him more intimately through His Word and through prayer. A desire to worship Him. A desire to fellowship with other followers of Christ. A desire to sin less and not let sin control or dominate us. A desire to live for God and to introduce others to Him. Sanctification has to do with our spiritual growth, maturity, and conformity to Christ.

The basic meaning of sanctification is that God sets us apart for Himself. Paul plainly teaches once we are saved, we are no longer our own, and our bodies become the temple of the Holy Spirit. The reason is we have been bought with a price (1 Corinthians 6:19–20). Consider the price God paid for your redemption. He gave His only Son as a sacrifice for your sins on the cross. He redeemed you with the precious blood of the Lord Jesus. Once saved, you belong to Christ. That has implications.

My twin sister and I were around eight years of age and living with our missionary parents in Bulawayo, a city in Rhodesia—now Zimbabwe. One day we suspected a visiting missionary family was using our toothbrushes. We set a "trap." They were. We were furious. Those toothbrushes were extremely personal. There was no way we would share them. We had set them apart for our exclusive use. We had "sanctified" them.

In the same way, God has a divine purpose for us and wants us to do His will and live for His honor, glory, and use. It's God's purpose that everyone who trusts in Christ become like Him and be conformed to His image (Romans 8:29). The apostle Peter made it clear we are to be holy in everything we do because God is holy (1 Peter 1:15–16). Peter quoted directly from the Old Testament where God said, "I am the Lord your God; consecrate yourselves and be holy, because I am holy" (Leviticus 11:44–45; 19:2).

The word *holy* (*hágios*) has the thought of being "set apart." When God saved you, He set you apart for Himself. Our response is to set ourselves apart for God. That's difficult to do when we are in a corporate board meeting, locker room, or classroom; at a bachelor or bridal party; on the sports field, military battleground, or in a hospital operating room. There cannot be a split allegiance. We are to live as those whom God has set apart. That makes a believer different and distinct.

Once saved, God does not leave us to our own devices. He gives the Holy Spirit to indwell those who trust in Christ for salvation. The Holy Spirit does several things in those who believe. For instance, He *enlightens* them and helps them understand God's Word and discover His will. He *equips* them to serve Him. He *empowers* them to live for Him. Allow the Holy Spirit to do in you and through you all God purposed for Him to do. He needs to do that without restriction and without reservation.

In his letter to the Thessalonian church, Paul made the ramifications of sanctification clear when he specifically declared God's will is that we should be sanctified; that we should avoid sexual immorality; that each of us should learn to control our body in a way that is holy and honorable, not in passionate lust like the pagans who do not know God. God did not call us to be impure. He called us to live a holy life. Paul continued to write that anyone who rejects this instruction is not rejecting a human being but God—the very God who gives us His Holy Spirit (1 Thessalonians 4:3–8). Wow!

This passage teaches several things.

First, it teaches that followers of Christ who engage in premarital or extramarital sex are living contrary to both God's Word and will. God called us to live a holy life. He set us aside that we might be different. Are you?

Sexual impurity is plainly outside God's will, whether it's having an affair, looking at pornography, participating in sexual harassment and misconduct, sharing off-color jokes, or entertaining impure and lustful thoughts.

Second, the passage teaches us the role the Holy Spirit plays in enabling us to live victoriously. We don't have to yield to temptation. God has made provision for us to soar like eagles (Isaiah 40:31).

I was getting a cup of coffee before a round of golf one morning, when I noticed a sign on the counter that read, *"May you be up to par today"*. I immediately told the attendant I had a better slogan that went like this, *"May today you fly with the birdies and soar with the eagles.*" Birdies and eagles in golf are better scores than par. Yes, we can soar like eagles. We don't have to be grounded all the time.

Third, the passage declares there are consequences for disobeying God's will in this matter. Have you ever wondered why so many things go wrong? Is it because you don't live right, that you haven't confessed your sin and experienced God's forgiveness and cleansing?

The apostle John tells us exactly what to do when we sin. We are to confess our sins. That's not a matter of just saying "I'm sorry." It is agreeing with God that what we did, or thought, was sinful. The process involves *conviction, contrition,* and *change.* Change involves repentance, an about-face, a new direction. When we do that, we will find God faithful and just to forgive us and to cleanse us from all unrighteousness (1 John 1:9).

Sanctification includes God's process of discipline. We are not to treat God's discipline lightly nor lose heart when He disciplines us. He disciplines us because He loves us. While God's discipline may be painful at times, its purpose is to train us so that it produces a harvest of righteousness and peace. Every athlete knows success and victory is the result of discipline, coaching, and training. There can be no gain without pain. Read Hebrews 12:5–11.

You could be responding right now, "Why are you hurling the Bible at me?" Because the Bible is our only authority for faith and practice. Without it, we have no navigational system. Many of the issues, problems, struggles, and pain we experience in life are self-inflicted because of our ignorance of God's Word. Worse than that is knowingly or stubbornly refusing to submit to and obey what God has clearly revealed in the Bible. It is imperative we live within the boundaries God has set. Failure to do that is equivalent to rejecting God. The adage is true. People reap what they sow.

God's will is that we live a life that is consecrated to Him.

God's will (thelema) is that those whom He saves and sanctifies should serve Him.

We all love to be served, wherever it is. We desire the finest possible service at the auto repair shop, store, or dentist's office. We readily embrace others doing something for us, but God expects followers of Christ to serve. We are saved to serve God and others.

The Lord Jesus became our prime example when He told His disciples He did not come to be served, but to serve, and to give His life as a ransom for many (Matthew 20:28; Mark 10:45). He was willing to lay down His own life for others.

On the memorable night of His betrayal, the Lord Jesus asked and answered a rhetorical question, "Who is greater, the one who is sitting at the table or the one who serves? Is it not the one at the table? But I am among you as one who serves" (Luke 22:27). Imagine the guest of honor serving while His disciples lounged at the table.

The apostle Peter expressed it succinctly in his first letter when he gave his readers three commands. They were to love each other deeply. Then they were to offer hospitality to one another without complaining. Thirdly, they were to use whatever gift they had received to serve others. In the process, they would become faithful stewards of God's grace in its various forms.

He then elaborated on what this would look like. When they *spoke*, they were to speak as if their utterances were the very words of God. When they *served*, it was to be with the strength God provides. The purpose was so that in everything God would be praised through Jesus Christ and that to Him would be the glory and the power forever and ever (1 Peter 4:7–11).

There is to be a spiritual and an eternal component to every act of service. God's fundamental purpose in saving us is that we serve Him and glorify Him in the process. That should be the motivation that drives us.

Worshipping and loving God is the greatest way we can serve Him. It is our highest vocation. Worship is a life lived for God's glory 24/7. God never intended worship to be limited to one hour a week in a church or listening to a Christian radio or television program, as convenient as that is.

Worship is a constant attitude. This means everything we do, whether it's at home, school, work, or play, should be for God's glory. We are to worship God whatever circumstance we encounter in life, as difficult as that may be. We are to worship Him in the good times as well as the bad times. We are to live, and if necessary, die for God. He is to be first in everything. Oswald Chambers summed it up well in the title of his classic devotional book, *My Utmost for His Highest*.

We can't serve others effectively if we don't worship God consistently and faithfully. Service flows from a worshipful heart. Worship is the responsive attitude of gratitude to God for all He has done for us. It determines our altitude.

Scripture teaches us to serve others. Paul reminded the Ephesian believers they were God's handiwork, and that they had been created in Christ Jesus for the purpose of engaging in the good works God had prepared in advance for them to do (Ephesians 2:10). He instructed Titus those who trusted in God should devote themselves to doing what is good (Titus 3:8).

Paul told the Galatians believers not to become weary in doing what is good. He gave the picture of a farmer who, because of his diligent labors in plowing, sowing, and cultivating, eventually reaped a harvest. It is this spiritual goal that compels us to take every opportunity to do good to all people, especially to those belonging to the family of believers (Galatians 6:9–10). Our goal is to reap a spiritual harvest.

The writer to the Hebrews challenged his readers to consider ways to reap this spiritual harvest by spurring one another on toward love and good deeds (Hebrews 10:24). We all need to be spurred on.

The fundamental aspect of service is that we first present ourselves wholly to God and place ourselves at His disposal so He can do His work in us and through us.

While the nature and sphere of our service may vary according to our natural abilities, spiritual giftedness, God-given passion, and calling, the meaning of it is always the same. Service begins with the worship of God. This necessitates the presentation of ourselves to Him (Romans 12:1–2). Worship is a life lived for God's glory. That means everything we do should be motivated by worship and be a reflection of worship.

The bottom line is every believer is called to serve God and, in the process, serve others. We are instructed whatever we do, whether in word or deed, it is to be done in the name of the Lord Jesus for the glory of God. It also has to be given with thanksgiving (1 Corinthians 10:31; Colossians 3:17). In a sense, we are saved to serve.

Whether we work in education, the military, corporate world, medical practice, or Congressional chambers, every follower of Christ should be exemplary because they give their best to glorify God. That is our calling. Christ's followers are obligated to do God's will. For this to occur two things are necessary.

God's will first needs to be known, understood, and obeyed. Secondly, the believer needs to be equipped to do or execute God's will through appropriate behavior and service. The writer to the Hebrews expressed this truth in his final benediction: "Now may the God of peace, who through the blood of the eternal covenant brought back from the dead our Lord Jesus, that great Shepherd of the sheep, equip you with everything good for *doing his will,* and may he work in us what is pleasing to him, through Jesus Christ, to whom be glory for ever and ever. Amen" (Hebrews 13:20–21; emphasis added).

Do you live for the praise and glory of God? Do people praise God for you? Allow God to do His work in you, and through you. Serve Him with a willing and pure heart.

Not only is it God's will (thelema) that those whom He saves be sanctified and serve Him, but that they should suffer for Him.

This is a hard concept to swallow. On the eve of His crucifixion, the Lord Jesus warned His disciples they would experience tribulation in the world. In encouraging them to be courageous, He reminded them of the fact He had overcome the world (John 16:33). This made a victorious life possible, even though it could involve martyrdom. Many a martyr has died triumphant, glorifying God to the end.

We all experience trials and tribulations of one kind or another. The choicest of saints suffer as the result of sin entering the world. Many suffer incredible pain and discomfort. Not all suffering, however, is the result of our sins, as Job in the Old Testament discovered. We live in a fallen world. Despite the tremendous advance of medical science, we will catch the common cold or contract fatal diseases.

During an early draft of this chapter, I met with the manager of a local bank in a small town in southwestern Pennsylvania. He was also the mayor of the town. He told me that within a twelve-month period a few years prior to my visit, fifteen of his forty staff contracted cancer. He believed his town had the highest cancer rate in the United States and attributed it to the community becoming the dumping ground for infectious contaminants transported from other districts in the northeast region of the country.

That's a man-made disaster beyond the seeming control of residents. However, I am thinking of suffering for Christ, suffering because we are His followers. Hard as it is to grasp, suffering is within the parameters of God's will.

The apostle Peter told his readers if it was God's will, it was better to suffer for doing good than for doing evil (1 Peter 3:17). He followed up by telling those who suffer according to God's will to commit themselves to their faithful Creator (1 Peter 4:19). Regardless of the circumstance, we are to be resolute, resilient, and resourceful.

Peter had earlier warned his readers they would experience unbelievable trials and persecutions. This was at the time resistance to Christians under Nero, the Roman Emperor, was beginning to ferment. Fires of persecution were burning on the horizon. Despite that, Peter commended them for their great joy, even though they were grieving because of all kinds of trials. He told them these trials proved the genuineness of their faith, which was of greater worth than refined gold. The end result would be praise, glory, and honor when Jesus Christ is revealed (1 Peter 1:6–7). That makes it worth it all.

Persecution and death are the ultimate sacrifice for allegiance to the Lord Jesus Christ. No matter how difficult and painful, martyrs accept death as their response to Calvary's love.

The finest characters are always forged in the furnace of affliction. Triumph can result from tragedy. Blessings can come from buffetings. Persecution tests our faith, and makes us stronger and purer. Millions of Christian martyrs throughout the history of the church, right up until the present time, testify to that.

I recommend you read *Foxe's Book of Martyrs* by John Foxe. The book is a history of the lives, sufferings, and triumphant deaths of early Christian martyrs.

Paul wrote to the Philippian church that it had been granted to them on behalf of Christ not only to believe in Him, but also to suffer for Him (Philippians 1:29). It is inevitable followers of Christ will suffer just because they are Christians. Paul told the

Christians in Thessalonica not to be unsettled by the trials they were experiencing for the simple reason they were destined for them (1 Thessalonians 3:3). No one said the Christian life is a bed of roses. Rose bushes have thorns.

Christians will suffer by virtue of following the Lord Jesus who was Himself despised, rejected, forsaken, and crucified by men who hated Him. Some believers suffer ridicule and ostracization because they are Christians. Former friends shun them because their new lifestyle and commitment is diametrically opposed to theirs. Others suffer loss of promotion or firing because of their Christian principles. Still others suffer persecution and death—the ultimate sacrifice for allegiance to the Lord Jesus Christ. No matter how difficult and painful, we should be willing to accept suffering as our response to Calvary's love. Peter made it clear any such suffering is solely on account of being Christians (1 Peter 3:14; 4:16).

Hebrews chapter eleven chronicles the lives of Old Testament saints who suffered unbelievable persecution, just as many do today. Count it a privilege if you are called to suffer that way.

God's will (thelema) is that those whom He saves and sanctifies, and who serve Him and suffer for Him should submit to authority.

The apostle Peter told his readers that, for the Lord's sake, they were to submit to every human authority—whether to the emperor as the supreme authority, or to governors who are commissioned by Him. This was for the simple reason it was God's will that, by doing good, they would silence the ignorant talk of foolish people (1 Peter 2:15). In other words, God's will is that a Christian's conduct removes any possible cause for slander or accusation. A believer is to live above reproach.

Paul makes this clear in his letter to the Romans when he told them everyone should be subject to the governing authorities because there is no authority God hasn't established. Consequently, whoever rebels against authority is rebelling against what God has instituted. To experience freedom from authorities, one generally only has to do what is right. Rulers are God's servants, agents of wrath, to bring punishment on the wrongdoer. For that reason we are to submit to the authorities—not only to avert punishment, but also as a matter of conscience (Romans 13:1–5).

We know all too well, however, that some rulers engage in the indiscriminate slaughter of innocent victims. Examples of rulers like that are Adolf Hitler in Germany in the 1930s and 1940s and Pol Pot in Cambodia during the late 1970s. Pol Pot ordered the slaughter of millions of his countrymen, mostly the educated, skilled, and urban dwellers.

There are more examples from the twentieth century when communist regimes were responsible for the brutal killing of millions of people. Today militant Islamists are just as vicious in their slaying of innocent people, many of whom are professing Christians. The despot Genghis Khan in the thirteenth century destroyed anyone and everyone who opposed him. His armies left deserts behind them in their campaigns across Central Asia into Europe. We know all too well many in local governments and in authority over us today are corrupt and ungodly and break the very rules they are supposed to enforce. Nevertheless, laws are for our benefit unless they violate God's rules.

Daniel's three friends—Shadrach, Meshach, and Abednego—refused to bow down and worship the golden image King Nebuchadnezzar had made and set up in the province of Babylon. As a result, they were thrown into a fiery furnace. They were willing to pay the supreme sacrifice for civil disobedience. They realized they served God, not a despotic king. In the end, God delivered them unharmed from their fiery ordeal. Read the entire story in the third chapter of Daniel.

Daniel himself was thrown into a den of lions for refusing to respond to a conspiracy against him. Fellow commissioners had the Persian king, Darius, issue a ban on praying to the God of heaven. That didn't deter Daniel from continuing to pray three times a day. Read that story in the sixth chapter of Daniel.

There are times when *civil* disobedience is necessary, when Christians have to take a stand for their faith, whatever the cost. Unlike many countries today, we in America are guaranteed freedom of speech by the Constitution. While many protests have become violent, Christians are required to always speak and act in conformity to the Word of God.

The book of Acts records the occasion when Peter and John refused to heed the proclamation of the Jewish leaders in Jerusalem, who forbade them preaching in the name of Jesus. This was *religious* disobedience. Read the account in Acts 4:14–20.

Martin Luther showed *ecclesiastical* disobedience when, on October 31, 1517, he nailed his ninety-five theses on the door of the Wittenberg Cathedral and started the Protestant Reformation which spread through Europe.

Oppressive communist regimes in Asia and Europe forced churches and Christians who refused to register with the authorities to go underground...until they were discovered. Many were jailed; some were killed.

There are times when followers of Christ must obey God rather than men and be willing to pay the price for doing so. With increasing opposition to God and the Bible, the church in Europe and now in North America has become less relevant to a secular society. Christian business owners are beginning to experience opposition and protests for their convictions. In the wake of increasing violent protests and rising anarchy in America, it is imperative followers of Christ not only be prepared to suffer for their faith but maintain the highest standard of Christian conduct, commitment, and charity.

God's will (thelema) is that those whom He saves and sanctifies, serve Him, suffer for Him, submit to authority, and be thankful.

Paul told the Ephesians they were to "always give thanks to God the Father for everything, in the name of our Lord Jesus Christ" (Ephesians 5:20). It is difficult to give thanks <u>for</u> everything. Paul meant what he wrote, though. Giving thanks is the zenith of Christian experience and commitment. You ask, "How is it possible to give thanks for adversity and trials, for sickness and pain?" It's only when we realize these things can, and should, bring us closer to God.

I am constantly amazed at how some believers rejoice in adversity. Only God, in His grace, can enable them to live triumphantly. The apostle Paul proved over and over again that God's grace was sufficient for every trial, burden, and pain he experienced. He bore the marks of his suffering in his body (2 Corinthians 12:9; Galatians 6:17).

James provides the answer to the question, "Why should we give thanks for adversities?" He told his readers to count it pure joy whenever they faced various trials because the testing of faith produces perseverance, maturity, and sufficiency (James 1:2–4). For that very reason we should thank God for adversity, conflict, and strife. They build faith and character.

Consider the Jewish believers to whom Peter wrote. They rejoiced greatly, even though they had to suffer grief in all kinds of trials. While they weren't pleasant, those very trials proved the genuineness of their faith. What made their faith invaluable was the fact it will result in praise, glory, and honor when Jesus Christ is revealed (1 Peter 1:6–7). Faith refined by fires of persecution is more precious than gold.

Peter continues this thought in his second letter. He wrote we are to add several things to our faith, such as goodness, knowledge, self-control, perseverance, godliness, mutual affection, and love. If we possess these qualities in increasing measure, they will keep us from being ineffective and unproductive in our knowledge of our Lord Jesus Christ (2 Peter 2:5–8). Turning trials into opportunities to glorify God makes us effective and fruitful. That's why we are to be thankful for everything. Some of life's greatest lessons are learned in the furnace of affliction.

It's equally difficult to give thanks <u>in</u> every situation. In exasperation, we may be tempted to say, "Lord, you have no idea what I am going through." You may just have been diagnosed with cancer or learned your spouse or child was killed in an auto accident. You may have unexpectedly lost your job or told your salary would be cut for the company to survive. You may have just learned your home was completely gutted by a fire or destroyed by a landslide.

Whatever the reason, God's will is that you be thankful. Giving thanks is one of the three evidences of being filled with the Holy Spirit (Ephesians 5:18a–21).

I have known many people over the years who became more effective for God and whose entire ministry perspectives changed as the result of illness, loss of a job, or the tragic loss of a loved one. God can and does use these things for His greater glory.

Paul gave the Thessalonian believers three staccato-like commands: "Rejoice always. Pray continually. Give thanks in all circumstances for this is God's will for you in Christ Jesus" (1 Thessalonians 5:16–18). This is powerful.

Interestingly, it is only through Christ we can rejoice. Joy is the fruit of the Holy Spirit, the result of His work in us. Psychologists and psychiatrists who know nothing about the working of the Holy Spirit are baffled when committed followers of Christ rejoice in adversity. To them, it is an inexplicable paradox. Giving thanks in every situation is extremely challenging. Followers of Christ learn to do this because it is God's will and because the Holy Spirit provides the enablement.

The Lord Jesus is always our prime example. We see this clearly on the night He was betrayed when He celebrated the Passover Supper with His disciples, and instituted what we now call the Lord's Supper, Eucharist, or Communion.

I refer you to Matthew's rendition of the event:

While they were eating, Jesus took bread, and when he had given thanks, he broke it and gave it to his disciples, saying, "Take and eat; this is my body. Then he took a cup, and when he had given thanks, he gave it to them, saying, "Drink from it, all of you. This is my blood of the covenant, which is poured out for many for the forgiveness of sins. (Matthew 26:26–28)

It is truly amazing as the Lord Jesus was anticipating the horrors of Calvary and the agonizing pain of crucifixion, He was giving thanks for it. He gave thanks for the bread, a symbol of His body about to be broken for us, and for the cup, a symbol of His blood about to be shed for us. What a legacy.

God's will (thelema) is that those He saves and sanctifies, who serve and suffer for Him, submit to authority, and are thankful should know His will.

Discovering God's will is difficult for most Christians because they don't go to the right place—the Bible. That's the first place to go because that's where we find ninety-eight percent of God's will outlined for us. However, we need to look and search diligently for it, even though it's there in plain sight. In the process, we will be greatly blessed, particularly as we bring our lives into conformity with God's expectations.

We have already noted the Holy Spirit is there to help us, lead us, and enable us to carry out God's will. Knowing God's will is much more than seeking His guidance as to which college to attend, which career to follow, which job to accept, which car or house to buy, or who to marry. God's will impacts our lives and our effectiveness in this life. Get the ninety-eight percent done and the rest will be much easier.

Two passages of scripture help make this clear.

> Show me your ways, Lord, teach me your paths. Guide me in your truth and teach me, for you are God my Savior, and my hope is in you all day long . . . Good and upright is the Lord; therefore he instructs sinners in his ways. He guides the humble in what is right and teaches them his way. All the ways of the Lord are loving and faithful toward those who keep the demands of his covenant. (Psalm 25:4–5; 8–10)

> I will instruct you and teach you in the way you should go. I will counsel you with my loving eye on you. (Psalm 32:8)

Let's summarize the implications of what we have considered in this chapter.

First, God desires men and women respond to the Gospel message, put their faith in Christ alone for salvation, and be saved. God's desire is so strong and His love for the world so great that while we are still sinners, He allowed Christ to die for us and bear our sins in His own body on the Cross at Calvary (Romans 5:8; 1 Peter 2:24).

This desire has world-wide implications. The Great Commission Christ gave to His disciples after His resurrection was for them to go into all the world, preach the Gospel, and make disciples of all nations. This involves baptizing them in the name of the Father, Son, and Holy Spirit.

Baptism is an act of obedience, an act of faith, and an outward sign of an inward belief. The commission also involves teaching disciples to obey everything Jesus commanded them. It was also given with the promise that He would be with them always, even to the very end of the age (Matthew 28:19:20; Mark 16:15; Luke 24:47; Acts 1:8).

This begs the question: Are you involved in the Great Commission? As followers of Christ, we need to align ourselves with God's plan of salvation and do what we can to ensure the Gospel is spread to as many nations and peoples as possible. You may never be a foreign missionary, but you can be a missionary where you are; whether it's in your home, school, place of work, or neighborhood. We are all to let our light shine for the glory of God. Be involved in missionary endeavors. This means participating in missions, praying for missions, and supporting missions.

Second, the fact God wants us to be holy means we need to do everything we can to set ourselves apart for God. God set us apart for Himself the moment He saved us. We need to make it a reality. To this end, we need to allow the Holy Spirit to do His conforming work in us, so we become more Christ-like. We need to read God's Word on a regular basis and learn to encounter Him through His Word and prayer. We need to obey the command to be holy.

The Harvey Weinstein scandal broke as I was first drafting this chapter. Harvey Weinstein is an American film producer and former film studio director. He and his brother, Bob Weinstein, co-founded Miramax, which produced several popular independent films. Winner of an Academy Award and seven Tony Awards, Weinstein is the epitome of what's wrong with Hollywood. In October 2017, the company's board of directors fired him following numerous allegations of sexual harassment and sexual assault against him.

Hollywood has long been antagonistic to Christianity, produces a ton of filthy movies, promotes biblically illicit lifestyles, and yet is "adored" by most Americans. The sad thing is so many followers of Christ know the movies they watch better than their Bibles. They know the actors better than Bible characters. They can tell you all about the movies they have seen but can rarely narrate Bible stories and passages. They are generally more influenced by Hollywood than a biblical worldview and a biblical lifestyle. This should be flipped. We need to take time to be holy.

The revelation of the Weinstein's scandals opened a Pandora's Box for leaders in the political, military, media, and corporate worlds to be publicly identified for their sexual abuses. This led to their firings, resignations, and shame.

As followers of Christ, we need to live above reproach.

Third, we need to serve God. We do this by offering ourselves completely to Him and praying, "Lord, what do you want me to do?" That leads to a willingness to do whatever He lays on our heart. As an old hymn says, "There's a work for Jesus only you can do." God has already equipped us to serve. He has made us unique and given us natural talents and spiritual gifts. These enable us to do whatever He has called us to do. But we need to develop those gifts, talents, and passions in order to serve Him effectively in whatever sphere He places us.

Fourth, as you take your stand for Christ, it is inevitable you will suffer persecution of one type or another. People may avoid you. Others may reject you and oppose you. Not because you are obnoxious, mean, or nasty, but simply because you are a follower of Christ. They just don't like what you stand for. Some people may hate you for aligning yourself with Christ. Some may kill you as a result, as many have experienced.

Fifth, you need to submit to the civil authorities God has placed over you, providing you don't compromise your faith or biblical conviction.

My one-time neighbor in Pittsburgh, who chaired the zoning board for the borough in which we lived, came to me for counsel one day. In putting a shed on his property, a minister of the Gospel had violated two ordinances. The shed exceeded the borough specifications. It was also placed on the boundary line, instead of seven feet inside his property. In several zoning board meetings, the minister argued God had told them that was the size of shed to purchase and he had placed it exactly where God had instructed him.

The zoning board was frustrated and began questioning whether they should argue with God, so strong were his assertions. I directed my neighbor to the passage in Romans 13 and recommended he confront the minister with it. He did. The shed was removed and replaced with one that complied with zoning requirements. The new shed was also placed the required distance inside the boundary line.

There's a sequel to that story, however. Several months later, my neighbor approached me again with another dilemma the zoning board faced. For ministry purposes, the same minister had requested a zoning exception allowing him to place a large satellite dish on his property in order to receive global television programs. Only a much smaller dish was permitted by the zoning laws. At my encouragement, the zoning board made an exception in this instance.

Sixth, the psalmists give us many reasons to be thankful. Take Psalm 107 for instance. The psalm begins with, "Give thanks to the Lord, for he is good; his love endures forever." The psalmist gives four word pictures of people crying out to the Lord in their distress. In each instance, the Lord heard their cries and delivered them. The psalmist then urged them to give thanks to the Lord for His unfailing love and His wonderful deeds for mankind.

How often are we ungrateful for God's goodness and unfailing love? Believers need to be thankful for all God has done and is doing on their behalf. We are to count our blessings each day.

Seventh, we need to discover God's will. That's what this book is all about, to help you *know, understand, and do* God's will. A line in the Lord's Prayer states, "Your will be done on earth as it is in heaven." Your response and mine should be, "Lord, let your will be done in my life.

With a little effort, anyone with serious intent can discover for themselves what the Bible says about God's will. You don't have to be a theologian to discover it.

I was teaching this course way back in 2005 and had concluded with the lesson on David asking God to teach him His will. I briefly covered the intent of the next week's lesson on God's revealed will. This prompted Chris Mason, a member of the class, to research the topic on his own.

Later in the week, Chris emailed me his findings and wrote, "Gordon, I found the will of God is clearly and explicitly revealed to us in the pages of sacred Scripture. God's will is that we be . . ." and he briefly covered the points in this chapter. Upon concluding my lesson the next Sunday, Chris commented, "Gordon, I can't believe you used my outline." I didn't. I had my lesson already prepared.

Chris then went on to ask the question, "How can I know the will of God? How can I know God's will for where to live, the right investment to make, the right job to take, or the right person to marry? The Bible does speak to these questions. God has given us principles in His Word to obey. By being diligent in the study of His Word, God will teach us to know His will."

Chris concluded by quoting 2 Timothy 3:16–17, "All Scripture is God-breathed and is useful for teaching, rebuking, correcting and training in righteousness, so that the servant of God may be thoroughly equipped for every good work." The thrilling thing was that with a little determination and research, Chris discovered these truths on his own. You too can discover them with a little effort on your part.

Can we discover every aspect of God's revealed will overnight? No. It takes a lifetime. My aim is to help guide you to pertinent passages of Scripture that highlight some of the things God has revealed. The rest is up to you to discover. That's your assignment until God calls you home.

We will be covering the questions Chris asked later on our journey. But first, we will work on discovering some divine imperatives in the Bible.

My Prayer

Dear Heavenly Father,

I worship You! I thank You and praise You for all You have done for me and for all You have revealed to me in Your Word. I thank You for bringing me to the point when I heard Your call and came running to Your Son, Jesus Christ. I thank You for the work of the Holy Spirit in my life. I thank You the Lord Jesus was willing to do Your will and give His life as a ransom for me. A thousand thanksgivings aren't enough. My only response is to say I am ready to do Your will. But there is still so much I need to learn about it.

Father, please help me fulfill the purpose for which You saved me. Help me to tell others about what Jesus can do for them. Help me to be holy and to serve You at home and at work, and to do everything for Your glory. Help me take a stand for You and to be uncompromising in a world that is antagonistic to You. I am willing to suffer for You if necessary. Make me a worthy ambassador as I represent You in my home, workplace, and community. Help me to be even more thankful than I am; I owe everything to You.

Dear Father, I pray all this in and through the name of Your dear Son and my Savior, the Lord Jesus Christ. Amen!

Application

We have covered a lot of ground in this chapter. Take each of the seven aspects of God's will that have been discussed and write out your action plan regarding each one. You may want to divide this into one, two, and three-year goals.

1.

2.

3.

4.

5.

6.

7.

Chapter Seven

Being filled with the Knowledge of God's Will

It is possible to feel brain-overload at times. We feel every-thing, including the kitchen sink, is being hurled at us. We try to remember every bit of trivia that comes our way. We attempt to absorb more than our brains seemingly can process. Our minds get cluttered with irrelevant junk, and we wonder what we can do with the massive amount of information our brains are accumulating. We leave little room for the important things of life. The mass amount of information becomes meaningless and useless. Yet we continue to cram everything we can into our craniums—everything *except* the Word of God.

We need to consider everything in light of eternity's values, not earthly ones. Then, we need to consider how we can use the earthly knowledge we have accumulated, in whatever field we are skilled, for the extension of God's kingdom and for His honor, glory, and praise.

Paul prayed that the Christians in Colossae be filled with the knowledge of God's will in all spiritual wisdom and understanding (Colossians 1:9). He gave his reasons why that prayer was so vital. Do you want to live a life worthy of the Lord Jesus? Do you want to please Him in every way? Do you want your service for God to be fruitful? Do you want to grow in the knowledge of God? Do you want to live above the daily grind and be empowered and enabled to patiently endure the struggles of life? Do you want to be able to give joyful thanks to your heavenly Father? Then make Paul's prayer your very own.

An excellent way to be filled with the knowledge of God's will is to discover the divine imperatives in the Bible. An imperative is something that is essential or urgent; it is a factor or influence making something necessary, not something to be avoided or evaded. The Bible is full of imperatives. Each imperative represents an aspect of God's will. The more imperatives we discover, the more knowledgeable we will become.

God's Word is His primary source of communication today. That's why it is so important to read the Bible. We should read it on a regular basis, not just as a matter of routine or duty. We need to "hear" what God is saying. While it's good to hear biblically based expository sermons and to read about the Bible, many Christians make that a substitute for reading the Bible for themselves. Personal Bible reading is the best way to get to know God, to develop personal intimacy with Him, to experience Him in daily life, and to talk with Him as one friend with another.

Our aim during this stage of our journey is to discover some divine imperatives. Prepare for an inductive Bible study as we consider four passages of Scripture. I will furnish the text and challenge you to discover the divine imperatives contained in the passage. Once you have identified them, the next thing to do is to prayerfully implement them into your life. The greatest thing we can ever do is to *know, understand,* and *do* the will of God.

Bible reading should never be haphazard, as one guy discovered one morning when he prayed, "Lord, show me what you want me to do today." With his eyes still closed, he opened his Bible and placed his index finger on Mathew 27:5 which read, "So Judas threw the money into the temple and left. Then he went away and hanged himself." Not sure if that's what God wanted him to do, he tried again. This time his finger fell on Luke 10:37 where Jesus told the expert in the law, "Go and do likewise." Confused, the man tried once more, this time resting his finger on John 13:27 where Jesus told Judas after he had taken some bread at the Last Supper, "What you are about to do, do quickly." Unfortunately, that's the way many people approach Bible study—a verse here and another verse there.

In my teenage years, I was encouraged to preface my Bible reading with the psalmist's prayer, "Open my eyes that I may see wonderful things in your law" (Psalm 119:18). Then I was taught to ask the following eight insightful questions whenever I read a passage of Scripture.

- Is there any reference to God, our heavenly Father, the Lord Jesus, or the Holy Spirit?
- Is there anything for which I should be thankful?
- Is there any sin for me to confess and forsake?
- Is there any restitution I need to make, such as an apology?
- Is there any example for me to follow?
- Is there any lesson for me to learn?
- Is there any prayer for me to pray?
- Is there any task God wants me to do?

Answering those questions lifts Bible reading to new levels, particularly as you let the truths learned transform you.

The first passage to consider is taken from the fourth chapter of Ephesians. Begin by asking God to open your eyes. You are in the process of discovering God's will for your life. Underline each imperative as you discover it. Finally, check your personal discovery against those I have identified.

Therefore each of you must put off falsehood and speak truthfully to your neighbor, for we are all members of one body. In your anger do not sin. Do not let the sun go down while you are still angry, and do not give the devil a foothold. Anyone who has been stealing must steal no longer, but must work, doing something useful with their own hands, that they may have something to share with those in need. Do not let any unwholesome talk come out of your mouths, but only what is helpful for building others up according to their needs, that it may benefit those who listen. And do not grieve the Holy Spirit of God, with whom you were sealed for the day of redemption. Get rid of all bitterness, rage and anger, brawling and slander, along with every form of malice. Be kind and compassionate to one another, forgiving each other, just as in Christ God forgave you. (Ephesians 4:25–32)

Have you done everything asked of you? Let's proceed and reflect on the fourteen imperatives I identified:

1. **Put off falsehood.** A falsehood is something false or untrue, the act of lying or making false statements, the lack of conformity to truth or fact; pretending to be what we aren't; a lack of transparency.

2. **Speak truthfully.** This is the standard judges require in our courts when we are under oath to speak the truth, the whole truth, and nothing but the truth. That's the standard Christ's followers should adhere to every day, not because we are under oath, but to demonstrate obedience to God's Word. Be a person of integrity. Never shade the truth or tell that "white" lie.

3. **Don't sin when you are angry.** This implies there is legitimate and illegitimate anger, or righteous and unrighteous anger. We need to deal with anger in a way that is holy and righteous.

Moses was justifiably angry when he descended the mountain where God had given him the Ten Commandments and saw the people worshipping a molten image (Exodus 32:19–20). Nehemiah was legitimately angry when, after an absence of thirteen years, he returned to Jerusalem and discovered people violating several of God's commandments (Nehemiah 13:6–29). Jesus was angry when He confronted merchants selling their wares in the temple precincts. In addition to price gouging, they were disrupting the worship of God (Matthew 21:12–13). His anger demonstrated righteous anger.

Righteous anger is the correct response to an injury suffered personally or by a third party. The injury could be physical, emotional, financial, or relational. It is legitimate for a woman to be angry when she is violated and raped, and for others to feel anger for the perpetrator. It is legitimate to feel anger when a loved one or friend is murdered, when people are oppressed, and when children are sold into slavery and abused by those seeking their own debauched pleasures. We should be angered by reports that one in three women in the United States have been sexually abused or assaulted. We should be angered when everyday thousands of babies die in the name of "freedom of choice."

The Lord Jesus cautions us against developing a seething anger in our hearts. Unrighteous anger leaves us bitter, seeking retaliation and revenge. But Jesus taught us to love our enemies, to reach out to those who hate us, to bless those who curse us, and to pray for those who mistreat us (Luke 6:27–28).

Paul specifically instructed the Christians in Rome not to take revenge but to leave things for God's appropriate response. He told them to give their enemies food and drink whenever they were hungry or thirsty. He summed up his injunction by telling them not to be overcome by evil but to overcome evil with good (Romans 12:19–21). While we may willingly accept this standard when mistreated and hated for Christ's sake, it may be difficult to accept if the injury or injustice is for another cause.

The apostle Peter reveals the response of the Lord Jesus to the personal injury He suffered on the Cross. "Christ suffered for you, leaving you an example that you should follow in his steps. . . . When they hurled their insults at him, he did not retaliate; when he suffered, he made no threats. Instead, he entrusted himself to him who judges justly" (1 Peter 2:21–23). On the Cross, Jesus prayed, "Father, forgive them, for they do not know what they are doing" (Luke 23:34).

The Lord Jesus had every right to be angry, but He knew exactly why He was suffering and was willing to experience it for you and for me.

4. **Don't let the sun go down while you are still angry.** This may be a problem in certain climates where the sun barely shines and during certain seasons when darkness falls early. Paul is simply telling us to get our anger resolved as quickly as possible—the same day if you can. Anger is like a cancer. It eats away the soul. Resolve issues quickly. Terrible things are born from anger. Anger ruins relationships, destroys the soul, and leads to things never imagined.

5. **Don't give the devil a foothold.** In military terms, it's called a beachhead. A beachhead is the area that is the first objective of a military force. It is the landing place on an enemy shore chosen to secure a position that will be used

for further advancement. The devil will take advantage of every situation you give him and will use it against you. Satan loves it when followers of Christ engage in questionable pursuits and activities, when they look at pictures and scenes that inflame the imagination, and when they frequent places their feet should never tread.

6. **Don't steal.** Stealing is more than shoplifting, cheating on expense accounts and taxes, embezzling, or robbing a bank. It includes stealing someone else's reputation, honor, dignity, virginity, and integrity. It also includes robbing God of the *time, talents,* and *treasures* due him.

   After withdrawing several hundred dollars from my bank ATM one day, I counted an extra twenty-dollar bill. When I went into the bank to report it, the teller's response surprised me, "No one has ever come in to say they received too much." It's hard to believe I was the only one to do so. I certainly didn't want bank robbery on my conscience or resume.

7. **Work. Do something useful with your hands.** We should all work and not rely on others. Idleness can lead to stealing, something we are taught to avoid. The underlying purpose in working is not only for the provision of our own needs but to have something to share with others in need— those less fortunate, privileged, and blessed. Our work should be useful, honorable, and legal. Instead of *taking*, we are *giving*. What a turnaround of thought.

8. **Don't say anything that is unwholesome.** In other words, watch your language. Avoid saying anything detrimental to anyone's physical or moral well-being. Don't be foul-mouthed or engage in indecent talk. Don't tell off-color jokes. Avoid expletives. Don't use "locker room" language. Avoid gossip. Let your conversation be above reproach. Be different. Let your light shine, even in the darkest situations.

9. **Let your speech be edifying.** Don't tear people down; build them up. Avoid harmful words. Look for something positive in a person's life, something God is doing, and give due affirmation and praise. Be an encourager, never a destroyer. Our tongues can be dangerous weapons.

10. **Don't grieve the Holy Spirit.** Like any person, the Holy Spirit, the third person of the Godhead, can be grieved by what we do and say. Here are three rules to follow: recognize His presence, respect His person, and rely on His power. Avoid anything and everything that restricts Him from working in your life. As believers, the Holy Spirit indwells us and follows us wherever we go. He enlightens, equips, and empowers us. Grieving the Holy Spirit restricts what He is willing, waiting, and wanting to do in us and through us.

11. **Get rid of all bitterness, rage and anger, brawling and slander along with every form of malice.** While that is a lot, it is essential we address these six sins because they are dangerous, devastating, and deadly.

    Like anger, bitterness also destroys the soul. Rage can have disastrous results. Brawling can lead to many a slugfest. Slander can ruin reputations and land the slanderer in court. Malice takes revenge.

    What's the answer? The Holy Spirit's control. He wants to produce His fruit in us. He anxiously waits to do so. Paul describes the fruit of the Spirit as "love, joy, peace, forbearance, kindness, goodness, faithfulness, gentleness, and self-control" (Galatians 5:22–23). This is the antithesis of what characterizes so many.

12. **Be kind.** We all need to be kind in word and action. What a different world it would be if we showed kindness. Think of the impact on our homes, schools, workplaces, churches, communities, cities, counties, and country. The anomaly is

that we crave God's loving kindness without demonstrating it in our own lives.

13. **Be compassionate.** Compassion is a feeling of wanting to help someone who is sick, hungry, or in distress. It is a feeling of deep sympathy and sorrow for someone stricken by misfortune. It is a strong desire to alleviate suffering whether physical, emotional, financial, or spiritual. The Lord Jesus was filled with compassion when He saw people living and wandering about as sheep without a shepherd. While some people are especially talented and gifted to be compassionate, this imperative is binding on every follower of Christ. We are to be tender-hearted, large-hearted, warm-hearted, and loving-hearted; not cold-hearted, cruel-hearted, or even heartless.

14. **Forgive as God in Christ forgave you**. You might say, "There's no way I am going to forgive him or her after what he or she did or said." You don't have an option because you are commanded to forgive. It is a divine imperative. Disobedience results in being out of God's will. We relish God's forgiveness on one hand but are often reluctant to forgive another.

What is your response now you have identified the divine imperatives in this passage? Are you still serious about *knowing, understanding,* and *doing* God's will? Relax; not every passage has as many divine imperatives, so don't be deterred from reading God's Word.

If you wish to do further research on your own, I suggest you start with the first verse of the fourth chapter of Ephesians and pick out all the divine imperatives leading up to the passage we have just considered. You will be amazed at the number of imperatives in this chapter alone. The Bible is full of them.

While the next selections will be shorter, there is enough in what we have just considered to keep you busy for quite a while. Don't skip over the passage too quickly. Ask God to search your heart. Pray the psalmist's prayer: "Search me, God, and know my heart; test me and know my anxious thoughts. See if there is any offensive (wicked or hurtful) way in me, and lead me in the way everlasting" (Psalm 139:23–24). Don't concern yourself with anyone else. Deal with the issues in your life first.

What problems in your life need addressing right now as a result of this first study? Maybe it's unresolved anger or the fact you are often untruthful or dishonest. It could be foul language from time to time. Maybe you have a problem with bitterness and rage. Maybe it's a lack of kindness and compassion. Or, maybe you have a problem forgiving someone, even yourself. It would be wise to address these issues before reading any further.

God's will is that we be conformed into the image of Christ. No amount of effort on our part alone will accomplish it. We need the divine enablement the Holy Spirit provides.

Imagine how different our lives would be if we were Spirit-controlled, if we prayed God would transform us and conform us by the renewing of our minds (Romans 12:1–2). The word *transformed* comes from the Greek word for metamorphosis. Metamorphosis is the process that leads to an outward, permanent change. Think of the process whereby an ugly caterpillar changes into a beautiful butterfly. That's the process God wants us to experience as He transforms us into someone beautiful.

Only God can make us into the person He wants us to be. Reliance on our own resolve and efforts leaves us frustrated. God wants to work in our lives. He gave the Holy Spirit to indwell us the moment we placed our faith and trust in His beloved Son. He never leaves us to our own devices. In addition, He has made every provision for us to live victoriously and to be more than conquerors through Him who loves us (Romans 8:37).

I often refer to five rules for reading the Bible, which has often been likened to a mine full of treasures. Are you looking for God's treasure in the Bible? Dig it up. Write it down. Pray it in. Live it out. Speak it forth. Make sure you pray into your life what you have just discovered from the passage we have considered. Then ask God to help you live out the truths you have learned. This way, you will realize the life-transforming power of God's Word.

In my book, *Authentic Christianity*, on page 307, I refer to the last two verses in this passage, and then suggest a prayer:

Lord, as I read your word, I am conscious of the fact that I am harboring some bitterness and anger because of the way "Jack" treated me the other day; it was totally uncalled for—I did nothing wrong, yet he lashed out at me. I realize bitterness and anger are sins, so I confess them to you right now. I ask you to forgive me and to help me love "Jack" despite what he did to hurt me. Help me to bear no malice toward him and enable me to freely forgive him if he ever asks for my forgiveness. Heavenly Father, I am so grateful that you forgave me my sins because of what Christ did on the cross for me. It would be unreasonable for me not to forgive "Jack" in return even though it is always difficult for me to forgive others. Help me to dismiss that incident from my mind so that I won't be bothered by it again. Lord, help me put the incident behind me and forget it.

Then, Lord, I realize that I am not always kind to people. I sometimes say unkind things. At times, my heart is hard and callous, and so I often take people for granted. Forgive me, Lord! I pray for a heart that's kind and tender, large, generous, understanding, and forgiving. I so much want to be kind-hearted, tender-hearted, and large-hearted. Lord, you know that I don't want to be cold-hearted, hard-hearted or cruel-hearted. Sometimes, Lord my heart is broken; please fix it.

Father, I thank you that I have learned so much from your Word today. Please help me to obey it and to practice it. I am amazed that you would forgive me and I am so thankful that you gave your Son for my sins. Help me to freely forgive just as you freely forgave me in Christ. I pray all this in the name of the Lord Jesus. AMEN!

It is time for our second passage.

In the fifth chapter of Matthew, we have what has become known as the Beatitudes. The Beatitudes are eight blessings recounted by the Lord Jesus in His Sermon on the Mount. Each beatitude is a proverb-like proclamation, without narrative. Each one is precise and includes a topic forming a major biblical theme. We pick up the passage at the tenth verse:

Blessed are those who are persecuted because of righteousness, for theirs is the kingdom of heaven. Blessed are you when people insult you, persecute you and falsely say all kinds of evil against you because of me. Rejoice and be glad, because great is your reward in heaven, for in the same way they persecuted the prophets who were before you. You are the salt of the earth. But if the salt loses its saltiness, how can it be made salty again? It is no longer good for anything, except to be thrown out and trampled underfoot. You are the light of the world. A town built on a hill cannot be hidden. Neither do people light a lamp and put it under a bowl. Instead they put it on its stand, and it gives light to everyone in the house. In the same way, let your light shine before others, that they may see your good deeds and glorify your Father in heaven. (Matthew 5:10–16)

Identify the two imperatives in this passage before reading any further. Then, you can proceed.

The first imperative is that you are to "*rejoice and be glad*" when people insult you, persecute you, and falsely accuse you because of your relationship to Jesus Christ. Persecution is not new. The prophets in the Old Testament were persecuted. Tradition has it that, with the exception of John who died of old age, every one of the apostles suffered martyrdom. This doesn't mean we will necessarily be martyred. It does imply some will be opposed, ostracized, and rejected because of their faith in the Lord Jesus. The injunction is that we rejoice under the circumstances.

Don't be mad. Don't be sad. Be glad! James instructed his readers to be joyful whenever they encountered various trials because adversities strengthen our faith and produce steadfast endurance (James 1:2–4). Peter picked up on this theme in his first letter when he commented on the Jewish believers who were experiencing various trials on account of their faith greatly rejoicing (1 Peter 1:6–7). This anomaly makes the Christian faith unique. Joy is the fruit of the Holy Spirit (Galatians 5:22).

The second imperative is that we *let our light shine* before others, so they will see our good deeds and glorify our Heavenly Father. Christ is the light of the world (John 9:5). Our planet would be really dark today had Jesus not come into the world on that famed Christmas night. Consider the impact the Gospel has made in countries where it has been proclaimed. Jesus brings light into the lives of those who trust in Him.

When we witness for Christ by life and by lip, we let our light shine for Jesus. Every believer should be a point of light in a world darkened and destroyed by sin and Satan. Satan's intent is to keep people blinded to the glorious message of the gospel lest they believe (2 Corinthians 4:4).

Imagine every believer in a community letting their light shine for God. It would be like a city on a hill that cannot be hid. The light that shines the furthest is the light that shines the brightest nearest home. So, let your light shine brightly for God. We may be the only gospel our friends, family, colleagues, and acquaintances ever read. Let people around you know you are a Christian. Often, you won't have to tell them. They will know it by your life and by your love. I heard someone say one time that there are five gospels—Matthew, Mark, Luke, John and us.

As a child I was introduced to the gospel song "This Little Light of Mine" written for children in the 1920s by Harry Dixon Loes. The song urges us to let our light shine for Jesus until He comes, and to let it shine around the world.

This song still impacts me today.

The implication of this imperative is clear. We are to let our lives shine for God's glory wherever we are, whatever our situation, and whatever our occupation. If necessary, be the single point of light in your home, neighborhood, and workplace. Let your life shine for Jesus.

It's time to consider our third passage. Turn to the thirteenth chapter of John's Gospel for our next imperative. You know the rule by now. Read the passage. Reflect on it. Find the imperative. Then pray it into your life.

When he was gone, Jesus said, "Now the Son of Man is glorified and God is glorified in him. If God is glorified in him, God will glorify the Son in himself, and will glorify him at once. My children, I will be with you only a little longer. You will look for me, and just as I told the Jews, so I tell you now: Where I am going, you cannot come. A new command I give you: Love one another. As I have loved you, so you must love one another. By this everyone will know that you are my disciples, if you love one another." (John 13:31–35)

Have you found the divine imperative in this passage?

We are to love one another as Christ loved us. Loving one another is not an option. It is a command. It is God's will. God loves us unconditionally. This means our love for others must be unconditional.

I have lifted the following thoughts from my book, *Authentic Christianity*, found on pages 53–55, where the Holy Spirit is addressing the Church in Ephesus.

"The Greek New Testament uses three different words for love; agape, phileo and storge. Eros, the common word describing a depraved and sensual love, was never used in the New Testament. It was too sensual and too erotic.

Agape is the highest and the noblest word for love in the Greek language. It expresses the essential nature of God (1 John 4:8, 16). The noun agape and verb agapeo describe God's attitude toward His own Son (John 17:26), toward mankind generally (John 3:16; Romans 5:8), and toward believers in the Lord Jesus Christ (John 14:21). Agape also determines the correct attitude of believers toward each other (John: 13:34) and the unsaved (1 Thessalonians 3:12; 1 Corinthians 16:14; 2 Peter 1:7). Agape love delights in giving and keeps on giving when the loved one is unresponsive, unkind, unlovable and unworthy. Agape love is unconditional.

Phileo, on the other hand, denotes a tender, affectionate love, and was generally the word for family devotion.

While phileo is also used of God's love for the Lord Jesus (John 5:20) and for believers, it is never used in a command for men to love God. We are to "agapeo" God! Phileo is a love that responds to kindness and appreciation shown.

Storge denotes natural affection or natural obligation. It is used of the affection one has for their spouse, child or pet.

Love can be known only from the actions it prompts. If there are no actions, there is no love. We know God is love because His actions demonstrated it and the giving of His Son on our behalf proved its sacrificial nature. God's love flows from His essential being and is the result of exercising His divine will in making a deliberate choice and decision to love.

Love for God is evidenced by actions and commitment to worship, to praise, to give thanks, to serve, to give sacrificially and to live in obedience. Love for others is demonstrated by ministering to various needs, engaging in deeds of kindness and by giving encouragement.

Christian love for others is not an impulse from feelings, a natural inclination or shown only to those for whom some affinity is present. Love is an attitude, a conscious choice, a deliberate decision, and always evidences itself in actions. That is why we are not only to love with words, but with deeds (1 John 3:18).

The Lord Jesus gave His disciples a new commandment to love one another, and His love for them was to be their constant pattern (John 13:34; 15:12, 16). The believers were to continually abide in Christ's love (John 15:9), because this was the only way they could prove to the world they were genuine disciples (John 13:35). It is impossible to love God and hate another person. In fact, if we don't love one another, we don't love God (1 John 4:20).

The apostle John clearly got the message and encouraged his own readers to love one another, because love is characteristic of God. Furthermore, loving with agape love is proof that one is born again and knows God (1 John 4:7). Because God first loved us, we are under divine compulsion to love one another (1 John 4:11).

Scripture outlines three tests of our love; loving God, loving fellow believers and obedience. Several times the Lord Jesus commanded His disciples to love one another—a single mention would have been sufficient to make it imperative (John 13:34; 15:12, 17). Christ then identified the ones who loved Him as those who obeyed His commandments (John 14:21). The apostle John wrote: "We know that we love the children of God when we love God and observe His commandments. (1 John 5:2)

Pray God will make you a loving person, that agape love will characterize you, and that you practice it every day because this is God's will. You are required to love God. You are also commanded to love your neighbor.

Madalyn Murray O'Hair (1919–1995) was an American atheist activist. She was the founder of the organization American Atheists, served as its president from 1963 to 1986, and is best known for the lawsuit that led to a landmark Supreme Court ruling ending official Bible-reading in American public schools in 1963. O'Hair became so controversial that in 1964 *Life* magazine referred to her as "the most hated woman in America."

O'Hair made a comment one time to the effect that the Lord's army was the only army she knew that kicked its wounded. As she observed the church, she saw nothing that appealed to her. Unlike the song, "They will know we are Christians by our love" she saw strife and division.

While there is enough here to keep you busy for quite a while, we will consider one more passage before we close this chapter.

Then the eleven disciples went to Galilee, to the mountain where Jesus had told them to go. When they saw him, they worshiped him; but some doubted. Then Jesus came to them and said, "All authority in heaven and on earth has been given to me. Therefore go and make disciples of all nations, baptizing them in the name of the Father and of the Son and of the Holy Spirit, and teaching them to obey everything I have commanded you. And surely I am with you always, to the very end of the age." (Matthew 28:16–20)

In these verses, known as *The Great Commission*, the Lord Jesus gave His disciples three imperatives before ascending back into heaven.

First, they were to go and make disciples of all nations. This imperative implies a clear presentation of the Gospel. Faith comes by hearing and hearing by the Word of God (Romans 10:13–17).

Second, they were to baptize those who believe in the name of the Father, Son, and Holy Spirit. Baptism is the outward expression of an inward faith. It is the badge of allegiance to Christ. It identifies a believer with Christ (Romans 6:3–5). In many countries, Christians are tolerated—until they are baptized.

Third, they were to teach believers to obey everything He had taught them. Luke records the practice of the early church, a practice that became a model for believers throughout the centuries. "Those who believed were *baptized* and they devoted themselves to the *apostles' teaching* and to *fellowship,* to the *breaking of bread* and to *prayer*" (Acts 2:41–42; emphasis added). These practices contributed to the incredible growth of the early church.

It is essential followers of Christ be well instructed in the Word of God and be grounded in the historic doctrines of the Christian faith. The Bible is foundational and transformational.

Fellowship is an attempted translation of the Greek word *koinonia* for which we have no English equivalent. The word means a sharing of one's self with another. It conveys a partnership. Just as Peter, James, and John were partners in their fishing business before Jesus called them, so believers are joint partners with God and with each other. The word implies community, hence the phrase "community of believers." As believers, we share in each other's joys and griefs, in the good times as well as the bad. Believers need each other. There is a bonding together. Each believer contributes to the spiritual, social, emotional, and physical welfare of another. They encourage one another.

Breaking bread refers to the sacred act of communion. In communion, we demonstrate the oneness we share in worshipping together. We also celebrate the life, death, resurrection, and ascension of Christ. We even look forward to His return.

The early church was a powerful church because it was a *pure* church and a *praying* church. There is nothing like the corporate prayer of a church. That's when things happen. The early church took every opportunity to pray in their homes and to participate in the public prayers of the church (Acts 4:31; 12:5). Prayer is to believing what breathing is to life. Christians and churches today desperately need prayer for spiritual life support.

The implications are clear. The Great Commission is Christ's mandate for the church today. We are to proclaim the gospel and disciple believers. We are to ground believers in the faith and equip them to disciple others who believe.

Look for the divine imperatives whenever you read God's Word. Underline them. Make comments in the margins. Make a list of God-glorifying goals, and then pray them into your life. Put them into practice. Reading God's Word should have practical outcomes.

Much of the Bible is written in narrative form and tells the story of God's dealing with mankind, largely through His chosen people Israel in the Old Testament. While many of God's commands in the Old Testament were written specifically to Israel to help them in particular situations, there are many valuable principles to be learned. The book of Proverbs, for instance, is full of advice and wisdom that will save us from heaps of trouble, despair, and brokenness. Much of the New Testament is also written in narrative form, especially the four Gospels and the book of Acts, but contained within those books are priceless principles we need to learn in order to be effective followers of Christ.

Get into the habit of reading God's Word daily; otherwise, the chances of personally discovering His will become extremely slim. Start with a few minutes each day. While helpful, don't rely on sermons and books. Go to the Book of books yourself. There is no way you will learn everything God wants you to know overnight. It takes a lifetime, and even then no one has "arrived."

The passages of Scripture we have explored together should keep you busy for quite some time. Discipline yourself to look for the divine imperatives when you read God's Word. Ask God to help you obey them.

Our journey so far has taken us into some of the mountain heights of Scripture where the climb has been steep. We have descended into the valleys where we experience the mundane situations of life. In the process, we have learned where God's will for our lives is to be found. The Bible is the only book that has withstood the tests of over three thousand years. No other book has been scrutinized and challenged as the Bible has been. Over the centuries the Bible has been banned, banished, and burned, yet it remains the world's best seller. No other book has transformed lives, communities, and countries the way the Bible has. The Scriptures testify of Christ (John 5:39). They have brought light into the darkest regions and hope into hundreds of millions of lives over the years. As archeology and science prove the Bible's accuracy and veracity, we can trust it as never before. It's the only place where we can find God's will outlined for us. That's why I have focused so heavily on God's Word.

The Bible is unlike any other book. It is truly unique. It is not just a book. It is a library of sixty-six books written over a period of fifteen hundred years in three languages by forty different authors living some sixteen hundred miles apart. One of its most remarkable qualities is the unity of its overall message.

Some have referred to the seven wonders of the Bible being its formation, unification, age, sale, interest, language, and preservation. The way in which it grew is one of the mysteries of time. It is the most ancient of books, the world's best seller, the only book read by all classes, written largely by uneducated men, and the most hated of all books. Yet it continues to exist because the Word of God shall stand forever.

Shepherds, kings, scholars, fishermen, a tax collector, doctor, prophets, a military general, a cupbearer, and a priest all penned portions of Scripture. Their purposes for writing differed. Some wrote to record history. Others wrote to offer spiritual advice, moral instruction, pronounce judgment, or predict future events. They wrote from palaces, prisons, places of exile, and more while recording history, laws, poetry, and proverbs. In the process they expressed their emotions, anger, frustration, joy, and love. Yet despite this marvelous array of topics and goals, the Bible maintains a flawless consistency and never contradicts itself or its common theme.

That's why I have directed you to the most precious of books, the only book that will withstand the passage of time.

This concludes the first half of our journey where we have learned that ninety-eight percent of God's will can be discovered in the divinely inspired Scriptures. We have by no means exhausted those Scriptures. I leave it to you to continue reading and searching for every aspect of God's will contained in His sacred Word. It involves serious reading and study. There is no greater thrill than to personally hear God speak through His Word. Seek the Bible daily. You will find it transformative, particularly as you prayerfully seek to implement what you learn. Don't just read the Bible. Apply it.

During the third stage of our journey, we will consider the practical aspects of knowing and experiencing God's will in the various circumstances of life. We will focus on guidelines for experiencing God's guidance and direction. We will consider the experiences and testimonies of others and help answer the many questions on your mind.

My Prayer

Heavenly Father,

I worship You and thank You for who You are. Your love is amazing, Your faithfulness is unchanging, and Your mercies are new every morning. I want to worship You 24/7. I do that by offering myself, everything I am, as a living sacrifice, holy and acceptable to You. I can only do that because Jesus loved me and gave Himself for me.

I confess my sins and every instance where I fall short of knowing, understanding, and doing Your will. I want to be more like You in word and in deed. I pray that my life will be a reflection of Yours.

Please make me a blessing to others as I live out Your will. May they, as they see Jesus in me, be drawn closer to You. I pray that those who don't know You will come to know You as I share the gospel with them. I pray Your Word will transform me the way a caterpillar is changed into a butterfly.

Consideration of the verses I have just studied has renewed my mind. Let them transform my life. I have learned so much I never knew before. I want to be the person You want me to be. I know I can never achieve that on my own, so I ask for Your help and for the enablement of the Holy Spirit. I want to take everything I have learned in this chapter to heart. I desperately want to do Your will. I have learned so many aspects of it that I never knew before, and have a much clearer understanding of what You want me to be and do. May Your will be done in my life.

Father help me spend more time praying these truths into my life before I continue the journey into the next chapter, as eager as I am to get there.

I pray and ask all these things in the precious and worthy name of the Lord Jesus. Amen!

Application

You may need to take a time-out to consider how to digest and apply what you have learned in this chapter. You may decide to reread the chapter. You will probably want to spend more time in prayer as you seek to respond to the divine imperatives and their implications. You may also want to seek the advice and support of a more mature believer to help you grapple with the truths encountered. You may need to reaffirm the relevance of the Bible to daily living and to *knowing, understanding,* and *doing* the will of God. You may even want to start rereading this book from the beginning. You are at a critical juncture in our journey together. Make the most of it before rushing into the next stage of the journey.

Part Three

Experiencing God's Guidance

Considering practical steps for experiencing God's direction on a daily and long-term basis.

Chapter Eight

The Secret to Experiencing God's Guidance

Serious followers of Jesus Christ want to know God is guiding them, as a shepherd guides his sheep. They yearn to know the secret of divine guidance. Many believers, however, seldom seek God's direction. They consider themselves self-sufficient and capable of determining their own destinies, believing they know best what makes them successful. Skeptics deny almost every possibility that God can or will direct their lives, even to the point of resistance.

The issue of divine guidance raises legitimate questions. "Is it really possible to experience God's guidance and direction? How can we possibly know what the right thing to do every time is? Why are things we never anticipated or planned happening to us right now when we asked God to guide us? How do we get out of the hole we dug for ourselves? Does God guide us without our knowledge? Does He ever overrule our decisions? Should we pray about every single decision?"

There are at least three popular misconceptions regarding divine guidance. The first is that God thinks solely in terms of geographic locations. Does He want us living in New York, Chicago, Dallas,

Los Angeles, or Miami; in North or South America, Africa, Asia, or Europe? The second misconception is that God only guides missionaries, pastors, and those in fulltime Christian service. Many consider God's guidance has little relevance to those in the marketplace, to professionals, and to stay-at-home moms. The third misconception is that God's will is so frustrating and elusive that it's not worth pursuing.

I recall sitting one Saturday afternoon with my parents in a Bible conference in Ayr, Scotland. Although I was only eleven years old at the time, I will never forget an illustration the preacher gave that day. He told the story of a Scottish sea captain who, despite violent storms, raging waves, and cloudy skies, successfully steered his ship into the harbor when others wrecked.

His secret was simple. He looked for three lights to guide him. One light was on a pier inside the harbor, the second outside the harbor precincts, the third on the hill overlooking the harbor. "My secret," he said, "is to steer my ship until I have those three lights in line."

The preacher went on to elaborate, "There are three lights to guide us in our Christian life. The first is the Word of God. The second is the deep inner peace generated by the Holy Spirit. The third is the unfolding of outward circumstances that confirm our deliberations and prayer requests. When those three lights are aligned, we know we are in the will of God."

The burning question on your mind right now may be, "How, then, does God guide me, and how do I align those three lights in my life?" In this chapter, we focus on the first light, God's Word. The Bible is our compass to navigate us through calm and stormy seas, our lamp to keep us from stumbling, our plumb line to keep us from leaning, and our anchor to keep us from drifting.

To help answer your questions, I draw your attention to two verses that have become life-verses for countless numbers of believers over the centuries and possibly millennia. Make these verses your divine compass.

Trust in the Lord with all your heart and don't lean on your own understanding; in all your ways submit to him, and he will make your paths straight. (Proverbs 3:5–6)

In order to better appreciate the wisdom contained in the verses, I combined several translations, including the Amplified Bible (AMP) Darby Translation (DARBY), The Message (MSG), and the Revised Standard Version (RSV), into the following rendition:

Trust, confide in, and confidently rely on the Lord with all your heart—from the bottom of your heart. Do not lean or rely on your own insight, intelligence, or understanding. In all your ways submit to him, recognizing and acknowledging Him. In other words, listen for God's voice in everything you do and everywhere you go. Then he will direct your paths making them straight, plain, and smooth as He removes obstacles blocking your way. He is the one who will keep you on track.

No wonder these verses have been called the "polar star" for every Christian. The polar star, also known as Lodestar, is a name of Polaris, the star seen with the naked-eye, closest to the earth's north celestial pole. Because of its property of remaining in a fixed position throughout the course of the night, the star is regarded as the infallible guide for those who use the stars for navigation. God's Word is infinitely more infallible than Lodestar and can, and should, be trusted as the guiding star for your life.

Our text contains a promise that God will guide us, direct our steps, and sovereignly cut out the path He wants us to take.

However, the promise is conditional. It is based on three prerequisites key to understanding the secret of God's guidance.

A prerequisite is something that is required as a prior condition for something else to happen or exist. Industry experience is needed to secure certain jobs. A college degree in a certain discipline is necessary to securing a position in a particular field. Board certification is required to practice certain professions. In the same way, certain prerequisites must be met before the promise that God will direct our paths takes effect. The prerequisites involve a decision, a danger, and a devotion.

There Is a Decision to Make

The decision centers on a command to be obeyed, on the prerequisite you trust in the Lord with all your heart. This imperative precedes the realization of the divine promise and calls for an implicit trust. Are you willing to trust the Lord? Are you really serious about trusting the Lord?

There is the *initial act* when we come before God for the first time, admitting we are sinners needing a Savior. It was at that moment we realized we would never make it to heaven on our own, and so we placed our faith and trust in Jesus Christ alone for salvation. We accepted His death and blood shed on a Roman cross as atonement, or payment, for our sin. That was the moment we exercised saving faith, when God saved us, forgave us, pardoned us, reconciled us to Himself, and justified us. Justification is the process whereby our holy God, on the basis of the meritorious work of Christ on the Cross, declares a guilty hell-deserving sinner not guilty. It was the moment when the Lord Jesus took up residence in us, and our bodies became the temple of the Holy Spirit (Ephesians 3:17; 1 Corinthians 6:19).

Trusting the Lord should be a *constant activity*. Having trusted Him for salvation, we now trust Him for our sanctification, the process whereby we are conformed into the likeness of Christ. This is an ongoing process as we allow the Holy Spirit to do His work in us and through us, to mold us and make us into the person God wants us to be.

Trusting the Lord should be a daily activity. We are to live each day by faith. We are justified by faith. The faith needed for our salvation is the faith needed for daily living, not saving faith—that was once for all—but living faith. Paul told the Colossian Christians, "Just as you received Christ Jesus as Lord, continue to live your lives in him" (Colossians 2:6). Those believers received Christ by faith. Now they were to live by faith. That requires trust.

Trusting God means having faith that He knows best. It means trusting His Word is never wrong. It means obeying His Word when it clashes with our own desires, instincts, beliefs, and culture.

If you have ever been involved in Christian camping, you probably participated in a "faith" walk. It can be a scary experience on a dark night, with rough terrain and terrifying obstacles. In addition, the participants are blindfolded and walk in single file as they anxiously grip the waist of the person in front of them. The leader is the only one who can see. Even then, he or she is carrying a flashlight. It is a tremendous lesson in trust.

In the same way, we are to follow the Lord and trust Him, even when we can't see the path ahead. We are to trust Him when the circumstances are bleak, like the unnavigable obstacles. We are to trust Him when we are experiencing our darkest days and nights. We are to trust Him when the days are bright and cheerful. The Lord is with us through every circumstance of life.

Trusting the Lord also calls for a *consistent attitude*. Whatever plans we make, we need to trust the Lord to lead us and guide us. He knows the way. It's easy to live each day without ever consulting God, following our own instincts and relying solely on the world's wisdom and way of doing things. We need the attitude of constant trust in the Lord, not just when we are in trouble and things are not going our way.

The apostle James states this philosophy well:

Now listen, you who say, "Today or tomorrow we will go to this or that city, spend a year there, carry on business, and make money." Why, you do not even know what will happen tomorrow. What is your life? You are a mist that appears for a little while and then vanishes. Instead, you ought to say, "If it is the Lord's will, we will live and do this or that." As it is, you boast in your arrogant schemes. All such boasting is evil. If anyone, then, knows the good they ought to do and doesn't do it, it is sin for them. (James 4:13–17)

There will be instances when we prayerfully make plans, trust God for the outcome, and then wonder why they are not materializing. We become frustrated and maybe angry, little realizing God may be overruling our decisions and leading us in a different direction. We need to trust Him through the darkest and most painful circumstances.

While it is essential that we trust God in every situation, there will be occasions when you must admit, "Lord, I know I can't do this on my own. I desperately need your help to get me through this ordeal." Quoting the Lord Himself, the writer to the Hebrews put it succinctly: "I will never desert you, nor will I ever forsake you, so that we confidently say, The Lord is my helper, I will not be afraid. What will man do to me?" (Hebrews 13:5–6).

The first prerequisite calls for an explicit trust and commitment. We don't have an option. Obedience is essential. Just as we are to give *thanks* with all our heart (Psalm 138:1) and *love* God with all our heart (Luke 10:27), so we are to *trust* the Lord with all our heart (Proverbs 3:5).

My point is simply this: trusting the Lord with all our heart does not mean we recklessly abandon common sense. I had a good friend whose niece got caught up with a wild charismatic group and believed God would miraculously save her if she drove her car at high speed into a tree. She tried it but was killed instantly. Common sense still prevails. We can't defy laws of gravity, such as jumping off a high rise building without a parachute and expect God to protect us.

Scripture specifically instructs us not to put our trust in human beings who cannot save for the simple reason that, on the day they die, their plans come to nothing. On the contrary, those whose help is the God of Jacob and whose hope is in the Lord their God will be blessed. He is the Maker of heaven and earth, the sea, and everything in them. He is forever faithful (Psalm 146:3–6).

We are to trust the Lord, not a political party or military power, as good as they might be. We are not to trust in people, as faithful and loyal as they might appear. We are not to trust in riches, pensions, investments, and IRA's, as secure as they might seem. Our trust must be in the Lord.

I tell the story of the father who endeavored to teach his young son a lesson in trust. He placed him on a high ledge and told him to jump into his outstretched arms promising to catch him. The little guy was understandably nervous and afraid. Finally, at his father's constant bidding, the boy jumped. But at the very last moment his dad took a step back letting him crash to the ground. Winded and wounded, the boy cried, "Daddy, why did you do that?" His father replied, "To teach you not to trust anyone—not even your father." That response prompts the inclination to rely on our judgment. It's difficult to trust the Lord when friends, family, and advisors have disappointed us.

Scripture teaches we need trusted counselors. Plans fail for lack of counsel but succeed when many advisors are involved (Proverbs 15:22). The counsel of godly men and women who live by biblical values is priceless. Never try going it alone. While surrounding ourselves with good mentors, our trust must ultimately be in the Lord. This calls for an unconditional surrender with no reservations, no back door exits, and no escape bridges. Are you willing to make a decision that momentous? William Borden did.

The following is a quote from my book, *Authentic Christianity*, found on pages 312–313.

Born in 1887, William Borden was the heir of the famous Borden Dairy estate. As a graduation gift from high school in 1904, his parents sent him on a world cruise. Borden had trusted Christ through the ministry of D. L. Moody, and as he traveled through Asia, the Middle East and Europe he was struck by the spiritual darkness in which people lived. In one of his earlier letters to his mother he wrote, "I think God is calling me to be a missionary." In a later letter he wrote, "I know God is calling me to be a missionary!" A close friend expressed amazement that he was literally throwing everything away.

Upon returning home, Borden enrolled in Yale University where he was instrumental in starting prayer and bible study groups on campus. He was active in street evangelism and greatly impacted the New Haven community for Christ. During his college years Borden wrote in his personal diary, "Say 'no' to self and 'yes' to Jesus." While still a student at Yale, Borden renounced his fortune in favor of missions and wrote two words on the flyleaf of his Bible—"NO RESERVES." He wanted to trust God for everything in his life.

Borden felt called to go to China and work with Muslims there. Upon graduation from Yale he received many lucrative job offers, including the opportunity to run the multi-million-dollar family business. But he was determined to follow God's call to the mission field. He again opened his Bible to the flyleaf, this time writing "NO RETREATS."

"On December 17, 1912 Borden set sail for China but stopped in Egypt to study Arabic to be better equipped to work with Muslims. While in Egypt, however, he contracted spinal meningitis and died on April 19, 1913 at age twenty-five. After years of schooling and training everything seemed wasted. However, after his death one of his friends received his Bible and turning to the flyleaf he found written under "NO RESERVES" and "NO RETREATS" were the words, "NO REGRETS."

While God may not call you to the foreign mission field, He is looking for a similar all-out commitment like that William Borden made to live for Christ. Are you ready and prepared to follow hard after God regardless of your job? Biblical standards apply there, too. It will be worth it all when one day we see Jesus!

While initially drafting this chapter, I happened to visit my good friend, Tim Colussy, in his office in Bridgeville, Pennsylvania. Tim is the president of Colussy Chevrolet, the oldest Chevrolet dealership in the USA, dating back to 1918. Upon graduating from college, Tim attended a Bible college for a year, thinking God might be calling him to foreign missions. Instead, he felt God calling him to be a "missionary" in the marketplace. He committed himself to the family business with the purpose of glorifying God there and using his influence to help expand God's kingdom.

Are you willing to trust God with your entire life? That's a decision only you can make. Regardless of your past—that's behind you—make the decision today to fully trust the Lord from this day forward. It's the first prerequisite to experiencing God's direction.

There Is a Danger to Avoid

Relying on our own resources and wisdom is dangerous. Scripture specifically tells us not to lean on our own understanding. This is variously translated as "do not rely on your own insight, understanding, or intelligence." That is so easy to do.

We are taught to think independently to reach the zenith of our chosen careers by relying on our own acumen, ingenuity, and hard work. Success seldom equates, however, to personal satisfaction. There's always more to achieve. Personal success is sometimes achieved at the expense of dishonoring God and failing to bring Him praise and glory. Success on its own cannot satisfy the deepest longings of the soul. Within the human heart there is a void, a cosmic loneliness, only God can fill. Many have amassed great fortunes, only to die miserable and penniless.

In 1923, there was a meeting of some of America's most powerful men. The venue was the Edgewater Beach Hotel in Chicago. The men were the leaders of their respective industries and some of the most successful businessmen at that time. The meeting was said to have been both a celebration of their success as well as an opportunity to plan their future exploits and dominance. Attending the meeting were eight financiers and power brokers who, it was reported, controlled more wealth than the United States Treasury at the time. Their success stories were published and inspired many to follow their examples. The list of men was impressive.

- Arthur Cutten, the nation's greatest wheat speculator.
- Albert Fall, the Secretary of Interior in President Harding's cabinet.

- Leon Fraser, the president of the Bank of International Settlements.
- Howard Hopson, the president of the largest utility company.
- Ivar Kreuger, head of the world's greatest monopoly.
- Jesse Livermore, the greatest bear on Wall Street.
- Charles Schwab, the president of the largest independent steel company.
- Richard Whitney, the president of the New York Stock Exchange.

Within twenty-eight years, all of these one-time successful men had met an unlikely end to their careers and lives:

- Arthur Cutten died abroad insolvent.
- Albert Fall was pardoned from prison so he could die at home penniless.
- Leon Fraser committed suicide.
- Howard Hopson was insane.
- Ivar Kreuger committed suicide.
- Jesse Livermore committed suicide.
- Charles Schwab was bankrupt and lived on borrowed money the last five years of his life.
- Richard Whitney was committed to Sing-Sing Maximum Security Prison, about thirty miles north of New York City.

The tragedy is professing Christians are not immune from disastrous consequences. Instead of following God's compass, many rely on their own resources, intellects, and pursuits. It is essential we acknowledge the Lord whatever road we travel, whatever path we tread, and whatever career we follow. That simply means we acknowledge Him as Lord of our lives, as our Commanding Officer or Supervisor. We are to do it in the best of times and in the worst of times. Life throws its bruising blows as we tread bumpy roads.

Disasters strike unexpectedly, and the Lord is often the last one we turn to when He is the only one who can prevent composure turning into confusion, hope into despair, and triumph into tragedy.

With its hills and valleys, Pittsburgh's winding roads create a constant challenge. They are often a nightmare to drive as lanes are closed for reasons ranging from accidents, tree-trimming, utility repairs, road construction, flooding, landslides, and inclement weather. I always try to get into the right lane—it could be the left lane—as soon as possible. If the delays are really bad, I'll take an alternate route. Getting into and staying in the lane of God's Word ensures a smoother and safer journey through life's struggles and challenges. Bad decisions create unnecessary anxiety, friction, chaos, turmoil, sadness, and regret.

We need an understanding *educated* by the Word of God and *regulated* by the Spirit of God. The Bible tells us that the one who trusts in his own heart is a fool, but the one who trusts in the Lord will prosper (Proverbs 28:25–26). Spiritual prosperity is to be preferred above anything else—even good health. The apostle John made that clear when he prayed his friend, Gaius, would enjoy good health, even as his soul prospered (3 John 2). Our greatest needs are always spiritual. When we put God first, everything else falls into true perspective.

We need counselors with a biblical worldview, opposed to opinions influenced by greed, eastern mysticism, new age philosophy, and materialism. Followers of Christ need to be different. We need to be salt and light in a confused and broken world.

The apostle James wrote about two distinct types of wisdom—one is from *below*, the other from *above*. Much of this world's so-called wisdom is derived from philosophers. Some of the most famous and influential of all time were from the ancient Greek world, including Aristotle, Plato, and Socrates. Aristotle had something to say on just about every subject, and modern philosophy almost always bases every single principle, idea, and notion on one of his teachings. His principles of ethics were founded on the teaching of good works, rather than being good. Plato taught it was only through philosophy that the world can be free of evils. Almost all of Western philosophy today can be traced back to Plato, a disciple of Socrates.

The apostle James described the wisdom from below as earthly, unspiritual, and demonic. It is characterized by envy, selfish ambition, disorder, and evil practices (James 3:14–16). We certainly live in a messy world. Many people are guided by their daily reading of horoscopes. Others rely on radio and television commentators voicing their opinions ad-nauseam on local news and talk shows. We often rely on brilliant educators, doctors, scientists, innovators, and industrialists whose own lives are, in many instances, broken and chaotic despite their education.

Instead of accepting what these pundits have to say, we are to filter what we hear through God's Word. The world is in chaos and seems to be getting worse. Commentators are struggling to decipher the confusion, unrest, violence, and heartache. There are people and organizations such as the Revolutionary Communist Party of the USA that is deliberately attempting to create violence and anarchy. Its manifesto clearly states this. The Bible, however, speaks clearly to end-time events.

From time to time I teach a seminar entitled *"What on Earth Is Happening?"* In the seminar, we consider current world events in light of biblical prophecy. For instance, Russia's role in the end times is no surprise as the Old Testament prophet Ezekiel foretold it over twenty-five hundred years ago. Just as the first advent of Christ was clearly foretold, so His second advent is clearly predicted. The Bible predicts future events and tells us that in the end times, things will become progressively worse.

The apostle John listed six things that will characterize that coming age—demonology, idolatry, murder, magic arts, sexual immorality, and thefts (Revelation 9:20–21). John's use of the

Greek words is revealing. For instance, *pharmakōn*, from which we derive our word for pharmaceutical, describes the use of drugs in practicing magic arts. *Porneias*, from which we derive the word pornography, is also used to describe everything from prostitution to every kind of unlawful sexual deviancy. These six things are increasingly rampant in the world today. They will "explode" in the biblical end times. It appears we are having a dress-rehearsal today.

Too readily, we listen to people whose own lives are in disarray. Consider some of the news anchors who have been fired because of sexual harassment and perversion. Others have been suspended for lying about their news stories. For some strange reason, we tend to admire movie stars and sports "heroes" who experience multiple marriages and drug and alcohol addiction even though they give generously to charity. All they do in reality is to exemplify Aristotle's philosophy—"You don't have to be good as long as you do good." We are taught "conventional" wisdom from childhood. Much of it is unspiritual and contrary to God's Word. Some of it is plainly demonic.

The apostle James describes the wisdom from above as pure, peace-loving, considerate, submissive, full of mercy and good fruit, impartial, and sincere. He states a principle that peacemakers who sow in peace will reap a harvest of righteousness (James 3:17–18). Paul taught an irreversible law of the universe when he wrote that we reap whatever we sow (Galatians 6:8). If we sow wheat, corn, or barley, we will reap accordingly. Sowing "wild oats" reaps nothing but trouble.

In his letter to the Corinthians, Paul provided an excellent commentary on the distinction between human and divine wisdom. He wrote:

Where is the wise person? Where is the teacher of the law? Where is the philosopher of this age? Has not God made foolish the wisdom of the world? For since in the wisdom of

God the world through its wisdom did not know him, God was pleased through the foolishness of what was preached to save those who believe. Jews demand signs and Greeks look for wisdom, but we preach Christ crucified: a stumbling block to Jews and foolishness to Gentiles, but to those whom God has called, both Jews and Greeks, Christ the power of God and the wisdom of God. For the foolishness of God is wiser than human wisdom, and the weakness of God is stronger than human strength. (1 Corinthians 1:20–25)

We need to check all our sources and resources, whether its literature, the internet, social media, the classroom, or counselors. Many of the greatest minds disclaim the Bible, disavow God, and discredit followers of Christ. Why listen to them?

A Bible college student of mine was a graduate of Iowa State University. She shared in class one time that on the first day of her philosophy class, the professor asked if there were any born-again Christians present. Nancy and one other student raised their hand. The professor then told them he would destroy their faith before the course ended. That is what we face today with liberal universities and secular professors. It is essential we rely on counselors with a solid biblical worldview.

Solomon rightfully articulated that the fear (reverential awe) of the Lord is the beginning of knowledge, but that fools despise wisdom and instruction (Proverbs 1:7). He warned us not to rebuke mockers lest they hate us. He continued to advise that the wise will love us when we rebuke them. They become wiser after listening to instruction, and they add to their learning when taught. Solomon concluded his comments by declaring the fear of the Lord is the beginning of wisdom and the knowledge of the Holy One is understanding (Proverbs 9:8–10). The psalmist later echoed those same thoughts in Psalm 111:10).

A friend in San Jose, California referred a young man to me. Alberto had trusted Christ and recently married. After his father-in-law died, his wife wanted to return to Pittsburgh. That's when I got to know him. I was struck by his seeming devotion to God and sincere desire to study the Bible. Finding it difficult to find a suitable job, Alberto joined the military. After serving stints in Iraq and Germany, he returned to Pittsburgh with his wife and three small children to live with his mother-in-law. He claimed to have read the Bible twenty-two times and could readily quote Scripture and reference its address. Sadly, though, he had knowledge without wisdom.

Upon arriving home from work each day, Alberto went straight to his room, read his Bible, and listened to Christian music. All to the neglect of his family. He often left it to his mother-in-law to cut the grass and shovel the snow. His failures led to estrangement, divorce, and the ultimate abandonment of his three young children. He remarried but quickly separated from his new wife. He continued to neglect his children. He was charged with failure to provide child support, and the last I heard of him, he was facing possible prison time. While Alberto had a heart for God, he had little to no idea how to relate his knowledge of the Bible to real-life situations. Wisdom is the application of knowledge.

We are to continually ask God to fill us with the knowledge of His will through the wisdom and understanding provided by the Holy Spirit. That is the only way we can live a life worthy of the Lord and please Him in every way. It is the only way to be fruitful and grow in the knowledge of God (Colossians 1:9–10). We are to *know, understand,* and *do* the will of God.

James tells us what to do if we lack wisdom. We should ask God for it daily. We need wisdom for every situation. Heavenly wisdom is infinitely greater than anything we can conjure up. The danger lies in relying on our own understanding.

We have intentionally spent a long time on this second pre-requisite for the simple reason this is where so many, including myself, fail.

It's time to consider the third requirement for experiencing God's guidance and direction.

There Is a Devotion to Cultivate

Solomon makes it clear in all our ways we are to submit to the Lord. We are to acknowledge Him and recognize Him as the One who chooses the paths we take straightening and smoothing the roads we travel.

We will inevitably encounter obstacles and rubble; however, God knows the road we should take. Sometimes He takes us through a situation, teaching us valuable lessons in the process. Other times, He leads us around the obstacles. More often than not, He tells us to back away, knowing the situation would be harmful to us. He removes barriers, stills the storm, and calms the wind. In every situation, He gives the needed grace to honor Him. He keeps us on track when we acknowledge Him.

The word *acknowledge* is from the Hebrew word *ada*, meaning to know by learning, observation, and experience. It includes an intimate knowledge and was used of Adam knowing Eve in sexual intimacy (Genesis 4:1). No relationship can be more intimate, providing it is done within the boundaries God has established.

We need to know God *intellectually, intimately,* and *experientially.* We need to acknowledge Him in every facet of our lives—whether it's personal, domestic, educational, vocational, or recreational. There should be no dichotomy between the sacred and the secular. Acknowledge the Lord whatever your career, pursuit in life, or daily activity. Live for God.

Three books have impressed me over the years. J. I. Packer's book, *Knowing God*, provides the intellectual knowledge we need to know about Him. Tim Stafford's book, *Knowing the Face of God*, shows how we can have an intimate knowledge of God. Henry and Richard Blackaby's book, *Experiencing God*, reveals how we can know God experientially. All three books are classics, in my opinion.

There is no greater thing than to know God and what He has done and can do. There is no deeper human longing than to know God is real and to meet Him face-to-face—to encounter Him in a personal relationship. There is no greater thrill than to experience God and His life-transforming power.

Acknowledging the Lord means submitting to His leadership and lordship. It means consulting Him and seeking His input and will on any given matter. It means being unafraid to stand up for Him and to acknowledge He is our God and Savior. It means avoiding independent decisions.

This intimate knowledge of God stems from developing a devotional life where we seek, practice, and acknowledge His presence. It takes time to be holy. We need to spend time in His presence each day. We need to be in His Word and allow Him to speak to us through it. We need to spend time in prayer and speak to Him as we would to a friend. The reason God often appears distant is because we keep our distance from Him. James tells us it is when we draw near to God that He will draw near to us (James 4:8).

Both the Old and New Testaments have a lot to say about seeking the Lord. The benefits of doing so are limitless. If we seek Him, we will find Him. Pick the time of day that best suits you. Some prefer the early morning hours. Others prefer evening or late-night hours. Give God priority and Christ first place. Seek to honor and glorify Him in all you do and say. Live your life for God's praise and glory. Not only is that His will; it's His purpose in saving us.

These, then, are the three prerequisites to experiencing God's guidance and direction. Let's highlight them again. The first prerequisite is that you trust in the Lord with all your heart, the second is that you avoid leaning on your own understanding, and the third is that you acknowledge the Lord in all your ways. These three prerequisites ensure the realization of a divine promise. When we do our part, God will do His! God's word is His bond.

There Is a Direction to Experience

The Bible is clear. If we do the first three things, God will do the fourth. He will direct our paths. That's a promise. The secret to experiencing God's divine guidance and direction is anchored in His faithfulness and ability to perform what He has promised. Nothing is impossible with God. The three prerequisites are fundamental in experiencing God's guidance. As a shepherd leads his sheep, so God will lead us. We need to trust Him, rely on Him, and stay close to Him. Sheep are prone to wander from the shepherd; so are we. The reason we find God's will so elusive is because we make it elusive.

Make the great decision to fully trust in the Lord. Follow it up by not leaning on your own understanding. Finally, cultivate a genuine devotion, and get to know God *personally, intimately,* and *experientially.*

God has promised to guide and direct us, and to keep us on track as we encounter Him through His Word, as we hear His voice and obey it, and as we develop an intimacy with him through prayer. Our part is to fulfill the prerequisites. God's part is to fulfill His promise. Both require trust, even when we question what He is doing to us and for us.

Literally, the concept is God will cut out the path He wants us to take, and He does it without our necessarily realizing it. He cuts the road over rugged terrain. He builds bridges across rivers, valleys, and water we think are uncrossable. He tunnels through mountains we think are impassable.

The Southern Beltway is under construction in the Pittsburgh area as I write. It has been in the planning stages for years and is slowly coming to completion. Lately, I was traveling an area where one road ran through a valley where massive reinforced concrete pillars were being built to support the overhead bridges soon be laid. I traveled another section where a complete hillside was being reshaped by massive earthmoving equipment. An interstate highway is experiencing delays as entry and exit points are being carved out of the hillsides. I talked to some local residents who complained about the noise and inconvenience experienced on a daily basis. Some had their homes and land seized under eminent domain laws.

One day it will be worth it all. We only see sections of the Beltway under construction. The surveyors, engineers, and contractors see the big picture and know the end results they are working hard to achieve.

It is the same when God is at work. We can only see the immediate things happening in our lives. We question the reason why. Despite the heartaches, upheavals, frustrations, and challenges, when we wholly trust the Lord, we can rest in the assurance that God is directing our steps and cutting out a path for us. Through it all, we should confidently rely on the fact God is already preparing the next section of the road ahead. We need to believe all things work together for the good of those who love God and who are called according to His purpose (Romans 8:28).

The process can be a thrilling experience as we trust the Lord to guide. The new job drops into our lap. The right life partner comes out of nowhere. The opportunity to serve God that we have been praying for becomes a reality. We trust Him to show us the light at the end of the tunnel, to reinforce the fact that there is no gain without pain.

The process can also be painful and bewildering at times, leading us to question God and say, "Lord, what are you doing to me?" We wrongly conclude God is unfair and unloving, even though we know that is not true. Life is not plain sailing. It can be stormy at times, often because of our own mistakes, stubbornness, and stupidity. God is somehow able to work all those things for our good and for His glory.

Three Old Testament individuals come to mind.

Joseph was hated by his brothers, sold into slavery, and bought out of the slave market by Potiphar, Pharaoh's right-hand man in Egypt. He was falsely accused by Potiphar's wife and thrown into prison where he was forgotten. All the while God had a plan for him. He was eventually promoted to become Pharaoh's chief of staff. Throughout his adversity, Joseph somehow had the quiet assurance that God was working for a greater cause.

Daniel was taken captive into the Babylonian Empire as a teen-ager. He eventually had the distinction of being a prophet—just read his amazing prophecies, some of which have already been fulfilled and others are awaiting fulfillment. He also had the distinction of being a key administrator in two world empires—first the Babylonian and then the Persian Empire.

Jonah survived a dramatic under water cruise in the belly of a big fish. God superintended every event in that story, so Jonah would eventually fulfill his commission and preach to the inhabitants of a wicked city within the brutal Assyrian Empire. The story teaches us that God sometimes breaks our obstinate wills in order to accomplish His purposes.

In all these instances we see God sovereignly working to achieve His plans. It's always best to submit to God in the first place rather than experiencing the tortuous results of disobedience.

Apart from being Jacob's favorite son and appearing some-what obnoxious when he shared his dreams, Joseph did nothing to deserve his brothers' hatred. Daniel was caught up in God's overall judgment of Judah when the Babylonians invaded Jerusalem. Jonah is a different story in that his experience was the result of deliberate disobedience and God's desire to give him a second chance.

God is at work in our lives, either disciplining or discipling us. His will is we trust Him implicitly, no matter how hard it is, so we don't rely on our own intellect and ingenuity, no matter how smart we are. His will is also that we acknowledge Him in every situation, no matter how unreasonable it seems. That sounds easy but doing it is something else. That's why we need Him. We need Him every hour because we can't do it alone.

Our next chapter underscores the fact that God created everyone unique with the divine purpose of glorifying Him and enjoying Him forever. Only a few realize that can only be accomplished through Jesus Christ. People use their mental and physical prowess to earn a living, to accomplish great things, to find satisfaction and fulfillment in life, and to reach the top of their careers without ever acknowledging God's role in their lives. It is incredible what people conceive and achieve. There seems to be no limit to human ingenuity. God's intent for your life is that you bring Him praise and glory in everything you do. That's His will.

My Prayer

Dear God:

First of all, I want to thank You for reaching out to me and saving me when I placed my trust in Your Son, the Lord Jesus, for salvation. I know that was the greatest decision I ever made, and I have no regrets, even though it has not been easy being a Christian.

I confess I have tried doing so much on my own. I have succeeded in everything I have attempted, I have reached all my goals, but I am finding it so difficult trusting You. I constantly lean to my own understanding and to conventional wisdom. I have learned I am not to do that. I need Your wisdom, something I greatly lack.

I realize I need to cultivate an intimate personal relationship with You. I know I can do that as I encounter You in Your Word and through prayer. Help me to place complete trust in You, knowing Your ways are perfect. Help me to put You first in my life. Help me to honor Your Son. Help me to be enlightened, equipped, and empowered by Your Spirit.

Father, please cut out the path of Your choosing for my life. Help me to meet the three prerequisites You have laid out, so Your promise will become a reality from day to day.

I pray all this in the worthy and precious name of my Lord and Savior, Jesus Christ. Amen!

Application

1. What do you need to do as a believer to demonstrate your trust in the Lord on a daily basis?
2. What do you need to do to display a greater reliance on the wisdom God provides?
3. What do you need to do to develop a closer walk with God each day?
4. List instances where you have definitely concluded it could only have been God who cut that path for you to follow.

Chapter Nine

Unravelling Who You Are

God created you a unique person. You are special. You are one of a kind, a fact David expressed poetically in a psalm describing God's omnipotence and omnipresence. He wrote:

> For you created my inmost being; you knit me together in my mother's womb. I praise you because I am fearfully and wonderfully made; your works are wonderful, I know that full well. My frame was not hidden from you when I was made in the secret place, when I was woven together in the depths of the earth. Your eyes saw my unformed body; all the days ordained for me were written in your book before one of them came to be. (Psalm 139:13–16)

God's formation of Adam and Eve, as described in the first two chapters of Genesis, was His crowning creative act. Adam and Eve were unique because they were the only creatures created in God's image. That doesn't mean they possessed all God's attributes. They were given a moral compass and were able to love, show justice, compassion, mercy, and grace. They were able to commune with God and with each other for purposes of companionship and community. They were given intelligence and wisdom. They were given dominion over the earth and were entrusted to care for every living thing ranging from animals, birds, fish, and plant life. They were given the ability and creativity to harness the world's natural resources for the common good.

Every human being has inherited these qualities to one extent or another. God, however, retained certain attributes, such as omniscience, omnipotence, and omnipresence which He didn't contribute to humans. The fact is every human being, including you and me, is created in the likeness of God. For centuries, theologians have called this the *Imago Dei*—the image of God. This is the reason human beings are uniquely distinct from all of creation.

David acknowledged God's observation of his formation in the womb, something ultrasound and sonograms do today. Then he recognized the days of his life were determined in advance. God had a purpose for him, just as He has a purpose for you and me.

The fact we are wonderfully formed is proven as medical professionals, researchers, and scientists learn more and more about the human body. Our intricate design attests to an intelligent design, one that could never happen by chance. Applying that to the whole of creation leads us to conclude we have an amazing God.

David expressed the wonder of our formation and composition some three thousand years ago, long before the era of modern medical science. That's why life is so precious, and why the Bible teaches the sanctity of life. Every life matters, even from the moment of conception.

Your uniqueness is established by your fingerprint and DNA. No one else in the world has your fingerprint, something forensic scientists use to their advantage. Just as it has been argued that no two snowflakes are alike, so it is argued no two fingerprints are the same.

Today, DNA typing is a powerful adjunct to forensic science. The method was first used in casework in 1985 in the United Kingdom and introduced to the United States by commercial laboratories in late 1986, and by the Federal Bureau of Investigation in 1988. I first became interested in the subject in 1985 after a Bible college student of mine was convicted of a murder he didn't commit. Eventually DNA typing helped exonerate him. I tell his story in my first book, *Innocence*.

How amazing is our Creator? Have you ever wondered why you are made the way you are? You inherited your parents' genes, chromosomes, and DNA. They inherited theirs from their parents, and so on.

DNA is popular today in helping people trace their genealogical and ethnic heritages. We resemble our parents in so many ways, whether it be appearance, mannerisms, intellect, or aspirations. Built into our uniqueness are our looks, natural talents, intelligence quotient, physical prowess, creativity, and potential abilities. Other than accidental cause, I can never understand why people undergo surgical reconstruction of their faces. Beauty is only skin-deep. My wife sometimes jokingly comments on my nose, but I laughingly respond, "I love it because that's the way God made me. It makes me distinctive."

This begs the question: Why are children born with deficiencies, such as Down syndrome? God is often labeled cruel for letting this happen. Cloe Kondrich has proved many people wrong. Born with Down syndrome, she has never let her diagnosis stand in the way of her aspirations. She is an amazing individual. She even has her own law, known as Cloe's Law, which ensures that parents of babies with Down syndrome have access to educational resources and support services. She also knows she is part of an endangered group in that the vast majority of preborn babies diagnosed with Down syndrome are aborted. Because of her father's commitment to the sanctity of life, Chloe has given hope to many. Sadly, because of abortion, European countries take pride in being almost free of Down syndrome.

Some deficiencies result from the mother's drug, alcohol, and nicotine use during pregnancy. Often the drug companies are to blame. Air pollution from auto and factory emissions is another culprit. Dangerous substances introduced into our atmosphere, soil, and water supplies cause allergies, disease, death, and harm to living organisms and food crops. Some see a correlation between the significant increases in arthritic diseases since the year 2000 with the introduction of genetically modified foods around the same time. The atomic bomb dropped on Hiroshima, Japan, on August 6, 1945, and Nagasaki three days later caused unprecedented and devastating pollution. The Chernobyl nuclear accident in Ukraine, formerly part of the Soviet Union, on April 26, 1986, was also catastrophic. Many wrongly blame God when man is the cause.

Wise parents recognize the positive traits in their children and steer them according—just as the Bible teaches in Proverbs 22:6. It's truly amazing how some children break out of the mold and accomplish things never imagined by their immediate family. Parents should certainly encourage their child to pursue legitimate innate desires. My mother was a nurse and midwife who trained in tropical diseases to help equip her for missionary service in Central Africa. From a young age, my twin sister had the same aspirations and, in due course, followed in mother's medical footsteps into the nursing profession.

For health reasons, my parents relocated to Johannesburg in South Africa when I was five years of age. The adjustment from life on a mission station in the Belgian Congo to suburbia wasn't easy. I was naïve, and my mind boggled at the new experiences. After my first visit to a circus, my ambition was to be a circus clown. Then, as I stood and watched the trains "speed" by on the main line from Johannesburg to Cape Town, I changed my mind. Seeing a guard sitting on the floor of the guard van by an open door, with his legs dangling over the edge, doing nothing was cool. I thought that was a great way to earn a living. Fortunately, my parents steered me in other directions.

Children display their innate desires from a young age. Some love to read, others love to play. Some are adventurous, others cautious. Some are musical, others theatrical. Some are leaders, others are followers. Some like making things, others like tearing things apart to see how they work. Some are friendly, others are loners. Everyone is wired differently.

As children grow up, some lean toward the arts, whether they be performing or visual. Others lean toward humanities, such as geography, history, languages and literature, philosophy, and theology. Still others are attracted toward the sciences, whether they be social, natural, or formal. Teenagers start gravitating toward professions, such as education, engineering, technology, legal, medical, financial, and business. Once in those fields, they specialize. It largely depends on their DNA and how they are structured.

What natural talents and aspirations has God given you? What are your innate desires? Some have the desire to wield power. This could potentially become dangerous as we consider the cruel and abusive leaders throughout human history. Others have a natural desire to come alongside those in need.

Legitimate desires need to be developed through education and training, whether it be self-study, technical school, college, or university. Entrepreneurial types, following their instincts, have become renowned for their inventions and patents. Others have built vast corporations. Some have taken us to regions and heights never thought possible of human attainment. Brilliant minds have accomplished what the average person thought impossible. As I watch programs like *Shark Tank*, I am amazed at what people dream of. Throughout history, we are indebted to the explorers, liberators, inventors, and entrepreneurs.

So where do you fit in? You are probably in the job you are in because it fits your natural instincts and innate desires, even though you have not realized your potential. You are probably doing what

God has wired you to do. Some may feel they are mired in the mud, however.

You may be asking the $64,000 question, "What is God's will for my life?" God's will is you become Christ-like and bring Him glory in all you do (Romans 8:29; 1 Corinthians 10:31). It's as simple as that. That should be your goal wherever you are in life. There is no higher calling than to be the very best you can be for the glory of God in whatever profession or job you are. You could be lawyering, building a corporate empire, saving a life in the emergency room, coaching a sports team, performing in some athletic endeavor, teaching in the classroom, driving a truck, managing an office, selling real estate, improving the internet, collecting garbage, or performing the work of a stay-home mom. God's will is you do all you do for His glory, to be the very best you can be for God.

You could, however, be asking a follow-up question, "How can I be the very best person I could be?" First, you need to ensure you have a personal relationship with Jesus Christ and are walking with Him each day. Then you need to allow the Holy Spirit to *change, instruct, equip,* and *empower* you. Finally, you need to know how God has wired you, so He can use you for His glory wherever you are.

Studies have helped people identify their strengths and weaknesses. I have used the DISC Profile Charts developed by Corexel to identify personality profiles. Other assessments address the likes of intelligence and creativity, for instance. Combined, these programs can be useful in helping a person better understand their complexities and uniqueness.

The DISC Profile is a blend of the four primary personality styles and their relationship to each other. DISC assessments are available online and are able to generate instant results. They help provide insights into an individual's natural and behavioral styles in relation to their workplace, leadership style, management approach, sales style, and other situations, as well as their relationship to each other. I recommend you take such assessments (there are many to choose from) as they help you recognize strengths to be maximized and weaknesses to be minimized. People score across the board and can be extremely high in one area and extremely low in another. Others might score more evenly across the four primary personality styles. Everyone is different. Spiritual assessments are also available and may be helpful in identifying spiritual giftedness in order to serve God effectively.

Each individual is composed of specific personality traits and talents. The four main types have been identified as pragmatic, extrovert, amiable, and analytical. Others refer to them as choleric, sanguine, phlegmatic, and melancholic. Still others refer to them as the driver, expressive, amiable, and analytical types. No one is a pure type. While we may be dominant in one type or another, we all possess characteristics of each type. The DISC profile charts identify the four basic personality traits as dominance, influence, steadiness, and compliance.

- **Dominant** (D) personality types tend to be direct and decisive — to the point of being demanding. They prefer leading to following and directing to receiving orders. They seek leadership and managerial positions. They are self-assured risk-takers and problem-solvers. This compels others to look to them for decisions and direction. They are self-starters, strong-willed, results-oriented, and determined. They think about the future, the big picture, goals, and tangible results. They are bottom-line organizers who can lead an entire group in one direction. They tend to challenge the status quo and think in innovative ways. They are highly motivated by new challenges, setting and achieving goals, and seeing tangible results. Freedom from routine and mundane tasks is important. Since repetition is boring and frustrating, changing environments in which to work and play can be highly motivating to them. They enjoy being in charge, having liberty to make decisions, and crave freedom from controls, supervision, and details.

Dominant personality types can be argumentative and unwilling to listen to the reasoning of others. They tend to ignore the details and minutia of a situation, even if it's important. They are inclined to achieve too much at one time, hoping for quick results. They crave to be in control of the situation and tend to become seagull managers who fly in, leave a mess, and then fly out again. In the process, they leave people frustrated and devastated, wishing they had never come.

- **Influential** (I) personality types are motivational, outgoing, encouraging, enthusiastic, optimistic, interactive, impressive, and friendly. They are good communicators and participative managers who are able to motivate, inspire, and influence others. They handle change well and respond positively to the unexpected. Their enthusiasm and sense of humor make them a focal point among others and provides them leadership opportunities. They express ideas well, work well with others, and are not afraid to offer opinions. "I" styles make great spokespeople, are persuasive, and are known for their positive attitude. They accomplish goals through people. They are extremely accepting of others and are strong leaders in brainstorming sessions. They function best around people, are natural problem-solvers, think outside the box, and will go out of their way to negotiate conflict and keep the peace.

Influential personality types see the big picture but also tend to avoid details and are therefore inclined to overlook important information and facts. They need others to do the research, to handle the details, to build their visions into a beautiful workable mosaic, and to ensure everything is organized. They excel most when they can be the talker, the presenter, the one who builds rapport and teamwork. They are not great listeners, and therefore give the impression of waiting to speak instead of listening. They are effective when presenting, motivating, and problem solving but sometimes may be slow to act. They could benefit from breaking big goals into smaller steps. "I" styles tend to be quick thinkers and need to slow down the pace for other team members.

- **Steady** (S) personality types are stable, predictable, even-tempered, friendly, amiable, accommodating, patient, humble, tactful, supportive, dependable, sympathetic, and sincere. They prefer close, personal relationships and are very open with loved ones. They are good listeners, encourage team harmony, strive for consensus, and try hard to reconcile conflicts as they arise. They are compliant toward authority and are loyal team players. They are naturally relational, creating a supportive and positive team environment. They tend to be realistic, well-grounded in common sense, and are able to see a simpler or more practical way to accomplish a goal. They are talented multi-taskers but will work at a slow and steady pace until something is completed. In striving for security and routine, they tend to resist change.

However, when change occurs, they acclimate best when given a long-enough period of time to adjust and an explanation of why the change is necessary. They view projects from both the overall big picture and the smaller steps to get there. They like tasks that can be completed at one time or seen through from beginning to end, and they enjoy practical procedures and systems. They are good implementers and managers. They tend to be peacemakers and nurturers in groups as they crave stability and predictability. They thrive in a team environment that's harmonious, with little change or surprises.

Because the Steady style is passive and avoids conflict, they tend to hold grudges when frustrated and are resentful instead of facing issues head on. They strive for positive environments and relationships and can be especially sensitive when it comes to criticism. Their desire to please makes it difficult for them to say no and causes them to be stretched too thin on occasions. They need affirmation, and truly appreciate recognition for their loyalty and dependability. They genuinely try to help with details and are a valuable support for team goals. If they have a concern or doubt, they will likely internalize it or hesitate to voice their feedback unless a safe environment has been created for dialogue.

- **Compliant** (C) personality types are accurate, precise, detail-oriented, and conscientious. They think analytically and systematically, and only make decisions after careful research and back-up information has been considered. They set high standards for themselves and others and tend to be perfectionists. Because they concentrate on details, they see things others don't.

  While reserved, compliant types tend to be calculating and condescending. They bring perspective to groups and tend to anchor reality in team thought. They think through every detail and process of a project and how it works. They make realistic estimates and will voice the problems they see with a plan or existing system. They will complete tasks they've committed to and will be thorough in the process. They are excellent in analyzing, researching, or testing information. They are conscientious and even-tempered. They do not need to be sociable at work. They enjoy working on their own. They are motivated by research, information, and logic.

Because of their attention to detail, "C" types excel in specialized or technical tasks. They will find mistakes that need to be corrected. They are effective trouble-shooters. They desire independence and autonomy, as well as a controlled and organized environment. They prefer exact job descriptions, with expectations and goals clearly laid out. They pay attention to details and concentrate on facts rather than people examples. They are instinctive organizers who can both create and maintain systems. They strive for consistency, logic, accuracy, and excellence. They ask important questions and talk about problems that could hold up projects. They are "do it yourself" managers who maintain focus on tasks and will see something through to completion. They emphasize quality, think logically, and strive for a diplomatic approach and consensus within groups.

"C" types tend to internalize their concerns and doubts, and also hesitate to verbalize their feelings unless they feel safe in doing so. They are passive and will avoid conflict rather than argue. They need clear-cut boundaries in order to feel comfortable at work, in relationships, or in taking action. For them, it's important to concentrate on doing the right things, rather than just doing things right. They need to focus more on people in order to build stronger relationships as they can leave the office without ever talking to another staff member all day. They need to push themselves to be decisive and take risks, especially if all the research isn't there to support it.

To summarize, the dominant and influential types, also known as Type A people, are active, aggressive, ambitious, controlling, competitive, preoccupied with status, workaholics, and impatient.

The steady and compliant types, known as Type B people, are passive, relaxed, less stressed, flexible, emotional, expressive, and have a laid-back attitude.

How do you see yourself in this mix? What is your personality profile? How God has wired you will help you determine your occupation and status in life? Discovering your personality profile will alert you to what God wants you to do for His praise and glory.

It's incredible what men and women have accomplished with their God-given talents and acumen. Amazing feats have been accomplished. Men built the pyramids in Egypt and the Great Wall of China. They learned navigation from the stars. Recent centuries have witnessed revolutionary inventions. In 1439, Johannes Gutenberg invented the movable-type printing press and started the printing revolution many regard as a milestone of the second millennium AD. In 1760, the industrial revolution began in Great Britain and then spread into Europe and around the world. The technological age soon followed. The twentieth century witnessed the birth of aviation, space travel, and the onslaught of the informational age.

Men have made amazing discoveries and navigated the oceans. They developed the steam engine, automobile, aircraft, and spacecraft. They discovered electricity, invented the light bulb, telephone, and internet. They have conquered the highest mountains and plumbed the ocean depths. They have built roadways and bridges spanning previously inaccessible terrain and water. They have put man into space, landed him on the moon, and engaged in extensive space exploration. They have turned rivers into manmade lakes, harnessed water for hydroelectric power, established power grids crisscrossing a country, and tapped into solar energy to power automobiles, homes, and factories. They have turned crude oil into a vast petrochemical industry. Medical science has helped curtail and even eliminate diseases, extending human and animal lifespans.

Spatial satellites have made knowledge instantly available and fingertip accessible. Knowledge can be instantly obtained by typing a few words on a keypad or speaking into an iPhone. Social media has taken off. All these accomplishments are revolutionary. No monkey, or any other animal for that matter, has been able to accomplish what human beings, created in the image of God, have accomplished. Place a monkey at a keyboard, but after punching the keys for a thousand years, it would not be able to produce a legible document, not even a sentence. Humans are in a unique category. God created them that way for a purpose.

Everything achieved by human ingenuity has been accomplished by men and women flawed by sin. The list includes atheists, agnostics, and those vehemently opposed to the Gospel. It includes those with little to no regard for God who live for themselves. It includes people with little to no intent of discovering God's will for their lives. They may be successful by human standards, but by eternal values they are unsuccessful even though they have made significant contributions to society.

The apostle Paul describes every unregenerate person as ungodly, even though they may profess belief in God. James tells us that even demons believe in God. They believe and shudder at the thought or mention of God's existence (James 2:19). Unregenerate people gratify the desires of their fleshly instincts, such as sexual immorality, impurity, hatred, jealousy, and selfish ambition. Read Galatians 5:19–21. The list provides a graphic picture of the culture that has existed for millennia. However, due to technology and the media, depravity is more blatant today.

The apostle Paul mentions another list in 1 Corinthians 6:9–10 but then adds: "And that is what some of you were. But you were washed, you were sanctified, you were justified in the name of the Lord Jesus Christ and by the Spirit of our God" (1 Corinthians 6:11). You may be in this group, and asking the question, "What happened?"

The change, sometimes dramatic, is the result of the saving work of Jesus Christ. Those with a biblical worldview claim Jesus Christ is the answer to every human problem and each dilemma the world faces. Amazing things happen the moment a person places their faith in Christ alone for salvation, is truly born-again, and seeks to become a faithful follower of Jesus Christ. Over forty things happen in the microsecond a person trusts Christ. They are forgiven, redeemed, reconciled to God, and instantly become His child. They are sealed to the day of redemption, indwelt by the Holy Spirit, and are spiritually gifted. In Christ, they become a new creation—God's handiwork (2 Corinthians 5:17; Ephesians 2:10).

This may be your testimony. Christ has changed your life. There is a hundred-and eighty-degree turnaround in your thinking. You are still a sinner, but one saved by God's grace. While the sin nature will never be eradicated this side of glory, you will sin less as your desire now is to become more like Christ each day, to exalt Him, and to glorify God.

The experiences of the early Christians in the book of Acts show us God has a mission, an essential mission, for all who trust Him. Every follower of Christ needs to know they are in full-time Christian service, whether it is in the home, marketplace, class-room, factory, hospital, laboratory, law court, military, prison, or someplace else—even if it's in a space station. You are Christ's ambassador, His representative in a world filled with confusion, hate, and evil. God's intent is you live each day for His praise and glory. That is His overarching will.

The purpose of this book is to help you discover God's will as it is revealed in His Word and to help show you how to experience His continual direction and guidance. It is the admixture of natural talents, spiritual gifts, and the work of the Holy Spirit that truly makes each follower of Christ distinct. We discover God has a far bigger purpose than we ever imagined.

Things change when God is at work in a person's life. Instead of the ugliness that characterizes the unregenerate person—despite all the good they may do and amazing things they may accomplish—God brings beauty out of ashes. Dramatic changes occur when a follower of Christ gives the Holy Spirit full sway and allows God's Word to transform them. It is the Holy Spirit who makes a believer in Christ fruitful and productive. Paul describes that fruit as love, joy, peace, forbearance, kindness, goodness, faithfulness, gentleness, and self-control (Galatians 5:22–23).

The apostle proceeds to teach that those who belong to Christ Jesus have crucified the flesh with its passions and desires. The true follower of Christ *is* different. Life takes on a new purpose—a divine purpose, one that pleases God and brings Him glory and praise. No longer does a follower of Christ live for time alone. He or she lives with eternity in view. Their perspective has entirely changed.

It is God's will that you display the fruit of the Holy Spirit in your life. It is what makes you different, more God-like, and holy. Add to that the spiritual gifts the Holy Spirit imparts at conversion, and you become a person not only able to please God but one able to bring Him the praise and glory He so rightly deserves.

Whatever your personality type and temperament, with all its strengths and weaknesses, displaying the fruit of the Spirit makes you distinctive. The distinction occurs when the Holy Spirit fills you and controls you. It is all the result of His enabling and equipping you to live the life God has planned for you.

You become loving instead of hateful, and joyful rather than sad, depressed, and melancholic. You promote peace as opposed to discord and unrest. Rather than being intolerant and writing people off, you put up with what you don't like in others. You become kind instead of unkind. You are patient rather than impatient, compassionate and considerate instead of demanding. You are faithful instead of unfaithful, whether it's in a spousal relationship, financial stewardship, or in merely doing what you say. You become gentle instead of harsh, abrasive, and abusive. You are self-controlled, whether it's with your passions, thoughts, tongue, attitudes, appetites, or anger. This is all God's will for you.

These amazing changes occur as you become God's handiwork, but only to the extent you cooperate with Him. Relying on your own strength, willpower, and perseverance will never produce such amazing results.

Love should always prevail. The apostle Paul provides a classic description of agape love that is God's love. Love is patient; love is kind. Love does not envy. Love does not boast. Love is not proud. Love is not rude. Love is not self-seeking, or easily angered. Love keeps no record of wrongs. Love does not delight in evil but rejoices with the truth. Love always protects, always trusts, always hopes, and always perseveres. Love never fails. (1 Corinthians 13:4–8).

What if we all loved like that? What if we all displayed the fruit of the Spirit in the home, school, and workplace? That's the kind of change God wants when you come to faith in Christ.

Martin Luther King Jr. was right when he said "Darkness cannot drive out darkness; only light can do that. Hate cannot drive out hate; only love can do that." Only the Holy Spirit can produce the type of fruit that makes us more like Christ.

I was blessed by reading Tim LaHaye's book, *The Spirit-Controlled Temperament*. It is a superb treatment of the basic human temperaments and how God can use them. Over one million copies of the book have been sold, and it was listed as a best seller. I read it in the 1980s, but still recall its overall impact. We are all born with distinct strengths but also weaknesses. God wants to transform our natural weaknesses and make us dynamic, effective Christians who live above anger, fear, depression, and selfishness. This book helps you discover who you are and, more importantly, who you can become through the indwelling Holy Spirit given to every believer who puts their trust in the Lord Jesus Christ

I trust that by now you are beginning to discover and understand the dimensions of God's will for your life. He wants you to be different, a difference that makes you attractive even to those who reject a biblical worldview and are convicted by your godly lifestyle.

One of the ways we experience God's guidance is through the natural talents we possess. You are probably doing what you are doing in your college disciplines, work, or profession because you followed your innate desires. You don't necessarily quit your job after trusting Christ, unless, of course, you are engaged in an illicit line of work. You stay where you are and live for Christ in that environment until God calls you out. He could lead you to another job, to another location, to a different profession—even to a foreign country. No matter where you are, God always wants you to be His ambassador.

Greg Brown (not his real name) was a graduate student at Northwestern University in Chicago when I first met him in the early 1980s. After seven years of study, he qualified as an architect, but his father encouraged him to one day lead an architectural firm. He needed management training. After earning an MBA, he got a job at the largest architectural firm in Chicago. No sooner had he started working there than the industry experienced a severe slump. Many employees, some with years of experience behind them, were released. To his surprise, Greg was retained. He was obviously viewed as a bright star on the horizon. However, a conflict was building within him.

Despite coming from a conservative Christian home, Greg barely knew about Christian missions—until he arrived in Chicago. His mind boggled at what God was doing around the world, and he wanted to be a part of it. But where?

Greg came to me for counsel. At the time, I was chair of the Chicago Missionary Study Class that represented a fellowship of over fifty churches located throughout the greater Chicago area.

Each month, we heard from missionaries and prayed for them. Greg was blown away. We discussed the global picture and then narrowed it down continent by continent. Eventually, Greg felt God calling him into the Muslim world. But where? After much prayer and waiting on God, he settled on a particular country and, with his wife, has served faithfully in that country for over thirty years. Greg has planted churches, participated in local radio programs, and lectured in local universities. In the meanwhile, he earned a doctoral degree in biblical studies.

During my initial meetings with Greg, I recall his increasing struggle with God seemingly calling him to surrender his career. After spending all those years earning his architectural and MBA degrees, and being a rising star in the workplace, why would God want him to make such a sacrifice?

We talked about C. T. Studd and others who had experienced similar struggles. I remember telling him God was not so much interested in his credentials as He was in making him the man He wanted him to be for the work He had planned for him. I referred to an anonymous poem that J. Oswald Sanders quoted in his book *Spiritual Leadership,* and that I had been quoting at the time.

When God wants to drill a man
And thrill a man
And skill a man,
When God wants to mold a man
To play the noblest part;
When He yearns with all His heart
To create so great and bold a man
That all the world shall be amazed,
Watch His methods, watch His ways!
How He ruthlessly perfects
Whom He royally elects!
How He hammers him and hurts him,

And with mighty blows converts him
Into trial shapes of clay which
Only God understands;
While his tortured heart is crying
And he lifts beseeching hands!
How He bends but never breaks
When his good He undertakes;
How He uses whom He chooses
And with every purpose fuses him;
By every act induces him
To try His splendor out—
God knows what He's about!

(Author Unknown)

God certainly knows what Greg Brown is about! Without him necessarily knowing it at the time, God had a plan and a specific purpose for him.

The moment a person trusts Christ, he or she is spiritually gifted to be what God has planned for them to be and do the work He prepared in advance for them to do (Ephesians 2:10).

After His ascension to heaven, the risen Lord Jesus appointed apostles, prophets, evangelists, pastors, and teachers to help equip His true followers to serve the growing body of believers, so they would grow in spiritual maturity (Ephesians 4:9–13).

Writing to the Corinthian church, the apostle Paul wrote about the Holy Spirit's role in sovereignly distributing spiritual gifts—the Greek word is *charismata*—to every true believer. While there is a variety of gifts, ministries, and effects, the triune God is overall in charge (1 Corinthians 12:1–11).

A spiritual gift is distinct from a natural talent. The combination of natural talents and spiritual gifts make you even more unique in God's sight. The way God has composed you relates to the way in which He, in His sovereignty, put you together as to likes and dislikes, looks, brains, and physical abilities. In addition, spiritual gifts serve as signposts pointing you in the direction God is leading and equipping you to serve Him.

Every true follower of Christ has at least one spiritual gift. In writing to the Corinthian church, Paul made that plain. No one, however, has all the spiritual gifts.

The take-away from this chapter is that God made you unique. Sin interfered with and curtailed God's purpose in creating you while still in your mother's womb. God's redemptive plan, as it unfolded in Jesus Christ, is that you do His will and live for His praise and glory.

D. L. Moody, probably the greatest evangelist before Billy Graham burst onto the world's scene, once said the world has yet to see what God can do with a man who is fully yielded to Him. Then he added, "By God's help, I aim to be that man!"

In his book, *Crucial Experiences in the Life of D. L. Moody,* Paul Gericke provides the context of that statement:

Henry Varley, a British revivalist who had befriended the young American in Dublin, recalled that in 1873 Moody asked him to recount words they had spoken in private conversation a year earlier, just before Moody's return to the United States. Varley provides this account.

During the afternoon of the day of conference Mr. Moody asked me to join him in the vestry of the Baptist Church. We were alone, and he recalled the night's meeting at Willow Park and our converse the following morning.

"Do you remember your words?" he said.

I replied, "I well remember our interview, but I do not recall any special utterance."

"Don't you remember saying, 'Moody, the world has yet to see what God will do with a man fully consecrated to him?'"

"Not the actual sentence," I replied.

"Ah," said Mr. Moody, "those were the words sent to my soul, through you, from the Living God. As I crossed the wide Atlantic, the boards of the deck of the vessel were engraved with them, and when I reached Chicago, the very paving stones seemed marked with 'Moody, the world has yet to see what God will do with a man fully consecrated to him.' Under the power of those words I have come back to England, and I felt that I must not let more time pass until I let you know how God had used your words to my inmost soul."

(Used with permission – Insight Press Inc.)

You probably have little concept of what God can accomplish when you are fully consecrated to Him. You don't have to be an overseas missionary, pastor, or in full-time Christian ministry for that to occur. God's will can play out regardless of your career. God is still looking for men and women who love Him with all their heart, soul, strength, and mind (Luke 10:27). Will you be that person?

My purpose in writing this chapter is to declare regardless of your personality type, natural talents, spiritual giftedness, skills and accomplishments, job position, and station in life God's will is that everything you do pleases Him. It doesn't matter if you are in the marketplace or in ministry; do everything for His glory. God's will is that you love, trust, and obey Him and that you be conformed into the image of His Son and bring Him praise and glory.

My Prayer

Dear God, I am truly amazed at Your creativity in making me the person I am. You have uniquely gifted me to reflect Your glory and to do Your will. I thank You for bringing me to this point in my life. Thank You for drawing me to Yourself through faith in the Lord Jesus. I want You to use me for Your praise and for Your glory. I recognize the strengths and weaknesses of my personality and pray You mold me into the person You want me to be.

Father, please help me in my job, profession, or ministry to always honor You. I pray my associates and colleagues truly see Jesus in me. I pray that I will use my time, talents, and treasures for Your glory. I pray in serving others I will serve You, whether it's in private where few see me or in public where my life is on open display.

I pray all these things in the precious name of the Lord Jesus. Amen!

Application

Take some time out to reflect on how God has uniquely made you. Then reflect on how your desires, passions, and goals may have changed since you first trusted Christ as you consider how your education, skills, and attainments can better serve God and bring Him the glory He so much deserves. Be open to God's leading as you become aware of the spiritual gifts He has given you. Then determine how you can be the person God wants you to be in the places and circumstances you currently find yourself. Ask God to show you how you can serve Him.

Chapter Ten

Becoming God's Masterpiece

One can only imagine what kind of genius thought of blowing down a metal tube and forming a bubble inside a molten blob of glass made from silica or sand, the most common material in the world, using human breath and fire to transform it from a solid to a liquid and back to a solid.

Dale Chihuly is a world-renowned entrepreneur in the field of glass sculpting. His exhibits in museums around the world leave people in utter amazement at the sheer beauty a craftsman can produce from mere sand. It reminds me of the Lord God who formed Adam from the dust of the ground in the garden of Eden and breathed into his nostrils the breath of life, making Adam a living being. No human being has replicated that marvel of creation.

I am fascinated when I see craftsmen at work. I can only imagine how someone sees potential in a block of wood or ice, paints a magnificent picture on a piece of canvas, molds a lump of clay into a beautiful vessel, sculpts castles and figurines from beach sand, or takes colored threads and weaves a beautiful tapestry. It reminds me of the chorus of Bill Gaither's gospel song, *Something*

Beautiful, which declares God can make something beautiful out of our confusion, brokenness, and strife.

Because of His saving grace and redemptive work, God can turn lives that are flawed, confused, broken, and messy into one of His masterpieces. The Bible affirms believers in Christ are God's workmanship, His handiwork, and that He is shaping and molding them into the vessel He wants them to be (Ephesians 2:10).

This presupposes two things: first, that God is indeed at work in our lives, and second that we are allowing Him to work without resistance or defiance. God's purpose is to prepare us for an eternity with Him and to conform us into the image of Christ. What does that image look like? Let's take a peek.

At the heart of being the person God wants us to be lies integrity. There was a time when it was rare for an American corporation to teach integrity. Integrity was pretty much taken for granted. Now the subject is high on the list of seminar priorities, and more companies are placing increasing emphasis on integrity and ethics in the workplace. While this is honorable, integrity must be reflected in every area of our lives. For instance, a doctor may demonstrate medical excellence and integrity and perform brilliantly in the emergency room but be engaged in an illicit affair by cheating on his spouse or tax returns. That belies a person of integrity.

Dictionary definitions of integrity vary from being entire or complete, morally sound, honest, free from corrupting influence and motives, uprightness, and rectitude to a rigid adherence to a code of behavior or the state of being unimpaired. Wikipedia, which is not always considered a reliable source for information, defines integrity as "the qualifications of being honest and having strong moral principles; moral uprightness." It goes on to say, "Integrity is generally a personal choice to hold oneself to consistent moral and ethical standards. In ethics, integrity is regarded by many as the honesty and truthfulness or accuracy of one's actions."

But integrity exceeds those definitions.

Several years ago, after teaching a Sunday school class in which the subject of integrity was discussed, Harry Obley, a good friend, gave me an article on ethics. It was written by an accountant for a conference of Certified Public Accountants in southern California where he was a guest speaker. I have never forgotten one point he made and the illustration he used. He wrote, "An ethical person is a person of integrity, which means they are true to their word."

He illustrated his point by telling the story of a wealthy farmer who challenged young men to jump into his outdoor swimming pool in which he had placed two hungry crocodiles. He promised three things to the man who was brave enough to dive into the pool, swim to the other end, and make his escape before a crocodile snapped its ferocious teeth around his body. He promised the courageous young man one million dollars, one of his daughters in marriage, and a brand-new house on his ranch in which the couple could live happily ever after.

He set the day and time. The event was widely promoted. A large crowd, including press, radio, and television reporters and cameramen, gathered around the pool. A loud splash was heard, and a man was seen swimming frantically for his life. Everyone stood with bated breath, fearing he would never survive the challenge as the crocodiles turned to make chase. Fortunately, he made it to the other end and climbed out of the pool as one crocodile was about to snap its jaws around his leg.

The crowd went berserk. Every camera focused on the young hero. Reporters rushed up to the adventurous man, as the farmer was heard shouting, "This is the man I want for my daughter," There was silence as one reporter asked the question, "How do feel after winning the three prizes? You must be one happy guy!" The young man responded with disgust, "I don't want any of that. All I want is to find the person who pushed me into the pool!"

The speaker at the conference touted the integrity of the farmer in his willingness to follow through with his verbal promises to compensate the successful contestant. "This was a man of his word," he said. But this raises a host of questions. What were the farmer's real motives? Would a person of integrity intentionally jeopardize a young man's life for a publicity stunt? Had he considered his daughter's willingness to gain a husband under these circumstances and one she could probably never truly love? Was the crowd showing integrity in wanting to see such a dangerous stunt? The real hero was the young man who refused the prize because he had no intention of competing for it in the first place. He was the one who showed integrity.

One can be true to their word but unethical in their demands and practices. That never makes anyone a person of integrity.

Integrity has to do with authenticity. People of integrity are free from duplicity. They don't confuse the sacred and the secular. They are not motivated by hidden agendas. What you see is what you get. Integrity also has to do with courage. People of integrity stand for their convictions, regardless of the consequences. They are also dependable and reliable. And, by the way, they are also true to their word which they regard as their bond.

Biblical integrity involves not merely acting according to one's beliefs and convictions but acting according to scriptural teaching and principles with the desire to please God and to glorify Him. This raises the subject of integrity to new heights. People of integrity are consistent as they "adorn the Gospel" and demonstrate a biblical lifestyle. They practice God's Word.

I will cover the subject of integrity under three headings—the basis, boundaries, and blessings of integrity.

The Basis for Integrity

Integrity flows from the character of God and nothing short of God's own nature. From a biblical perspective, integrity involves living in a way that our lives mirror God's nature and character.

We discover integrity as we observe how God acts toward us. God made a special covenant with Israel, for example, and remained steadfast and faithful even in the face of constant rebellion. He never wavered in His love for them. Jeremiah captured this attribute of God when he wrote, "Because of the Lord's great love we are not consumed, for his compassions never fail. They are new every morning; great is your faithfulness" (Lamentations 3:22–23). These verses became the theme of Thomas Chisholm's great hymn, "Great is Thy Faithfulness," which is loved, sung, and quoted by so many.

Because God is faithful, He is trustworthy. Knowing He is true to His promises, we can trust Him with every facet of our lives. Because God is trustworthy, He is also just. God's justice reflects three other qualities. First, He is fair. For example, He causes the sun to rise on the evil and the good and sends rain on the righteous and the unrighteous (Matthew 5:45). Second, He is impartial in that He offers salvation to all people regardless of race, ethnic origin, social status, gender, or transgender (Galatians 3:28–29). Third, God's justice entails compassion.

God will never act inconsistently with His character. While He is holy and hates sin, His justice demands the sinner be brought to account and punished. This raises the question, "How then can a holy and just God punish sin and yet be merciful to the sinner without compromising His holiness and justice?" Love found a way.

God calls us to be like Him. We are to be holy because He is holy. As imitators of God, people of integrity are faithful and therefore trustworthy. Following God's example, they act justly, are impartial in their dealings with others, act compassionately toward others, and walk in love—as God loves them.

Integrity begins with a heart that is right toward God. The prophet Micah declared, "He has shown you, O mortal, what is good. And what does the Lord require of you? To act justly and to love mercy and to walk humbly with your God" (Micah 6:8).

The Boundaries of Integrity

Integrity has broad boundaries which flow into all dimensions of life, including the vocational, financial, sexual, and domestic realms.

Integrity in the Vocational Realm.

Vocational integrity means we model our lives after God's own example of holiness, faithfulness, justice, love, and compassion.

As employees, integrity begins with viewing our vocations, not as a vacation, but as a way of bringing glory to God and serving others. When we work sincerely and wholeheartedly as unto the Lord rather than unto men (Ephesians 6:5-7), our job is transformed into a ministry as we fulfill our assigned tasks for the Lord's sake. People of integrity become model workers—conscientious, punctual, hardworking, honest, trustworthy, and faithful.

As employers, integrity involves treating employees justly. This includes paying fair wages and paying them on time. It also means seeking to provide a safe environment that promotes integrity.

Way back in 1980, William Pollard, a senior vice-president in the ServiceMaster Corporation at the time—he later became president and then chairman—invited me to attend one of their quarterly three-day seminar/workshops for managers and franchise owners. Several things about that seminar stick in my memory. First, the company had an enviable track record in that, over the prior twenty-one years, each quarter's profits exceeded the previous quarter. The second thing that impressed me was the company's mission statement which incorporated four stated objectives. They were to glorify God, strive for excellence, develop people, and make a profit. Their stated goal was to never make a profit at the expense of people or excellence. Neither would they undertake any business transaction, no matter how profitable, that would dishonor God.

Integrity in the marketplace means refusing to align with dishonest, shady, and unethical practices, even though standing firm for our convictions could result in losing the contract or being fired. Ultimately, it's the praise of God we seek, not the praise of men.

In one of his books, Harry Ironside (1876–1948)—the beloved pastor of Moody Memorial Church in Chicago—told the story of a commuter train ride into the city on a cold, windy, and icy day. Every passenger was wrapped in their winter coats, scarves, and gloves when the conductor came by to examine their tickets. Everyone grumbled and complained because he knew them all. He saw their tickets every day. "Not today," they said. "Don't make us take off our gloves and open our coats to get our tickets out." Finally, amid the rising complaints, one passenger shouted, "You are not very popular today." The conductor immediately responded, "Head office thinks very highly of me!" It's what God thinks of us, not what men think, that matters. That's the bottom line.

Integrity in the Financial Realm.

Financial integrity covers a wide spectrum. For one, it refuses to let economic criteria and success measure human worth because as the Lord Jesus said, "Watch out! Be on your guard against all kinds of greed; life does not consist in an abundance of possessions" (Luke 12:15).

A person of integrity resists every temptation to advance their financial status through dishonesty, injustice, oppression, or deception. Solomon provides the reason, "Better the poor whose walk is blameless than the rich whose ways are perverse" (Proverbs 28:6).

Integrity means we don't steal from our employers, whether it be inventory, office supplies, time, intellectual property, or resources. It means we don't cheat on our income taxes, fudge expense reports, or defraud creditors. It also means we pay our bills on time and, when we experience unexpected financial restraints, we immediately notify our creditors to work out a plan, not evade them.

Financial integrity also means being good and faithful stewards of the resources God has entrusted to us, including time, talent, and treasures. While it is not widely accepted, there is nothing we have that we didn't receive from God. He gave us bodies and brains, and the skills and stamina, to earn wages and make a living. The believer recognizes all the earth's resources belong to God, from the cattle on a thousand hills to the wealth in every mine. Believers belong to God because we have been bought with the price of the precious blood of Jesus Christ. For that reason, we are to glorify God in our bodies (1 Corinthians 6:19–20).

Integrity in the Sexual Realm.

God's universal gold standard is clear: "Marriage should be honored by all, and the marriage bed kept pure, for God will judge the adulterer and all the sexually immoral" (Hebrews 13:4).

Sexual intimacy is only pure when exercised appropriately. For the single person, it means a willingness to wait until marriage for sexual intimacy and intercourse. God's call to virginity before marriage is unequivocal. For a married person, it means being faithful to one's spouse alone, and avoiding things like pornography and places like massage parlors and strip bars. Sexually transmitted diseases are just one price people pay for breaking the boundaries God has established. Others suffer broken marriages, devastated families, blackmail, job loss, and public disgrace.

Purity also means obeying Jesus's command not to lust after that which is not ours (Matthew 5:27–28). This means, men, that we do not put ourselves in a position to use or abuse women sexually, either by thought or by action. It also includes the exploitation of women for sex. For the single man, it means treating every woman in a manner that respects and preserves her virginity for her future husband. The same is true for Christian women. Women lust after men, dress provocatively, engage in sexual fantasies, and make irresistible advances.

The temptations for both men and women are legion. For married people, sexual purity means reflecting God's absolute faithfulness to their spouses. You can probably bet your bottom dollar that when a man or woman cheats in the most sacred and intimate human relationship, they are also cheating in other areas. An axiom I used in the corporate world was: "If you are cheating on your spouse, you are probably cheating on your company." For that reason, at a time when it was permissible in south-central Africa, when hiring senior executives, I would inquire about their intimate relationships.

Integrity in the Domestic Realm.

A fourth dimension of integrity is living with integrity in the home. Away from home, we can easily put on a charade. However, we cannot fool those with whom we live. They see the inconsistencies between what we say and do.

People of integrity mirror God's nature to their families. They say with the psalmist, "I will be careful to lead a blameless life . . . I will conduct the affairs of my house with a blameless heart" (Psalm 101:2). They live out this commitment in the big and little occasions of family life. They seek to be faithful, just, and compassionate in all they say and do.

In addition to the four areas mentioned above, integrity also flows into the realms of ethical and moral conduct. Do we really understand the importance of moral and ethical purity in the marketplace, in the classroom, in the emergency room, and on the factory floor? In His teachings, the Lord Jesus made a direct connection between Christianity and morality. Who we are has a direct impact on what we do. While people stiffen, become uncomfortable, even begin to sweat at the mention of morality, we must avoid all immorality.

The Bible commands us to become holy and blameless (Ephesians 1:4), to live a life worthy of our divine calling (Ephesians 4:1), to be imitators of God (Ephesians 5:1), to keep ourselves pure (1 Timothy 5:22), and to keep ourselves from being polluted by the world (James 1:27). That's what being a person of integrity means.

In both Hebrew and Greek, the word *holy* refers to something or someone set apart for God. Purity is one of the major characteristics of a holy man and woman. Something pure is spotless, stainless, free from what weakens or pollutes, and free from moral fault. That's our calling in Christ.

As people of integrity, we wrestle with issues such as breaking the code of silence, doing what is right rather than expedient, and being brutally honest when we see our company incurring unnecessary cost overruns, doing something illegal, or just plain wrong.

Integrity also flows into our verbal communications. Our word is to be our bond, even if it proves costly. A verbal agreement should be as legally binding as a written contract.

Over the years, I've told the story of the building contractor whose business collapsed due to a housing slump. He lost his own home in the economic downturn. He professed to be a follower of Jesus Christ. His family was desperate, and he let it be known he was praying for a job.

Learning of his need, a wealthy man in his church came to him and told him he wanted a house built and asked him to build it. He gave him the plan. It was to be a magnificent home. "I want it built with the finest materials and labor, no matter the cost," he said.

Handing the contractor the architectural drawings, he asked for a quote. The contractor costed in the best materials and workmanship, and to his surprise the quote was accepted. However, he determined to cut costs, use the cheapest materials and labor, and to skimp everywhere he could, pretty sure it would never be discovered.

Eventually the house was finished. Gleefully, the contractor sought the final contractual payment, knowing full well he had cheated, saving himself a substantial sum of money.

The family had been living in a dingy and cramped apartment all this time and had looked forward to the final payment that would help get them out of the hole they were in. What happened next was beyond his wildest imagination.

The benefactor handed the contractor the title deeds to the new home, telling him he had intended giving it to him from the outset. It was a bittersweet moment. The contractor was awestruck, thrilled on the one hand, but dismayed on the other, knowing he could have owned a home built with the finest materials and labor.

To what extent are we like that with God? Instead of building our lives with gold, silver, and precious stones, we use wood, hay, and stubble with no lasting value. Paul addressed this in 1 Corinthians 3:12–15. It is easy to shortchange God and deny Him our best.

The Blessings of Integrity

The Bible does not promise being a person of integrity will be easy. There's often a cost involved. The Lord Jesus Christ proved that as He encountered misunderstanding, ridicule, and opposition — even to the point of persecution and crucifixion. Nevertheless, we are called to integrity. The blessings far outweigh the buffetings.

Integrity brings security. Three scriptures affirm this. "Whoever walks in integrity walks securely, but whoever takes crooked paths will be found out" (Proverbs 10:9). "The integrity of the upright guides them, but the unfaithful are destroyed by their duplicity" (Proverbs 11:3). "Righteousness guards the person of integrity, but wickedness overthrows the sinner" (Proverbs 13:6).

As I write this, in addition to the Harvey Weinstein scandal, breaking news focused on sexual misconduct involving some five hundred senior military personnel, some posing severe security risks. In addition, industries ranging from tech to finance, from Hollywood to the news media, have been rocked by sexual harassment and assault scandals that have led to the ouster of top executives. Then reports of sexual scandals among some of the highest offices in the country broke as politicians were forced to resign. The cover-up of churches for the sexual abuses by priests has also been exposed. Understandably, there have been cries for reform — but reform will never cut it. Only the saving grace and keeping power of Jesus Christ will.

With the haunting fear of being caught, the lack of moral integrity leaves perpetrators extremely insecure. Not so the righteous person who walks according to God's Word. From a child, my mother taught me that the best pillow is a good conscience. That certainly ensures a good night's sleep. As a result, I have endeavored to live without the daunting fear of constantly looking back over my shoulder to see who is coming after me.

Integrity is also exemplary. Even though we may be subject to ridicule and persecution, we leave a lasting impression on colleagues and co-workers. Many have acknowledged their lives were incredibly changed because of the influence of authentic followers of Christ who were not afraid to let their light shine. Peter put it succinctly in his first letter, "Live such good lives among the pagans that, though they accuse you of doing wrong, they may see your good deeds and glorify God on the day he visits us" (1 Peter 2:12).

Most importantly, *integrity pleases God.* If our lives please God, we know we will stand before Him one day without shame. The psalmist expressed it well, "Because of my integrity you uphold me and set me in your presence forever" (Psalm 41:12).

In Psalm 15, David asked the question, "Lord, who may dwell in your sacred tent? Who may live on your holy mountain?" He then provided the answer:

> The one whose walk is blameless, who does what is righteous, who speaks the truth from their heart; whose tongue utters no slander, who does no wrong to a neighbor, and casts no slur on others; who despises a vile person but honors those who fear the Lord, who keeps an oath even when it hurts, and does not change their mind; who lends money to the poor without interest; who does not accept a bribe against the innocent. Whoever does these things will never be shaken. (Psalm 15:1–5)

The benefit is: "Whoever does these things will never be shaken"

I am not for one moment suggesting living a life of integrity is a means of salvation, even though it saves us from many situations. We are saved by God's grace through faith in Christ alone. Integrity shines for all to see. More importantly, it glorifies God and exalts the Lord Jesus Christ, who by His amazing love and sacrificial death at Calvary made it possible to live such a life. For this reason, above all others, we commit to being a reflection of our God and Savior.

You may be wondering why I am spending so much time on a chapter such as this when discovering God's will is your pursuit. You may be asking, "Why don't you get down to where the rubber meets the road?" I am! Living a life of integrity *is* God's will for you.

It is disturbing so many find God's will elusive. They find God's will elusive because of the lives they live and by the state their lives are in. While God is the God of the miraculous and nothing is too hard for Him, we sometimes make it almost impossible for God to do His work in us. We need to be like pliable clay in the potter's hands.

God has a wonderful plan for our lives. Paul declared we are God's handiwork, His workmanship, His masterpiece, created in Christ Jesus to do good works, which He prepared in advance for us to do (Ephesians 2:10).

Some other versions help bring out the concept the apostle is conveying. The Message paraphrase of that text reads, "He creates each of us by Christ Jesus to join him in the work he does, the good work he has gotten ready for us to do, work we had better be doing."

The Amplified translation, sometimes referred to as the magnified version, reads "For we are His workmanship [His own master work, a work of art], created in Christ Jesus [reborn from above— spiritually transformed, renewed, ready to be used] for good works, which God prepared [for us] beforehand [taking paths which He set], so that we would walk in them [living the good life which He prearranged and made ready for us]."

J.B Phillips put it this way, "The fact is that what we are we owe to the hand of God upon us. We are born afresh in Christ and born to do those good deeds which God planned for us to do."

God is at work in your life whether you realize it or not, and whether you cooperate with Him or not. God never gives up on you once you place your faith in Christ alone for salvation. As your loving heavenly Father, He coaches and trains you in righteousness. The training can be tough at times. Every serious athlete knows there can be no gain without pain.

Like a master workman, God uses His hammer to knock us into shape, His chisel to chip away unnecessary and unproductive things, and His sandpaper to smooth the rough edges. All the while, His Word is there to light our path. The Holy Spirit is present within us to *enlighten, enable, equip,* and *empower* us. The Lord Jesus, to whom we constantly look, is there to be our example.

One time, artists from around the world assembled to display their art. The show was held in a facility with a mezzanine floor. The crowd had gathered on this floor to watch one artist put the finishing touches on a beautiful picture. He made the last few strokes of his brush and then slowly stepped back for one final look, never realizing that with the next backward step he would fall over the low railing and crash to the floor below.

A visitor noticed his imminent danger, rushed to the painting, picked up a brush, dipped it in the paint, and then smeared the picture, completely destroying it. The process literally took milliseconds. Furious, the artist rushed toward his masterpiece screaming, "You destroyed my picture." The man responded, "Yes I did, but I saved your life." There are times when God has to destroy our works of "art" to save our lives and overrule our plans in order to make us His masterpiece. A loving God can never be cruel or unwise.

On a recent trip to Florida, I bumped into over three hundred wood-turners who were meeting for their annual convention at the same conference center where I was staying. My wife and I visited their display one evening and stayed for their final award ceremony.

I was literally blown away by the sheer beauty of their work— all intricately carved or machined from pieces of wood. I thought to myself, "If people have the patience, skill, and imagination to produce such works of art, what could God do with us who are marred and stained by sin as He molds, shapes, and makes us into the vessels He wants us to be?"

The big difference is that unlike the pieces of wood, which offer no resistance, we resist God even to the point of fighting what He wants to accomplish. If those wood artists can turn the knotty imperfections of wood into a beautiful object, just imagine what God can do with lives that are flawed.

You may well be broken and crushed by your sin, by the choices you have made, and by the directions you have taken. Some of these may be irreparable despite having confessed them to God and experiencing His forgiveness. That may be your story. Determine from this point on to be in the will of God. He can and will make something beautiful of your life. God has a wonderful plan. He has a divine purpose in saving you. Make a renewed commitment to fully surrender your life to Christ.

The final take of this chapter is that you make it your priority to become the person God intends you to be. That's His will. When your priorities are right, the rest will more readily fall into place. Surrendering your life to Christ will not immunize you from the inevitable challenges that arise. Your faith will still be fully tested through the vicissitudes of life. But, like the believers Peter and James wrote to, you too can be joyous in the midst of adversity and suffering (1 Peter 1:6–8; James 1:2–3). That in itself is a marvel of God's grace.

My Prayer

Dear heavenly Father, thank You so much for putting up with me and tolerating me. While I feel my life is so messed up at times, I know You are at work. I have changed so much since I first trusted Christ. I want to become Your master-piece, the vessel You want me to be. Mold me and make me after Your will. I abandon myself to You. I know it's not a reckless abandonment because I trust You. I know I won't be perfect this side of eternity, but I want to be as perfect as I can be.

I want to be a person of integrity, to be known as a person of faith, a vibrant faith.

Father, there are so many pieces of my life that need chiseling or to be sawn off. There are rough patches needing to be smoothed. Please make me pliable, so You can mold me after Your will. I want to be a vessel of honor, so I can demonstrate to a lost and broken world what You can do with a person fully consecrated to You. I want to be a shining light in my home, in the workplace, and in the world, so people will be attracted to You. I want to dwell in Your sacred tent and live on Your holy mountain so when I come down to the valley, I will be a blessing to all I come into contact with.

I pray all this in the name of Your Son, Jesus Christ. Amen!

Application

Prayerfully consider what you need to do to become the person God wants you to be. List five action steps.

1.

2.

3.

4.

5.

Chapter Eleven

When God Is in Charge

G uy H. King, a clergyman of the Church of England, was greatly loved in the parishes he served. His ministry extended to a much wider circle of evangelical Christians, including me. He was one of my heroes. His preaching and teaching were greatly appreciated at the renowned Keswick Convention in England's Lake District. His devotional commentaries for Scripture Union were read by millions around the world. His weekly Bible studies at Christ Church, Beckenham, where he served as vicar for twenty-one years until his death in 1956, became the basis for several books. His expositional commentaries on both Paul's letters to Timothy were a compelling read. Guy King titled Paul's first letter to Timothy, to whom he was passing the baton, "A Leader Led." Every developing leader needs to be led. Some people, however, can't bear the thought of taking orders from others.

Compasses, maps, and global positioning systems provide navigational direction. Ancient mariners sought direction from the stars by night, while the sun guided others by day. Some people rely on horoscopes and mediums for guidance. Others wander aimlessly through life, never knowing where they are going. Companies pay consultants a fortune for their expertise and knowledge. The Bible, however, is the only infallible source to find the directions we really need in life.

What if we took orders from God and let Him direct our steps each day? What if we were insubordinate and refused God's direction?

Some three thousand years ago King Solomon wrote, "In their hearts humans plan their course, but the Lord establishes their steps" (Proverbs 16:9). Someone commented, "Man proposes; God disposes." The Scottish poet Robert Burns (1759–1796) expressed it well when he wrote, "The best-laid plans of mice and men often go awry."

The theme of this chapter is taken from a text in the thirty-seventh Psalm which addresses the issue of God's involvement in our lives. It also raises intriguing questions. How can the sovereign God of the universe take charge of our lives and direct our steps? Why doesn't He prevent bad things from happening to us? Why does God have to superimpose His will on mine?

Imagine yourself praying God guide and direct you through the next twenty-four hours. What would that guidance look like?

As a starter, He would direct you to His Word and to prayer. Then He would direct you into doing His will. He would direct you along paths of righteousness. He might direct you to some other person to whom you could share the gospel. He would direct you to honor Him at home, school, work, or play. On particular days, He would direct you to His "house" where you would assemble with other believers for purposes of worship, teaching, connection, and prayer (Acts 2:42). We can only imagine what He would do.

Imagine experiencing an impulse to be somewhere at a certain time, only to "bump" into a friend, pastor, or counselor you hadn't seen for a while and whose advise or help you really needed. Imagine feeling prompted to call someone only to learn they were in dire need of help. Imagine feeling an urge to attend a church you hadn't visited for a while and heard a message that spoke directly to your present need. Imagine tuning your car radio or television to a Christian station and hearing a verse of Scripture, song, or message that grabbed your attention.

Were these instances coincidences? Or, was God sovereignly directing your steps? The Lord directs the "feet" of those who commit their ways to Him. It is possible to regularly experience God's direction and guidance. It is possible for our daily Bible reading to relate to something that occurs later in the day. It could be a specific prayer that is amazingly answered.

While in my mid-twenties, my practice was to read five Psalms and one chapter of Proverbs each day. I read the Psalms to develop my devotional life and Proverbs to gain wisdom and understanding.

One morning, I read Proverbs chapter six, and for some reason was particularly struck by the following verses:

My son, keep your father's command and do not forsake your mother's teaching. Bind them always on your heart; fasten them around your neck. When you walk, they will guide you; when you sleep, they will watch over you; when you awake, they will speak to you. For this command is a lamp, this teaching is a light, and correction and instruction are the way to life, keeping you from your neighbor's wife, from the smooth talk of a wayward woman. Do not lust in your heart after her beauty or let her captivate you with her eyes" (Proverbs 6:20–26).

That passage put me on guard. Later in the day, a woman stormed into my office. She had received a letter from our accounts receivable department demanding immediate payment of her delinquent account. She wanted my intervention. She was well dressed and well perfumed. Her flirtatious attitude immediately made me wary. Her compliments, fluttering eyebrows, eyelids, and eyelashes were all an obvious attempt to weaken my resistance. I believe my reading that morning provided the wisdom I needed to counteract her. It wasn't a coincidence. I truly believe many issues are resolved in advance by obeying instructions God provides in His Word.

We know God is good, kind, loving, and patient. That doesn't mean immunity from illness, pain, and disaster. We live in a sinful world. Notwithstanding our sinful nature, we know God desires the very best for us. He has planned that we are not left to our own devices. The indwelling Holy Spirit is proof of that. However, it is possible to ignore Him, to grieve and restrict Him, and to prevent Him from doing in us and through us what God intends Him to accomplish.

We are left perplexed as to why our lives are frequently barren, and our spiritual growth is stunted. We legitimately question why so much seemingly goes wrong and why we are stressed and lack the peace we crave. We even question God's love. We are confused as to why our prayers aren't being answered, forgetting that certain conditions must be met for God to answer prayer.

God hears and answers every prayer, even though His response may not be what we prayed for. Our requests could be *denied,* and God just says "No!" There are times when God's response is *delayed* as Daniel discovered (Daniel 10:1–21), and *different* as Paul learned (2 Corinthians 12:7–12). There are also occasions when the answer is *direct* and even exceeds our expectations.

We constantly hear the cry, "Why isn't God answering my prayers?" I have asked that question many times myself.

God always answers the sinner's prayer for salvation. In Luke 18:9–13, the Lord Jesus told the parable of the Pharisee and the Tax Collector. God rejected the Pharisee's prayer but heard and answered the tax collector's cry when he prayed, "God, have mercy on me, a sinner." Jesus said he went home justified before God. The apostle Paul affirmed that whoever calls on the name of the Lord will be saved (Romans 10:13).

There are a "baker's dozen" reasons why He doesn't seem to hear and answer our requests.

- Not asking in Jesus's name and for God's glory (John 14:13–14; 1 Corinthians 10:31).
- Not praying to God through the Lord Jesus Christ (John 14:6; 1 Timothy 2:5).
- Not asking in accordance with God's will (Matthew 6:10; Luke 22:42; 1 John 5:14–15).
- Living in disobedience and rebellion (1 John 3:22).
- Failing to abide in Christ as He taught His disciples to do (John 15:7).
- Not believing God will answer our prayers (Mark 9:23; 11:22–24; Hebrews 11:6; James 1:6–8).
- Asking with wrong or impure motives (James 4:2–3).
- Harboring unconfessed sin in our hearts (Isaiah 1:15; 59:1–2; Psalm 66:18—read the context, verses 16–20).
- Being unwilling to forgive others (Mark 11:25–26).
- Neglecting to abide in God's Word (Proverbs 28:9; John 15:7).
- Lacking persistence and ceasing to pray when the answer doesn't come immediately (Matthew 15:21–28; Luke 11:5–10; 18:1–8).
- Becoming impatient and frustrated at God's response, or lack of it (Psalm 27:14; 37:7; Isaiah 64:4).
- Not delighting in the Lord (Psalm 37:4).

These thirteen reasons flow out of not trusting the Lord with all our heart, by relying on our own understanding, and by failing to develop personal intimacy with God. Problems inevitably storm into our lives. Sometimes God keeps us from the storm; other times He deliberately takes us into the storm and through it—as He did with His disciples one time (Mark 4:35–41).

All this is a preamble to where I want to take you during this stage of our journey, which is based on Psalm 37.

David wrote the psalm which overflows with wise exhortation and counsel. While the psalm is an acrostic poem with each stanza beginning with successive letters of the Hebrew alphabet, I have merged them into a single document.

The psalm contrasts the significant difference between the righteous and the wicked. We live in a sinful world where the wicked seemingly prosper, and committed Christians find it impossible to compete if they follow hard after Christ. God knows the world we live in and how difficult it is to maintain righteous standards. However, as followers of Christ, we live with eternity's values in view.

David lived in a fallen world. Despite his sin and failures, he was a man after God's own heart (Acts 13: 22). While far from perfect, he was nevertheless a righteous man.

We pick up the thirty-seventh Psalm at the third verse and follow it through verse forty:

Trust in the Lord and do good; dwell in the land and enjoy safe pasture. Take delight in the Lord, and he will give you the desires of your heart. Commit your way to the Lord; trust in him and he will do this: He will make your righteous reward shine like the dawn, your vindication like the noonday sun. Be still before the Lord and wait patiently for him; do not fret when people succeed in their ways, when they carry out their wicked schemes. Refrain from anger and turn from wrath; do not fret—it leads only to evil. For those who are evil will be destroyed, but those who hope in the Lord will inherit the land. A little while, and the wicked will be no more; though you look for them, they will not be found. But the meek will inherit the land and enjoy peace and prosperity. The wicked plot against the righteous and gnash their teeth at them; but the Lord laughs at the wicked, for he knows their day is coming. The wicked draw the sword and bend the bow to bring down the poor and needy, to slay those whose ways are upright. But their swords will pierce their own hearts, and their bows will be broken. Better the little that the righteous have than the wealth of many wicked; for the power of the wicked will be broken, but the Lord upholds the righteous. The blameless spend their days under the Lord's care, and their inheritance will endure forever. In times of disaster they will not wither; in days of famine they will enjoy plenty. But the wicked will perish. Though the Lord's enemies are like the flowers of the field, they will be consumed, they will go up in smoke. The wicked borrow and do not repay, but the righteous give generously; those the Lord blesses will inherit the land, but those he curses will be destroyed. The Lord makes firm the steps of the one who delights in him; though he may stumble, he will not fall, for the Lord upholds him with his hand. I was young and now I am old, yet I have never seen the righteous forsaken or their children begging bread. They are always generous and lend freely; their children will be a blessing. Turn from evil and do good; then you will dwell in the land forever. For the Lord loves the just and will not forsake his faithful ones. Wrongdoers will be completely destroyed; the offspring of the wicked will perish. The righteous will inherit the land and dwell in it forever. The mouths of the righteous utter wisdom, and their tongues speak what is just. The law of their God is in their hearts; their feet do not slip. The wicked lie in wait for the righteous, intent on putting them to death; but the Lord will not leave them in the power of the wicked or let them be condemned when brought to trial. Hope in the Lord and keep his way. He will exalt you to inherit the land; when the wicked are destroyed, you will see it. I have seen a wicked and ruthless man flourishing like a luxuriant native tree, but he soon passed away and was no more; though I looked for him, he could not be found. Consider the blameless, observe the upright; a future awaits those who seek peace. But all sinners will be destroyed; there will be no future for the wicked. The salvation of the righteous comes from the Lord; he is their stronghold in time of trouble. The Lord helps them and delivers them; he delivers them from the wicked and saves them, because they take refuge in him.

I want to focus on verses 23 and 24. The King James Version translates them "the steps of a good man (or woman) are ordered by the Lord: and he delighted in his way. Though he fall, he shall not be utterly cast down: for the Lord upholdeth him with his hand." I took these two verses to heart as a young man and made the commitment to trust the Lord to order my steps, to overrule my decisions, and to keep me from falling.

While other versions translate the verses differently, they all convey the concept the Lord does special things in the lives of the righteous who are clearly defined in the psalm. Here are how some other translations of verses 23 and 24 read.

The steps of a man are established by the Lord, and He delights in his way. When he falls, he will not be hurled headlong, because the Lord is the One who holds his hand. (New American Standard Bible)

The steps of good men are directed by the Lord. He delights in each step they take. If they fall, it isn't fatal, for the Lord holds them with his hand. (Living Bible)

The steps of a [good and righteous] man are directed and established by the Lord, and He delights in his way [and blesses his path].When he falls, he will not be hurled down, because the Lord is the One who holds his hand and sustains him. (Amplified Bible)

The psalm portrays a picture of God responding positively to a certain group of people, which brings me to the first of seven points I wish to emphasize.

The Person God Describes

The psalm highlights the contrast between righteous and unrighteous people. There is a stark difference. The righteous person is characterized by certain qualities, which David clearly highlights in the psalm. One take from the psalm is that God's favor rests on the righteous and that He personally watches over them.

However, you may respond, "Wow, that's cool, but I am carrying a lot of baggage in my life right now. I know God has forgiven me, but I am still so far from what I should be and want to be. There's no way God is going to look favorably on me." Wrong! God wants to make you the person He wants you to be. You are His workmanship and masterpiece (Ephesians 2:10). Tell God right now you want to be that person and will cooperate with Him by submitting to Him and trusting Him, and by following hard after Christ.

The moment you placed your faith and trust in Jesus Christ alone for salvation, God imputed His righteousness to you and made you righteous through Christ. That's *positional* righteousness. However, it is also God's will that you be sanctified—holy and separated for His pleasure and use. That's *practical* righteousness. We are not to live like pagans and unrighteous people. So that you know what God expects of a righteous person, I highlight fourteen characteristics David outlines in the psalm. The righteous person:

- Trusts in the Lord and does good (v. 3)
- Delights in the Lord (v. 4)
- Commits his or her way to the Lord (v. 5)
- Is still before the Lord and waits patiently for Him (v. 7)
- Refrains from anger and turns from wrath (v. 8)
- Hopes in the Lord (v. 9)
- Reflects true humility (v. 11)
- Accepts the bare necessities of life are better than the wealth of the wicked (v. 16)
- Spends his or her days under His care (v. 18)
- Gives generously (v. 21) and lends freely (v. 26)
- Speaks wisdom and justice (v. 30)
- Hides God's Word in his or her heart (v. 31)
- Keeps the way of the Lord (v. 34)
- Takes refuge in the Lord (v. 40)

This gives you something to aim for. Don't rely solely on your own efforts. Rely on the Holy Spirit to develop within you the desire to be the person God wants you to be and to display the characteristics the psalm portrays. The change will come as you encounter God through His Word and through prayer.

I arrived in the United States with my wife and two daughters on September 22, 1973, and immediately experienced my first autumn season. When the snow began to fall, I shook the branches of the trees in the front yard, trying my hardest to get the remaining dead leaves to drop, so I could gather them up before they were buried. A neighbor spotted me and laughingly told me not to bother. I ignorantly questioned why. "Because in the spring, when the sap flows through the branches, the new leaves will knock off any dead leaves remaining on the branches," he replied.

It is like that in the Christian life. As you spend time in God's Word, in prayer, and obeying God's commands, you will experience the old desires and habits falling away. You will discover that you have become a new person, or a new creation in Christ, just as Paul wrote to the Corinthian believers (2 Corinthians 5:17).

I was paying for a cup of coffee at a convenience store one day, when I noticed a young woman walk through the door. As she headed for the coffee station. I couldn't help but notice her shirt. In big bold letters were the words, I AM A BIBLE-BELIEVING CHRISTIAN—I was unable to read the words in smaller print at a glance. I approached her and thanked her for her boldness. Her response thrilled me.

"The Bible has transformed me," she said.

Among other things, she was a recovering alcoholic and drug addict. The Bible is powerful—just as the writer to the Hebrews declared. The Word of God is alive and active. It is sharper than any double-edged sword. It penetrates soul and spirit, joints and marrow. It judges the thoughts and attitudes of the heart (Hebrews 4:12).

God's Word is transformational when you let Him work in your life. Let Him transform you as no one else or nothing else can.

The Purpose God Reveals

The psalmist declared the Lord firms up the steps of those who delight in Him—He establishes and directs their steps. The truth that God is sovereignly at work in the lives of the righteous and orchestrates their moves gives hope. It builds confidence. It also requires continual trust.

Someone rightly commented that God not only directs our steps, He also determines our stops. We might have been planning an event when suddenly circumstances changed. The deal we were negotiating unexpectedly fell through. The romance was broken off. The vacation never materialized. The anticipated promotion vanished like the morning mist. It is hard to accept God was sovereignly at work overseeing and overruling in accordance with His will. It is difficult to accept disappointments when our heart aches and tears flow, when something we were hoping for never materialized. However, we can readily resign ourselves to disppointments after praying His will be done and trusting Him to guide and direct us.

The following passages reinforce the truth concerning God's desire to guide us:

- "Trust in the Lord with all your heart. Don't lean on your own understanding. Submit all your ways to him" (Proverbs 3:5–6). He will then straighten your paths, or literally cut a path for you.
- "He guides you along the right paths, the paths of righteousness, for His name's sake" (Psalm 23:3). As a shepherd guides his sheep, so the Lord guides those who put their trust in Him. When we are inclined to stray from the path God has chosen, our divine Shepherd nudges us. He sometimes stops us in our tracks. He redirects us—often to our consternation.
- "He guides the humble in what is right and teaches them his way" (Psalm 25:9). The Lord Jesus taught that those who exalt themselves will be humbled, and those who humble themselves will be exalted (Matthew 23:12). The Lord is our teacher as well as our guide.
- "The Lord will guide you always" (Isaiah 58:11). We can always count on God's continual guidance, providing we are trusting Him to direct us.

God's purpose in guiding us is that we do His will. He is constantly at work within us. Our challenge is to cooperate and follow His leading. The paths God takes us down are the paths He wants us to take.

The Procedure God Adopts

God guides us through His Word; through a still, small voice; through the voice of conscience; through circumstance; and through the Holy Spirit. He also guides us through "sanctified" common sense. This is different from earthly wisdom.

God has a plan for our lives. However, He doesn't hand us an exact blueprint like an architect or mechanical engineer does for a contractor to follow. He has given us His Word to read and obey. We considered the big picture in earlier chapters. God's overall plan is we be conformed into the image of His Son and bring Him praise and glory.

God generally leads us one step at a time. He doesn't reveal the next step until we respond to the step He has already revealed. So, how does God guide us?

God Guides Us through His Word

The Bible is sufficient for faith and practice. As we pray for God's guidance and study His Word, the very answers we are praying for often jump out at us in that day's reading. For instance, you may be struggling to forgive someone who has hurt you, and that very day your scheduled Bible reading touches on the subject of forgiveness. Or, you may hear a sermon on forgiveness in church or on the radio. The timing is no accident and proves God is working in you.

God Guides Us through a Still, Small Voice

A verse in Isaiah reinforces this truth: "Whether you turn to the right or to the left, your ears will hear a voice behind you, saying, "This is the way; walk in it" (Isaiah 30:21). We may be praying about something specific, uncertain about which way to go or what to do, when we hear a voice, a "knowing," behind us. We instinctively know it is God's voice because of the deep peace we experience when we respond positively.

This is an entirely different scenario from the demonic voices Nikolas Cruz, the high school shooter in Parkland, Florida on February 14, 2018, claimed to have heard. God promotes life, liberty, and justice. The devil's only intent is to harm, captivate, destroy, and kill.

A Bible college student of mine called for help one Sunday afternoon. He had been witnessing to a man in the adjacent park and had brought him into the student lounge, supposedly for further dialogue. The student bolted as soon as I arrived and left me with the stranger. I immediately learned why. The guy was hearing "voices," telling him he was Elijah the prophet and that he was about to embark on a mission to rescue the Iranian hostages. He truly believed he was about to travel to Iran on a flying saucer and dramatically rescue the hostages single-handedly.

The hostage crisis occurred when Muslim student followers of the Imam's line held sixty-three diplomats and three other United States citizens hostage inside the American Diplomatic mission in Tehran. The crisis lasted for 444 days from November 4, 1979, until January 20, 1981. Unfolding events eventually led the Iranian government to enter negotiations with the United States, with Algeria acting as a mediator. The crisis ended when the hostages were formally released into United States custody the day after the signing of the Algiers Accords—just minutes after the new American president, Ronald Reagan, was sworn into office.

The stranger I met that Sunday afternoon had nothing to do with the release of those hostages. He was mentally deranged. Listen for God's voice. He will never instruct you to do anything contrary to His Word. He will never instruct you to do evil.

While drafting this chapter, I was awaiting a phone call giving me thirty minutes' notice to meet someone at a certain place. So as to be close, I drove into the vicinity to get a cup of coffee at Starbucks and wait for the call. That was my plan. However, as I drew close, I felt a sudden urge to go to McDonald's instead. On arrival there, I purchased a coffee, sat down at a table, and began texting. I then spotted a guy reading his Bible and writing in a notebook. I approached him and said, "Good book you are reading."

"I live by it," he said.

I responded, "So do I."

For his devotions, he was reading in the book of Ezekiel. After discussing some of the future events recorded in the book, such as the coming Russian invasion of Israel predicted in the thirty-eighth and thirty-ninth chapters, we eventually shared our backgrounds. We discovered we attended the same mega-church. We immediately bonded. But that is not the end of the story. As news of this encounter spread, several friends came up to me in the ensuing weeks and said, "I believe you met Kevin at McDonalds. He was telling us about it."

I believe God directed my steps that day and prompted me to suddenly change course and go to McDonalds instead of Starbucks. Meeting Kevin was a highlight of that day and proved the truth of Genesis 24:27 where Abraham's servant proclaimed, "As for me, the Lord has led me on the journey to the house of my master's relatives." The King James Version translates it, "I being in the way, the Lord led me."

God Speaks through the Voice of Conscience

Conscience plays an important role in experiencing God's guidance. When we find ourselves going down a particular path that would prove harmful and displeasing to the Lord, conscience kicks in and says, "No!" We need a sensitive conscience—one *educated* by the Word of God and *regulated* by the Spirit of God. We need a conscience that immediately strikes when we are about to do or say something wrong. The greater our knowledge of God's Word, the more sensitive our conscience becomes. Pray for a tender conscience. It saves us from unnecessary struggles and debacles.

God Guides Us through Circumstances

I will develop this thought in greater depth in a later chapter, but I want to reference it here. Things happen. This raises the agonizing question as to why bad things happen to good people.

As I worked on my first draft, the worst hurricane in a couple of decades to hit the USA hammered Texas with devastating results. No sooner had Hurricane Harvey hit, than Hurricane Irma clobbered Florida. Then California experienced the worst-ever wildfires killing scores of people.

On top of all that, there was the massacre in Las Vegas when a lone gunman unleashed a rapid-fire barrage of bullets from the 32nd floor of a Las Vegas hotel, killing at least fifty-nine people and injuring more than five hundred attending a country music festival below.

Then, as I was reworking this chapter, Hurricane Florence brought torrential rain and historic flooding to North Carolina. Then even worse fires ravaged California, causing devastating damage to the town of Paradise.

We question why disasters happen.

In Luke 13:1–5, the Lord Jesus clearly stated such calamities do not necessarily represent God's judgment. He gave two scenarios. The first involved some Galileans whose blood Pilate had mixed with their sacrifices. The second occurred when a tower in Salem collapsed on a group of people, killing eighteen. Jesus said the victims were not worse sinners than other Galileans just because they suffered, and that those killed when the tower fell on them were not guiltier than other residents of Jerusalem.

Calamity is no respecter of people. Both believers and unbelievers experience the forces of nature and the fury of man. Earthquakes occur. Buildings and bridges collapse because of architectural, engineering, and construction deficiencies. Cancer strikes unexpectedly.

So the question is: How does God possibly guide people through those types of situations when many lose everything they possess? In many of these circumstances, many people are compelled to reevaluate possessions. Some come to faith in Christ. Others make a deeper commitment to Christ. God uses all these circumstances to "speak" to us, to draw us closer to Himself, and to manifest His amazing grace.

God Guides Us through the Holy Spirit

Paul writes about us walking by the Holy Spirit and being led by the Holy Spirit (Romans 8:14; Galatians 5:16–18, 25). There's nothing more powerful than witnessing a Spirit-led believer.

The Pleasure God Experiences

Allowing God to lead and direct us, following His way, and walking in His paths, causes Him to delight in us just as parents do when their children are obedient, respectful, and helpful.

We please God when we obey His Word, do His bidding, and walk in the paths He has chosen for us. It is God's will we live a life worthy of the Lord and please Him in every way (Colossians 1:9–10).

Pleasing the Lord should be the goal of every follower of Christ, every day, as it is His will. Then, as believers, we look forward to the day we hear His "Well done, good and faithful servant." We bring glory to God when our ways, actions, and thoughts please

Him. As the Westminster Shorter catechism says, "Man's chief end is to glorify God, and to enjoy Him forever."

Furthermore, we find special favor with God when we walk in the paths of righteousness, in the paths He has chosen for us to tread. Solomon wrote: "When the Lord takes pleasure in anyone's way, he causes their enemies to make peace with them" (Proverbs 16:7). I like the way the Message Bible states it: "When God approves of your life, even your enemies will end up shaking your hand."

Psalm 37 outlines fifteen amazing things God does for the righteous who delight in Him and follow His ways. The Lord:

- Gives them the desires of their heart (v. 4)
- Accomplishes their way (v. 5)
- Causes their righteousness to shine (v. 6)
- Grants those who wait patiently for Him to possess their possessions (v. 9)
- Sustains the righteous (v. 17)
- Oversees the way of the righteous (v. 18)
- Provides in times of shortage (v. 19)
- Establishes their path (v. 23)
- Delights in the way of the good man (v. 24)
- Strengthens and encourages the righteous (v. 24)
- Never forsakes the righteous (v. 25)
- Preserves the godly ones forever (v. 28)
- Steadies the righteous (v. 33)
- Protects the righteous (v. 33)
- Saves, helps, and delivers the righteous (vs. 39–40)

We should be encouraged and thrilled our heavenly Father truly watches over us and has our best interests at heart. Granting the desires of our heart does not mean God gives us everything we want. We should never allow our desires to conflict with God's direction. Fleshly, selfish, greedy, and impure desires never emanate from God.

The Possibility God Foresees

The righteous are not perfect. They are still sinners. You and I are sinners by nature. We were sinful at birth, even from the time of our conception (Psalm 51:5). We are also sinners by practice. God knows that.

Two passages of Scripture I fall back on many times are in Psalm 103 where David tells us just as a father has compassion on his children, so the Lord has compassion on those who fear Him. That is because He knows how we are formed. He remembers that we are just dust (Psalm 103:13–14).

> The Lord is compassionate and gracious, slow to anger, abounding in loving kindness (Psalm 103:8). This is after telling us "God will not always accuse, nor will he harbor his anger forever. He does not treat us as our sins deserve or repay us according to our iniquities. For as high as the heavens are above the earth, so great is his love for those who fear him; as far as the east is from the west, so far has he removed our transgressions from us" (Psalm 103:9–12).

God foresees the possibility of our stumbling and falling. Every one of us will fail, falter, and fall sometimes as we live for Christ.

Many things cause us to stumble. The apostle John aptly summed it up when he wrote:

> Do not love the world or anything in the world. If anyone loves the world, the love of the Father is not in them. For everything in the world—the lust of the flesh, the lust of the eyes, and the pride of life—comes not from the Father but

from the world. The world and its desires pass away, but whoever does the will of God lives forever. (1 John 2:15–17)

We can be easily lured by the world: by its *passions*, the lust of the flesh; by its *possessions*, the lust of the eyes; and by its *positions*, the pride of life. Adam and Eve were tempted by these three things in the Garden of Eden (Genesis 3:6). So was the Lord Jesus in the wilderness (Matthew 4:1–11). Adam and Eve sinned. The Lord Jesus didn't.

If we are not careful, we are dazzled by the "attractiveness" of the world and all it has to offer. We fall prey to the schemes of the devil. That is why we need to wear the entire armor of God (Ephesians 6:10–18). It is easy to stumble, but as the psalmist affirms in our text "The Lord makes firm the steps of the one who delights in him; though he may stumble, he will not fall."

God has made provision for our failure. When we fail, we need to be contrite and confess our sin. When we do so, God is faithful and just to forgive our sins and to cleanse us from all unrighteousness (1 John 1:9). The apostle Jude plainly tells us God can keep us from stumbling (Jude 24). God makes firm the steps of those who trust in Him and delight in Him.

In Psalm 23, David acknowledged God's role in his life when he used the compound name Jehovah-rohi; rohi meaning shepherd. Because of his personal relationship with God, David could justifiably say, "The Lord is my Shepherd." As his Shepherd, God attracted his faith; provided his food, directed his feet, dispelled his fears, overcame his foes, and assured his future. God always leads us in the paths of righteousness.

However, we should never forget the lessons of Hebrews 12. Training in righteousness can sometimes be painful, but as the axiom goes, "there is no gain without pain." Rightly accepted, the pain produces a harvest of righteousness and peace for those who have been trained by it (Hebrews 12:10–11).

The Protection God Promises

The promise of God's protection is expressed in the words, "Though he may stumble, he will not fall, for the Lord upholds him with his hand." (Psalm 37:24)

The New American Standard Bible translates it "When he falls, he will not be hurled headlong, because the Lord is the One who holds his hand." The Living Bible puts it this way, "If they fall, it isn't fatal, for the Lord holds them with his hand." The Amplified Bible expresses it, "When he falls, he will not be hurled down, because the Lord is the One who holds his hand and sustains him."

Stumbling impedes our Christian walk. While we need to walk circumspectly, uprightly, and firmly, we can be easily tripped. Falling can be hurtful.

We are constantly bombarded with temptations through the media, advertising, and our own sinful thoughts. The world has its allurements, but as Paul wrote to the Corinthians, "No temptation has overtaken you except what is common to mankind. And God is faithful; he will not let you be tempted beyond what you can bear. But when you are tempted, he will also provide a way out so that you can endure it" (1 Corinthians 10:13).

James tells us that; "When tempted, no one should say, 'God is tempting me.' For God cannot be tempted by evil, nor does he tempt anyone; but each person is tempted when they are dragged away by their own evil desire and enticed. Then, after desire has conceived, it gives birth to sin; and sin, when it is full-grown, gives birth to death" (James 1:13–15).

It is possible to fall pretty hard sometimes, and our lives, as well as the lives of others, can be devastated. Consider an illicit affair, whether it is premarital or extramarital, scandalous action, an alcohol or drug addiction, corporate embezzlement, or something much more serious. Don't boast if none of these things have never happened to you—it is only because of God's grace.

You could be in any one of these situations right now and wondering, "How on earth did I get to this point?" The good news is that recovery is possible, and you aren't alone. God is the God of the second chance as David, Jonah, and Peter discovered. However, recovery involves a process. You may be absolutely crushed and broken, but you aren't abandoned. You could be serving a life sentence. Whatever your circumstance, God has a plan for you.

This brings me to my final point.

The Power God Supplies

David declared a glorious truth. Though we stumble and fall, we are not hurled headlong. We do not suffer a fatal wound because the Lord is there to hold our hand regardless of how crushing and devastating the experience. We don't have to jettison our faith. Recovery is possible because the Almighty God, the Creator and Sustainer of the universe, the One who has done great and mighty things, is there holding our hand. That brings amazing consolation and comfort.

- Reflect on David after he had an illicit affair with Bathsheba, a married woman, and then ordered her husband sent into the front lines of the battle where he was killed by enemy fire. David struggled with the secret sins for almost a year until the prophet Nathan exposed them. He had to live with the dire consequences for the rest of his life (2 Samuel 12:1–23).
  Psalm 51 records David's contrition, confession, and cleansing. Despite his mistakes, the direction of David's life was Godward. His heart for God is clearly evidenced in the psalms he wrote. Psalm 78:72 testifies to David's leadership of Israel as he shepherded them with integrity and

guided them skillfully. God Himself testified David was a man after His own heart (Acts 13:22).

- Imagine how Jonah felt after he slipped up and fell into the belly of the big fish God had ordered. He realized God wasn't finished with him. He had resigned his commission, but God re-signed him and recommissioned him. God is the God of the second chance.

- Consider the time Peter stepped out of the boat to walk on the water toward Jesus. He was doing fine until he felt the wind and saw the waves. He became fearful, took his eyes off the Lord, and began to sink. Matthew tells the rest of the story as the Lord stretched out His hand and saved him (Matthew 14:31).

  Peter failed again after the Lord Jesus warned him He had given Satan permission to test him, to sift him like wheat. Jesus assured him of His prayer that his faith would not fail and that he would be restored to effective ministry after denying Him. "Not me, Lord, I'll never deny you. I'm ready to follow you to prison and to death," Peter boasted (Luke 22:31–34).

  Peter did follow Jesus as He was led to Pilate's judgment hall, but he followed at a distance. It was there in the court-yard that he vehemently denied the Lord three times. Just as Jesus had predicted, Peter heard a cock crow. Jesus also heard it. He turned and looked at His disciple. Crushed, Peter left the courtyard and wept bitterly.

- God's strong arms are seen at the time Moses, just before his death, pronounced a blessing on the Israelites. When he came to the tribe of Asher, he told them "The eternal God is your refuge, and underneath are the everlasting arms" (Deuteronomy 33:27).

This same truth is found in another favorite passage of mine when, through the prophet Isaiah, God told Israel, "Do not fear, for I am with you; do not be dismayed, for I am your God. I will strengthen you and help you; I will uphold you with my righteous right hand" (Isaiah 41:10).

Several lessons can be learned from this. First, when we stumble in our Christian walk, God's hand is there to steady us. Second, when we fall, God's hand picks us up. Third, when we crash, we crash into God's arms. There is no greater security. Our fall doesn't need to be fatal to our Christian experience. God is there to catch us, comfort us, and strengthen us. After that, He is eager to re-sign and recommission us to His service, as He did Jonah.

The sixty-four-thousand-dollar question is this: Would you like God to direct your steps? Others might ask if you want God to be your pilot or co-pilot. Are you willing to let the Lord Jesus Christ have first place and be president, not just a resident in your life?

No matter your status or sphere in life, are you willing to follow God's direction and guidance, or do you want to determine your own destiny in life? Millions have chosen that path, built successful companies, amassed great fortunes, and achieved notoriety and fame only to disown their families and end their lives in shame. We cannot be labeled successful if we fail in the most intimate relationships of life. Success in one sphere and failure in others does not warrant the title successful.

The good news is that when we fail, God is there to help us recover. We will deal with that process in chapter 13.

In the next stage of our journey we will get more practical and examine some principles to help you discern God's will in areas that are not specifically revealed in His Word.

My Prayer

Dear God, I am learning so much about You I never knew before. You truly are an amazing God. Again, I worship You with my whole being. I am so thankful You are willing to guide me, as a shepherd guides his sheep. I am tired of just wandering around aimlessly at times when You have a divine purpose for me. I ask You to direct me so that I may feel Your hand upon me.

Father, I confess I often slip, stumble, and fall. Please make my steps firm, and keep me from stumbling and falling. Keep Your hand on me, and let me constantly feel Your strong embrace. May I become more aware of Your presence within me and around me. Help me know each day You are with me, guiding me.

Then, Father, give me a greater desire to daily read Your Word. Help me to devote more time to prayer. Make me the person You want me to be. Help me live like the righteous person You have in mind. I so much want to please You.

Father, please help me to honor You in my home, in my schooling, occupation, and recreation. Help me use my career for Your glory. Help me be successful by Your standards, not the world's. Then help me use all the resources You have so graciously given me to extend Your kingdom for Your honor, praise, and glory. Help me reflect You wherever I am, that people will see Jesus in me.

Father, help me to trust You to accomplish what You want to do in me and through me. I belong to You; I want people to know that!

I again ask all these things in the worthy name of the Lord Jesus. Amen!

Application

Determine who you want to lead you. It's great having a godly mentor. It's tremendous having another believer you look up to, someone you seek to follow, and whose wise counsel you seek. But ultimately, never take your Christianity from others; take it direct from Christ. Determine how you wish to be led. Write your thoughts below.

Chapter Twelve

Discovering God's Circumstantial Will

G od has promised to direct our paths when we trust Him with all our heart and meet the three prerequisites covered in chapter 8. We have seen what happens when God directs our steps. The big challenge is detecting God's will in the varied circumstances of life, being confident of His guidance, and being assured of His presence as we seek to walk with Him.

The Bible tells us Enoch walked with God for three hundred years—that was before the Great Flood when longevity was the norm (Genesis 5:22).

Walking with God involves commitment, communion, and companionship. It's hard to keep pace with God. He moves with majestic strides, making it almost impossible to keep up with Him sometimes. Other times, He seemingly moves at a snail's pace, and we impatiently run ahead of Him. That is much more common. The goal is keeping step with God as He leads us along the paths of righteousness. How do we do that?

The prophet Amos asked the question, "Do two walk together unless they have agreed to do so" (Amos 3:3)? There must be mutual concurrence to walk with God. We keep pace with God as we encounter Him each day through His Word and through prayer. We walk with God as we practice His presence throughout the day. This is the only way to build an intimate and personal relationship with Him. This is the only way to experience God in the daily routines of life.

We have learned 98 percent of God's will is contained in His Word. What about the remaining 2 percent? That's the big question on our minds right now. How do we know what career path to pursue, what college to choose, what job offer to accept, what person to date or marry, what house to buy, what church to attend, what investment to make, or how to spend our free time?

Without necessarily addressing those situations, the Bible provides principles to guide us in making decisions that are not only right but wise.

Many people make decisions based on intuition. Intuition is the ability to understand or know something without any direct evidence or reasoning process. We all probably admit to making certain decisions because they felt good. But intuition and feelings alone are never a reliable basis for decision-making. We can do due diligence, weigh the pros and cons, and still see decisions go awry.

Some people play life by chance, hoping to hit the jackpot. Others flip a coin, like the student who was taking a true and false test. The professor watched him flip a coin as he nervously answered each question. He sat upright in his chair when he was done. The professor understood the process—the student didn't have a clue. However, his curiosity was piqued when he observed the bewildered student repeating the process. Approaching him, he asked why he was doing it a second time. "Just checking my answers," the student replied. Many are that flippant when it comes to decision-making.

Don't be satisfied with just making good decisions. Make excellent decisions. Take to heart Paul's prayer for the believers in Philippi that they would discern what was best, or excellent (Philippians 1:10).

We need to prayerfully wait on God, even though doing so may stretch our patience to the limits. The prophet Isaiah wrote, "Those who wait for the Lord—who expect, look for, and hope in Him—will renew their strength. They will soar on wings like eagles; they will run and not grow weary, they will walk and not be faint" (Isaiah 40:31).

Before playing a round of golf one day, I got a cup of coffee at the cafeteria. On the counter was a sign that read "May your day be up to par!" I told the attendant I had a better slogan, and I wrote it out for her. "May today you fly with the birdies and soar with the eagles!" For those who aren't golfing enthusiasts, a "birdie" is one stroke under par; an "eagle" is two strokes under par. A golfer's aim is to play a round of golf in the fewest number of strokes. Learn to soar through life like eagles.

Not only do we need to use the brains God gave us, we need spiritual acumen and understanding. While it is essential we commit our plans to the Lord and wait on Him, there will inevitably be occasions when quick thinking and spontaneous decisions are required. Nehemiah learned this when Artaxerxes, the Persian king, expected an instant response to his question in 445 BC.

Nehemiah was the king's cupbearer and had just received devastating news concerning the defenseless condition of the city of Jerusalem after the Jewish return from the Babylonian captivity. His sad countenance showed as he served the king. This was an offense often punishable by death. Artaxerxes asked why he was sad. Nehemiah related the plight of his people, because the walls surrounding the city were broken and left the residents open to enemy attack. They needed help.

The king asked what he was requesting. Caught completely off guard, Nehemiah did the only thing he knew to do. There was no time for reflection or consultation. His response had to be immediate. In that crucial moment, he lifted his eyes toward heaven and prayed to the Lord God Almighty. It was possibly the shortest prayer in the Bible as he cast himself upon Jehovah. God inspired his answers. The king amazingly gave him everything he requested, and Nehemiah faithfully acknowledged God's goodness (Nehemiah 2:1–8).

An old hymn written by James Montgomery (1771–1854) expresses Nehemiah's prayer that day:

> Prayer is the soul's sincere desire,
> Uttered or unexpressed,
> The motion of a hidden fire
> That trembles in the breast.
> Prayer is the burden of a sigh,
> The falling of a tear,
> The upward glancing of an eye
> When none but God is near.
> (Public Domain)

You may be at a juncture where you are thinking, "What a relief, all that stuff you have covered is fine and dandy, but I have major decisions to make. I need to decide my college major. I would like to get married. I have two job offers; how do I know which one to accept? I need to decide where to relocate. I need to know whether or not to finalize a deal or buy a new car.

I have consistently emphasized God has already revealed ninety-eight percent of his will in His Word and all we need do is to prayerfully read the Bible, discover what it is, and then obey it. I can't stress that point enough. However, we get things backward and spend most of our time worrying about the nitty-gritty decisions of life, as important as they are. Some people worry about insignificant things in life, like whether to bake a chocolate cake or apple pie, or what color scheme they should choose to wear that day. There are much greater decisions in life.

Sir Alexander Fleming FRS FRSE FRCS (1881–1955) was a Scottish physician, biologist, pharmacologist, and botanist who is famous for discovering penicillin. This discovery began the era of antibiotics, which has been recognized as one of the greatest advances in therapeutic medicine.

Fleming enjoyed a distinguished career and was duly acknowledged for his remarkable achievements. He was knighted by the king of England in 1944, and the following year shared the Nobel Prize in physiology and medicine. In 1999, he was named in *Time* magazine's list of the 100 most important people of the twentieth century. In 2002, he was chosen in the BBC's television poll for determining the 100 greatest Britons. Then in an opinion poll in 2009, he was voted third "greatest Scot" behind only the poet Robert Burns and William Wallace. Wallace was one of Scotland's greatest national heroes. He was the leader of the Scottish resistance forces during the first years of the long and ultimately successful struggle to free Scotland from English rule.

It was 1949. I was twelve years of age and living with my missionary parents in Bournemouth, England—they were on furlough at the time. I distinctly remember listening to Alexander Fleming being interviewed on the British Broadcasting Corporation one evening. I found the interview fascinating, if only for the reason penicillin probably saved my life after being bitten by a dog in Africa and suffering severe septicemia that left me bedridden for several months.

The interviewer asked Fleming what he considered his greatest discovery of which penicillin was only one. I will never forget Fleming's unequivocal response. "My greatest discovery," he said, "was the day I realized I was a sinner in need of a Savior, and trusted Jesus Christ as my Lord and Savior." That is indeed the greatest discovery and decision anyone can make.

Countless decisions confront us on a daily basis, many of which are deeply significant and have life-long consequences.

We will consider eight principles to help you make right decisions. In the process, you will discover answers to those aspects of God's will you find elusive—decisions such as job selection, marriage, geographic location, Christian service, community involvement, and more.

While all the principles are important, we will devote more time to some. We will "flesh out" others in a later chapter. The eight principles should be considered in context of each other, not in isolation.

I offer the principles in the form of an acrostic using the word DISCIPLE. There is the Discipline of Prayer, Integrity of Scripture, Stirrings of the Holy Spirit, Circumstances of Life, Insights of Friends, Possession of Natural Talents and Spiritual Gifts, Lordship of Christ, and Experience of Peace.

Discipline of Prayer

Prayer is communication with God and is a two-way street. God communicates with us through His Word. "All Scripture is God-breathed and is useful for teaching, rebuking, correcting and training in righteousness, so that the servant of God may be thoroughly equipped for every good work" (2 Timothy 3:16–17).

Listening to God speak through His Word is essential. We communicate with God through prayer. Prayer is talking to God, chatting with him. Prayer is imperative. Real prayer is not just a hurried blurb.

It is important we interact with God and tell Him about our dreams, desires, frustrations, problems, and weaknesses. Tell Him you love Him and want to glorify Him by doing His will. Take everything to God in prayer. Prayer is as vital as the air we breathe.

It is the lifeline to God. Prayer is not a long-distance call. We have immediate access to an omnipotent God.

Spend time conversing with God. Prayer involves *adoration,* being in awe of God for who He is and worshipping Him. It involves *confession,* keeping short accounts with God, not letting anything come between you, and securing His forgiveness which is contingent upon confession (1 John 1:9). Prayer also involves *thanksgiving,* giving thanks for everything—for blessings as well as for buffetings, for tests and for trials. We are also to give thanks in whatever situation we might be in. We easily become ungrateful. Gratitude determines our attitude, which in turn determines our altitude. Finally, prayer involves *supplication* where we submit our own needs and requests to God, as well as the needs of others. This is known as intercession.

Paul told the Philippians to be anxious for nothing, but in everything by prayer and supplication to let their requests be made known to God (Philippians 4:6).

Dr. George Carson was elderly when I first met him, and, over the years, we became good friends. He began his career as a dentist and then switched to radiology—a subject he taught at the University of Pittsburgh before he retired. He was an usher at the church I attend and was always very particular about his dress. One day I approached him and asked, "George, did you pray about which tie to wear today?" He stood upright, squared his shoulders and replied, "No, I didn't." Touching his tie, I jokingly responded, "Well, if you had, you wouldn't be wearing this one."

It is OK to pray about the little things in life because God is concerned about the things that concern us.

I am often reminded of the incident in the Old Testament when the "sons" of the prophet Elisha came to him saying they needed a new residence. Their present living quarters were somewhat cramped. They obtained the prophet's permission to cut down some trees beside the Jordan River in order to provide the lumber to build a larger facility.

As one student was felling a tree, the axe head accidentally flew off the handle and landed in the river. Distraught, he ran to the prophet and cried out, "Oh no, my lord! It was borrowed!" Imagine being that careless to lose a borrowed item. Elisha asked where it fell, cut a branch, and threw it where the ax head had landed. It immediately floated to the surface. The student reached out and recovered it.

Not only does the incident reveal God's miraculous power, it demonstrates His concern when someone is distressed over losing a borrowed axe head. Read the account in sixth chapter of 2 Kings.

Tell God what you are going through. Tell him your needs. He is the greatest friend you can ever have. Ask Him for the wisdom needed to make the right decisions, and to discern His will. Ask God to guide and direct you. Sometimes He may lead you in directions you may not have considered or even conceived. He may even guide you into making decisions you might baulk at and shy away from.

Too often, we become impatient and run ahead of God. We want immediate answers, and when they don't come, we proceed as we think best. Sometimes God needs to change us, reshape our circumstances, and bring us into alignment with His will. So keep praying and waiting until the answer arrives.

We noted earlier the answer may be delayed for a number of reasons—timing may be one. Other times God may deny our requests entirely because they conflict with His will, are not in compliance with His Word, or are not in our best interests. Then God may respond differently to our requests. He knows best. Oftentimes the answer is direct—the words are hardly out of our mouths before the answer comes.

From Psalm 37:4–5, we learned when we delight ourselves in the Lord, He gives us the desires of our heart. That occurs because

God tunes our heart so our desires become His desires. We also learned when we commit our way to the Lord and trust in Him, He will do it. Again, we need to be careful not to let our desires conflict with His direction.

We need to engage in personal prayer. Take time to pray. It could be throughout the day. The first stanza of the anonymous children's worship song *"Whisper a Prayer"* put it this way, "Whisper a prayer in the morning. Whisper a prayer at noon. Whisper a prayer in the evening, to keep your heart in tune." In other words, be in constant touch with God on His throne. Hebrews 4:16 describes it as a throne of grace. You may approach God any time. You don't ever have to stand in line. Prayer reveals our dependence upon God. Prayerlessness is proof we are attempting to go it alone, without God.

We also need prayer partners. Invite trusted friends to pray with you and for you. Ask your accountability group, small group Bible study, or Sunday school class to pray for you, even though you feel uncomfortable doing so. There will be times when you need the prayer support of your entire church and wider circle of friends. Don't go it alone!

But you say, "My life is so messed up. I am experiencing so much pain. I can't believe I got myself into this situation." That's because you didn't talk to God about it. The very first thing you should do is pray, then pray some more, and then pray again until God clearly leads you one way or the other.

Integrity of Scripture

Scripture is informational, instructional, and inspirational. Spend time in God's Word. This calls for sacrifice and discipline. Many benefits, including wisdom, are derived from spending quality time in the Bible.

A good start is to read one chapter of the book of Proverbs a day. That way you will cover the book in a month. Repeat that for a year, and you will be amazed at the wisdom you derive. Prayerfully read 1 Corinthians 13 for a month and note the difference in your life. Memorize key verses and note how God brings them to mind at the exact moment you need them.

I have driven this principle throughout the earlier chapters, so it will suffice to merely reiterate what we have already considered.

Ninety-eight percent of God's will for our lives has already been revealed in His Word. By now, if you diligently considered the passages referred to and done the assignments, you will have discovered many aspects of God's will you never realized were within the circumference of His plan for your life. There is no point in asking God for special guidance on issues which Scripture already provides clear-cut answers. All you need to do is pray God will help you obey the injunctions, practice them, and follow the path He has outlined for you.

Anything contrary to God's Word is outside His will. The Scriptures are sufficient for faith and for practice. Bind this principle around your neck. Let the Bible be your guide.

Stirrings of the Holy Spirit

The stirrings of the Holy Spirit might also be called the promptings of the Holy Spirit. The Holy Spirit is eager to lead and to guide you. In fact, the apostle Paul envisioned followers of Christ being led by the Spirit (Galatians 5:18).

The Holy Spirit will never lead you to act contrary to God's Word. He will never prompt you to steal, lie, commit adultery, or form an unequal yoke. The promptings of the Holy Spirit reveal God's intentions for you. They indicate how He is guiding and directing you at a particular moment in time.

Let me give you three examples of the Holy Spirit's promptings. You then can reflect on your own.

The first example involves Rodney "Gypsy" Smith (1860–1947). I generally get a blank stare whenever I mention Gypsy Smith. Only a few Americans have ever heard of him.

Born in a gypsy tent six miles northeast of London, at Epping Forest in England, Gypsy Smith received no education. His family made a living selling baskets, tin ware, and clothes pegs. His conversion to Christ as a sixteen-year-old resulted from a combination of three things: the witness of his father, hearing Ira Sankey sing (he was D. L. Moody's soloist), and a visit to the home of John Bunyan in Bedford. Bunyan was the author of *Pilgrim's Progress*, probably the greatest allegorical story ever written. It was there, at the foot of John Bunyan's statue, he determined he would live for God.

A few days later, he attended the Primitive Methodist Chapel in Cambridge. The preacher gave an invitation, and as Rodney went forward to receive Christ, somebody whispered, "Oh, it's only a gypsy boy." That was November 17, 1876. He ran home and told his father he had been saved. He obtained a Bible, an English dictionary, and a Bible dictionary and carried them everywhere he went. People laughed at him, but he responded, "Never mind, one day I'll be able to read them." He then added, "God has called me to preach, too."

He taught himself to read and write, and practiced preaching by going into the fields and speaking to the trees. At seventeen, he stood at a street corner some distance from the gypsy wagon and gave a brief testimony. This was his first attempt at public speaking. His preaching soon drew the attention of William Booth, founder of the Salvation Army, and on June 25, 1877, Smith accepted Booth's invitation to be an evangelist with the Mission. He subsequently made over forty evangelistic trips abroad to such countries as the United States, Australia, and South Africa. Some regard Gypsy

Smith as the best loved evangelist of all time. Crowds packed the halls and auditoriums whenever he told his life story.

Many stories have been told about Gypsy Smith. In fact, books and booklets have been written about him. The following is one story I heard which illustrates my point about being prompted by the Holy Spirit.

Gypsy had been invited to speak somewhere in northern England. This necessitated a train ride from London to his destination. However, it required a two- or three-hour stopover in Manchester, where he would change trains. His intent was to remain within the enclosed station precincts and pray. Instead, he felt a strong urge to exit the building. Not understanding why, he walked toward a nearby park. As he strolled through the park, he heard someone sobbing. Nearby, he spotted a homeless man seated on a bench, utterly forlorn and hopeless.

Gypsy approached the stranger, put his arm around the man, and offered to help him. "No one can help me," he cried.

"Oh yes there is," Gypsy responded, and began telling him about the Lord Jesus.

"No, He can't help me," the homeless man repeated. "Only one person in the world can help me, and I will never see him again."

Gypsy Smith replied, "Tell me who he is, maybe I know him."

"No, you would not know him," the desperate man cried.

"Tell me about him," Gypsy Smith pleaded.

"Well, years ago I went to a tent meeting to hear a man preach. He was convincing, but when he gave the altar call, I refused to respond. Oh, I wish now I had accepted his invitation to receive Christ, but it is too late. I will never see that man again. He's the only one who can help me."

"Do you remember his name? Maybe I could locate him," Smith asked.

"Gypsy Smith," the man sobbingly blurted out.

"I am Gypsy Smith. I am that man. Let me help you now!" Suffice it to say, Gypsy led the stranger to the Savior that day.

Was the prompting Gypsy Smith had to leave the precincts of the train station coincidence or was the Holy Spirit leading him? Obviously, the Lord led him. You may well have had similar experiences.

The second example concerns John and Maryann Bell in Pittsburgh, Pennsylvania. They had both recently trusted Christ and had become involved in a local church located in the "south hills" region of the city. They committed themselves to serve the Lord.

God laid prisoners on their hearts, and in due course, they established a prison ministry, which they named *Life's Key*. I was privileged to serve on their board for a few years. The Bells quit their jobs in order to give themselves full time to the ministry, which is still going strong after nearly forty years. It was a venture of faith, for without any salary, pledges, or guaranteed income, the Bells determined to trust God to supply their financial needs. It wasn't easy.

A few years passed. The ministry was making a significant impact in the lives of prison inmates and their families in a multi-state area.

In the course of chatting with John one day, he told me about the time their mortgage was due, but they were two hundred dollars short. Packing their children off to bed early, they fell to their knees and prayed for a miracle. They prayed desperately and earnestly until well after midnight. They were still praying, when they heard a rattle at their rear screen door. John ran to see who it was, only to see the taillights of a car disappear out of their driveway without being able to read the license plate or recognize the vehicle. As he turned to reenter the house, he noticed an envelope inside the screen door. He opened it and inside were ten twenty-dollar bills, the exact amount they had been praying for. He had no idea who the donor was. The gift was completely anonymous. It was an amazing answer to agonizing prayer.

Several years passed, and I was having breakfast with David Good, a good friend, and a founder and elder at the Bell's church. We were sharing stories, and Dave told me about the time he awoke around midnight, unable to sleep. He kept feeling an urge to give some money to the Bells. The urge grew stronger. Believing he was being Spirit-led, he dressed, drove to the bank, withdrew two hundred dollars from the ATM, put the notes in an envelope, and then drove several miles to the Bell's home. He dropped the envelope behind the screen door, never realizing John and Maryann were still on their knees praying for God to miraculously provide the funds needed to pay their mortgage.

The third example is a personal story of how my wife Nancy and I experienced God's leading one Saturday morning. It was 1968, and we were still living in Africa. I had gone to my office to complete a project. Around midmorning, I felt a strong urge to buy some meat for a missionary family in the area. Archie and Virginia Ross were "faith" missionaries, serving without a guaranteed salary or pledged support, and their conviction, like George Mueller, was only to tell God of their needs and those of their four children. I dismissed the notion, but the prompting grew stronger and stronger. Finally, I drove into the city to buy a good-sized beef roast. Then for some inexplicable reason, I told the butcher to throw in some steaks, a shoulder of pork, a leg of lamb, lamb chops, ground beef, and finally several pounds of bacon and sausage.

I drove straight to the Ross's home to deliver over thirty pounds of meat. Two cars pulled out of the driveway as I approached the house. Then to my surprise, I spotted Nancy's car among others still parked in the yard. After socializing for a while, the remaining friends left. Nancy and I were left alone with Archie and Virginia. They shared their amazing story.

A missionary family of five was scheduled to arrive later that day from neighboring Zambia, but the Rosses had insufficient food for their week's stay. They also lacked the resources to buy the necessary supplies. Confidently expecting God's provision to arrive in that morning's mail, they waited for the mail carrier to come and go. They ripped open the few envelopes, but there were no checks.

"No problem," they thought, "the answer may be lying in our post office box." To save gas, Archie rode his bicycle three miles to the post office in the heart of the city, confident he would find some checks he could cash before the banks closed. Again, there were no checks in the mail at the post office box. It was around ten o'clock in the morning when Archie arrived back home and reported the dire situation to Virginia. They did the only thing they knew to do under the circumstances; they dropped to their knees, desperately asking God to provide for their urgent needs.

It was at that moment I was stirred to buy meat. Nancy had the urge to buy groceries. Others had the prompting to buy vegetables and fruit. One teenage boy had been sent on an errand to buy bread, but for some reason bought more than his mother had requested. He thought to himself, *Mother will kill me if I bring all this bread home. I'll take some loaves to the Rosses.* Within a couple of hours, God had provided enough food for eleven people for a week. What an amazing God!

That is how the Holy Spirit stirs and prompts followers of Christ to respond when their minds are open to God's leading and will. The Holy Spirit will never lead anyone to do something rash, harmful, or evil. He is the Holy Spirit.

Circumstances of Life

The circumstances of life are also known as the providences of life. Things happen for a reason. For the believer, there is a direct correlation between obedience and guidance. Obedience to

Scripture places us on the path to experience God's guidance and direction. As the prophet Samuel told King Saul, "Obedience is better than sacrifice" (1 Samuel 15:22).

We can confidently expect God to guide us when we put Him first, honor the Lord Jesus, and walk in the Spirit. He shapes our circumstances. It is then we happen to find ourselves in the right place at the right time. God does shape our circumstances, as Joseph, Moses, Elijah, Daniel and Jonah discovered:

- God had a plan for Joseph's life, so he allowed his brothers' hatred to get him to Egypt where the rest of the story is history.
- For forty years, Moses's experience looking after his father-in-law's sheep in the Arabian wilderness equipped him to lead the children of Israel during their wanderings in the area he knew like the back of his hand. As one writer put it, Moses spent forty years in an Egyptian palace, learning he was everything. Then he spent forty years in the wilderness, learning he was nothing. The next forty years, while leading the children of Israel in the desert, he learned God was everything.
- God took Elijah out of obscurity into history when he told him to announce to King Ahab there would be a severe drought in the land of Israel. God then ordered him to hide by the brook Cherith to avoid detection. There he spent some eighteen months in isolation, learning to trust God for every provision. During that bleak time in his life, he learned to trust in God. This experience prepared him for the extreme challenges that lay ahead.
- God allowed the Babylonians to take Daniel captive as a teenager, so he could fulfill His bigger and perfect plan within both the Babylonian and Persian empires.

- God worked in Jonah's life, causing him to repent of his disobedience and ultimately fulfill his commission to preach to the inhabitants of Nineveh.

Consider your circumstances. What is God teaching you? Is He telling you anything? Maybe your circumstances are such that you need to jettison unnecessary baggage in your life. The writer to the Hebrews expressed it perfectly when he advised his readers to lay aside everything that hinders and the sin that so easily entangles. Then he added they were to run with perseverance the race marked out for them, fixing their eyes on Jesus, the pioneer and perfecter of faith (Hebrews 12:1–2).

Maybe you need the council of trusted friends. Maybe you need to get back into the Word or back to church. Maybe you need to talk to God in prayer.

Unbeknown to you, God is providentially shaping your circumstances. Maybe you have wanted to change your job for some time but never actively pursued other possibilities. Then one day, you are unexpectedly released. God is certainly telling you the time has come to make the change you desired.

In 1975, while serving as Director of Emmaus International, as it is now called and based in Oak Park, Illinois at the time, I received a request from a young man in Yangon, Myanmar (formerly Rangoon, Burma) to distribute our Bible courses in his country. Needing to check him out, I wrote to a Scottish missionary, Peter Ferry, who was currently based in Thailand. He made frequent trips to Burma and was an ideal person to report back to me. He immediately recommended someone else—a Ronnie Tin Mung Tun, whom I duly appointed our Burmese director. At the time, I was planning a trip to India and neighboring countries, so I decided to include Rangoon in my itinerary. It was one of the highlights of my overall trip.

Ronnie impressed me as a man of tremendous faith. His life story thrilled me. He was the Assistant Manager of British Airways in Rangoon. He was also actively serving the Lord when off duty.

He was a Bible teacher on the Far East Broadcasting Company in Manilla, Philippines. FEBC is an international radio network airing Christian programs to countries throughout Southeast Asia, including Burma. Ronnie recorded his messages in a studio located in the home of a former Burmese attorney general. He then sent the tapes to Manilla, from where they were broadcast back into Burma. Ronnie's ministry "Witnessing for Christ" followed up all the contacts. It was a vibrant ministry, which had, at the time I met Ronnie, participated in planting some eighty churches among the Chin tribe's people in the northern territory.

Ronnie felt a strong calling into full-time ministry but didn't want to outrun God. He and his wife prayed earnestly and waited for independent confirmation of God's will before resigning his position with British Airways. One day his boss told him, "Ronnie, I have bad news for you. I have just received word from London we need to cut expenses, and they want to terminate your position."

"Praise the Lord," Ronnie shouted. He had received the outside confirmation he had prayed for. The story doesn't end there, however. Two weeks later, Ronnie's boss called him back into his office and excitedly informed him he had received good news from London. The directors realized their mistake. He was sixty years of age and due to retire shortly. Ronnie was only forty years old and still had twenty years ahead of him. They had humbly retracted their prior decision.

"No way," Ronnie retorted. He had gotten the leading he had prayed for. Like Elisha in the Old Testament, he realized his commitment was being tested. He replied, "Thanks, but no thanks!" God certainly shaped, and maybe even orchestrated, the circumstances giving Ronnie the needed independent assurance of his call into full-time ministry.

Maybe you can relate to Ronnie's story and can testify to how God shaped your circumstances without you necessarily realizing it. You received that job offer you prayed for, met your future spouse, or received an invitation to go on a foreign missions trip that completely changed your perspectives.

Insights of Friends

Be open to wise council. Allow others to point you in the right direction. Maybe it's your parents who have known you since birth and know your strengths and weaknesses. It could be your boss who knows what you do best. Be wary of a promotion beyond your level of competence. Seek the advice of a close and trusted friend who has your best interests at heart and who is willing to pray with you. It could be your pastor. It should certainly be your spouse if you are married or fiancé if engaged. It could be a stranger who God brings into your life at exactly the right moment and who you will never see again, someone who appears like an angel and then disappears.

God guides and leads us into the knowledge of His will through the Scriptures, through the Holy Spirit, and through His servants who help provide wisdom and confirmation of our prayers.

You could be praying about enrolling in a graduate course when a friend says to you one day, "You know, I have been praying for you, and was thinking you should go back to school to get that master's degree." Someone else might say, "I have been watching you talk to those little kids and think you would make an excellent preschool teacher." Someone else might say, "Have you noticed how those teenagers rally around you? You would make a great youth worker or high school counselor." Another person might say, "You are so compassionate. Have you ever considered ministering to shut-ins, homeless people, or refugees, or even being a nurse?"

Sometimes that's all the confirmation we need. If you are consistently receiving advice or input from trusted friends and counselors that is contrary to your own plans, it behooves you to listen. God could be answering your prayers for guidance.

Possession of Natural Talents and Spiritual Gifts

We have already learned God made each one of us unique. Each personality type has its own strengths and weaknesses, abilities and disabilities. These help identify what we do best and what we should avoid lest we become a "square peg in a round hole."

That metaphor was originated by Sydney Smith in a series of lectures on moral philosophy that he delivered in 1804–06. He wrote, "If you choose to represent the various parts in life by holes upon a table, of different shapes—some circular, some triangular, some square, some oblong—and the person acting these parts by bits of wood of similar shapes, we shall generally find that the triangular person has got into the square hole, the oblong into the triangular, and a square person has squeezed himself into the round hole. The officer and the office, the doer and the thing done, seldom fit so exactly that we can say they were almost made for each other."

Dr. Willard (Will) Reitz, a retired psychiatrist, is a good friend—we have been in the same Sunday school class and small group Bible study for years. He told me of the occasion when a young man came to him totally perplexed. He came from a family of doctors. His parents had sent him to medical school, and the pressure to succeed was relentless. But his heart was not in the medical profession. He came to Will for counsel.

As Will worked with him, he discovered how God had uniquely talented and wired the young man. He was extremely artistic. Will guided him in that direction. He quit medical school, enrolled in art school, and became a professional artist. While he never made the money he would have made in the medical profession, he found satisfaction using his artistic talents.

In addition to the natural talents God has endowed us with, he bestows spiritual gifts to believers in Christ. Amazing things happen the moment a person comes to faith in Christ for salvation and is saved, converted, born-again, and becomes a child of God.

Four passages in the New Testament address the important subject of spiritual gifts.

The apostle Peter divides spiritual gifts into two basic categories—speaking and serving. Those who speak should do so as if they are speaking the very words of God. Those who serve should do so with the strength God provides. The purpose of both speaking and serving gifts is that God be praised and glorified in everything through Jesus Christ (1 Peter 4:11).

Writing to the Ephesian Christians, the apostle Paul outlined the foundational gifts to build up the church. Christ Himself gave some to be apostles, some to be prophets, some to be evangelists, some to be pastors, and others to be teachers to equip His people for works of service, so that the body of Christ (the church) would be built up in the faith and in the knowledge of the Son of God (Ephesians 4:11–13).

Writing to the Romans, Paul revealed we have different gifts, according to the grace given to each of us. If our gift is prophesying, then we are to prophesy clearly in accordance with our faith. If it is serving, we are to serve lovingly. If it is teaching, we are to teach enthusiastically. If it is encouragement, we are to encourage frequently. If it is giving, we are to give generously. If it is to lead, we are to do it diligently. If it is to show mercy, we are to do it cheerfully (Romans 12:6–8).

Finally, in his letter to the Corinthians, Paul identified another set of spiritual gifts, or manifestations, of the Holy Spirit. He told the believers there are different kinds of gifts, but it is the same Spirit who distributes them. There are different kinds of service, but the same Lord. There are different kinds of working, but it is the same God at work in each instance.

In 1 Corinthians 12:4-11, Paul states the various manifestations of the Spirit are given for the common good, not for the sole benefit of the one possessing the gift. To one believer there is given through the Spirit a message of *wisdom*, to another a message of *knowledge* by means of the same Spirit, to another *faith* by the same Spirit, to another gifts of *healing* by that one Spirit, to another *miraculous powers*, to another *prophecy*, to another *distinguishing between spirits*, to another speaking in *different kinds of tongues*, and to still another the *interpretation of tongues*, or languages. Paul concludes by emphasizing all these manifestations are the work of the same Holy Spirit who distributes them to each one as He determines.

Later in chapter twelve, Paul emphatically states the Holy Spirit gifts people differently. There is no single gift that is given to every believer. We all have a unique blend of gifts. Every believer has at least one gift. Some have several gifts. No one has all the gifts.

The combination of natural talents and spiritual gifts makes each believer even more unique in God's sight. The way God has composed you and wired you relates to the way in which He, in His sovereignty, put you together as to likes and dislikes, looks and brains, and physical abilities. In addition, a believer's spiritual giftedness is a signpost pointing in the direction God is leading him or her to serve Him. God created you for a divine purpose. The way He composed you with your natural talents and abilities, and gifted you spiritually, helps you identify the areas He wants you to serve Him.

Spiritual giftedness is attributed to Christ and to the Holy Spirit. Its fulfillment is dependent on His power, enabling and equipping you. Spiritual giftedness wins people for Christ, builds them up in the faith, shepherds them through life, and ministers to their needs, whether it's for purposes of biblical knowledge, wisdom, encouragement, or leadership. Relying solely on natural talents to speak for God and to serve Him will never match the results achieved by the Holy Spirit's equipping, enabling, and empowering.

Lordship of Christ

Preachers in the early twentieth century popularized the thought of practicing the presence of Christ. That simply means living as if the Lord Jesus was physically present. If that were the case, we would monitor what we said and did, and where we went. Just as we would not wish to intentionally offend those we love, we need to be careful how we live in Christ's presence.

The fact is, as born-again Christians, Christ lives within us. Paul made reference to this in his letter to the Colossians when he informed them that Christ was in them (Colossians 1:27). He also revealed to the Ephesian believers the wonderful truth of the indwelling Christ (Ephesians 3:17).

It is unwise to proceed with any plan if we lack the confidence the Lord is with us, approving our decisions. While it's true He has promised to never leave us or forsake us, we need to remain close to Him. We should seek His blessing in regard to every decision we make. Don't proceed with a decision if you do not sense the Lord is with you in it.

The whole question of divine guidance is not our relationship to the issues, but our relationship to the Lord Jesus. The apostle John made it clear to his readers that our vertical relationship to God determines our horizontal relationships. We will be out of touch with others if we are out of touch with God (1 John 1:3–4). Why should we expect God's guidance and blessing if our relationship with Him is distant, interrupted, blurred, or broken? There's a reason why prayers are seemingly unheard and unanswered. We covered that in an earlier chapter.

As the Lord Jesus was being escorted toward the cross on the night He was betrayed, Peter denied him. Admittedly, he was

241

following the Lord, but at a distance. Earlier that night in the upper room, Jesus told His disciples He was the vine; they were the branches. He promised them if they remained in Him, and He in them, they would bear much fruit. Apart from Him, they could do nothing (John 14:5–6). Peter was going it alone and, on that dreadful night, ceased abiding in Christ.

Clearly our fruitfulness is contingent upon staying close to Christ and abiding in Him. Make Him Lord of your life.

Experience of Peace

Paul gave the Philippian Christians wonderful advice when he instructed them not to be anxious about anything. The antidote to anxiety in every situation is to present our requests to God through prayers and petitions offered with thanksgiving. Paul told them when they did that, the peace of God, which transcends all understanding, would guard their hearts and minds in Christ Jesus (Philippians 4:6–7).

The peace of God is like a barometer. A barometer is a scientific instrument used in meteorology to measure atmospheric pressure. In the same way, the peace of God and the tranquility it produces, is a measurement of God's approval.

Like a stop sign, lack of peace is a clear indication not to proceed with our intentions. Risk takers are willing to take a chance. Introverts often have a difficult time making up their minds about most things. Regardless of our personalities, if we are praying for God's guidance, a lack of peace is a sure sign He is "telling" us to continue waiting on Him. Wait until the answer comes.

John Heick was the founder and president of the Heick Die Casting Corporation in Chicago, Illinois. He was also a devout follower of Jesus Christ. In addition to his business acumen, at least in the years I knew him, he ran his company on prayer— often to the aggravation of his senior staff. The company purchased metals months in advance on the futures market. However, despite the pressure of his buyers, John's practice was to only buy after much prayer, and only when he felt at peace about it. He had the uncanny knack of buying when the price was low and expected to drop even further, only to find it rose unexpectedly. He also had the uncanny ability to make decisions contrary to prevailing conventional wisdom in the marketplace. He told me of an instance he wanted to wait to buy but regretfully listened his staff, only to lose a quarter of a million dollars as the price unexpectedly dropped instead of rising. He always credited God for guiding him.

John Heick's maxim was, "Never proceed if you are lacking the peace God provides." Allow the peace of God to rule in your life.

These eight steps are a lot to learn, but they are all markers or signposts to guide us along our earthly pilgrimage. When they are in line, we can confidently drive down bumpy roads or sail across turbulent seas with the assurance God is with us because our hope and trust is in Him. They are all part of true discipleship, which comprises a personal relationship with Almighty God through faith in His beloved Son. They also embrace a fellowship as we commune and walk with Him on a regular basis. Finally, they represent a stewardship as we wisely use the talents and gifts God has given us for His praise and glory. That ultimately is God's will. That is His purpose in creating you and saving you.

My Prayer

Heavenly Father:

I again thank You for Your incredible love in reaching down to me and saving me. You have created me for a divine purpose. That purpose is a lot clearer now. I want to live my life for Your honor and glory. I want to walk with You along life's narrow way. I want to please You in everything I do because I love You so much.

Help me, Father, to be more devoted to prayer and to obey Your Word. Help me to not act contrary to its teachings. Help me to recognize when the Holy Spirit is stirring me and prompting me to do something. Give me faith to respond accordingly. Help me to recognize how You are shaping my circumstances to bring me into conformity with Your will. Help me to gracefully accept the godly insights friends and counselors provide. Help me to use my natural talents and spiritual gifts for Your glory, whether it's at home, school, work, sports field, or church. Help me make Jesus Christ Lord of my life so that everyone knows my allegiance to Him. I pray that the peace of God that passes all under-standing fill me from day to day as I obediently seek to live for You and do Your will.

Father, I pray You will bless me so that I may be a blessing to others, and bring praise, glory, and honor to You.

I pray all this in and through the precious name of the Lord Jesus Christ. Amen!

Application

There is a lot to absorb after reading this chapter. I suggest you start with prayer, probably the most important of the eight aspects we considered. Prayer relates to every area of our lives. Prayer is communication. But remember, communication is a two-way street. God communicates with us through His Word. We communicate with Him through prayer.

How do you see God working through the circumstances you are facing or experiencing? List the lessons you think God might be teaching you.

1.

2.

3.

4.

5.

6.

Chapter Thirteen

Praying for Special Guidance

rayer is often like former Boston College quarterback Doug Flutie's pass to wide receiver Gerald Phelan in 1984 as time expired at the end of the game. Using Roger Staubach's famous quote, famed broadcaster Brent Musburger called it a "Hail Mary." It lifted the Eagles to a thrilling upset of Miami, the defending national college football champion. Now, the term is used to describe a long, typically unsuccessful pass made in a desperate attempt to score late in the game. That's how many people pray—only when they are desperate and late in the game.

The Bible tells us to pray without ceasing (1 Thessalonians 5:17). That simply means prayer should pervade our lives, be an integral part of our day, and declare our dependence upon God for His guidance and blessing. This doesn't mean there won't be times when we send a "mayday" signal to God.

The question is how and when to pray, and what to pray for. Circumstances will arise that necessitate prayer for God's special guidance. Maybe you feel it is time to change your job or career—your company has made some questionable decisions that make you feel uneasy, you have received a job offer in a different city or state, or you are in a job where your skills are not being fully utilized. You could be looking for a spouse, contemplating a major investment, or even considering a new avenue for serving God. You may even be thinking about how much to give to your church and to Christian ministries and missions.

To help you think through various scenarios, I will first draw your attention to a biblical example of how to pray, then show how God used that passage in my life, and finally share a personal testimony of how God changed the course of my life by calling me into fulltime ministry.

Backtrack nearly four thousand years to the events recorded in the twenty-fourth chapter of the book of Genesis. While part of antiquity, the chapter reads like a modern romance thriller. It all starts in the town of Nahor in the northwestern region of ancient Mesopotamia, now Iraq. Genesis 11 records the migration of Terah and his family from what became known as Ur of the Chaldees in the south to Haran in the north where they eventually settled.

Abraham was the son of Terah. Abram, as he was called then, was seventy-five years old when God appeared to him one day and gave him a command, which He followed with a promise:

Go from your country, your people and your father's household to the land I will show you. I will make you into a great nation, and I will bless you; I will make your name great, and you will be a blessing. I will bless those who bless you, and whoever curses you I will curse; and all peoples on earth will be blessed through you. (Genesis 12:1–3)

God would never violate that promise.

The command was explicit. Abraham was to leave his country and kindred behind. This meant his wife Sarah would be the only relative accompanying him. The promise implied he would have a son who would procreate into a great nation uniquely blessed by God.

Some twenty-five years elapsed before Isaac was born. In the meanwhile. Abraham ran ahead of God. Frustrated with God's timing, and at Sarah's insistence, he had an illegitimate relationship with her maid, Hagar. This resulted in Ishmael's birth, unmanageable tensions in the home, and the beginning of the Arab-Israeli conflicts that still plague the Middle East today. Ishmael was never part of God's plan. God's plan was that Abraham and Sarah would have the promised son.

This was Abraham's second major mistake. When God called him to leave his country, relatives, and his father's house to proceed to the land He would show him, he obeyed. The writer to the Hebrews describes that obedience, "By faith Abraham, when called to go to a place he would later receive as his inheritance, obeyed and went, even though he did not know where he was going" (Hebrews 11:8). But it was only a partial obedience. He took his nephew, Lot, with him. God had distinctly told him to leave every family member behind. His partial obedience also led to conflict and strife within his household. Read the thirteenth chapter of Genesis.

By the time we pick up the story, Abraham is old, well advanced in years. The Jews divided old age into three stages. They called sixty to seventy "the commencement of old age," the years from seventy to eighty the "hoary-headed age," and after eighty a man was said to be "advanced in years." Abraham was one hundred and forty years old at the time. He was well-advanced in age. Isaac was around forty years old. Abraham concluded the time had come for Isaac to marry.

Abraham, at the time, was living in the Negev in the southern region of the Promised Land. He commissioned his senior, most-trusted servant to find the bride for Isaac. The servant, unnamed in the story, was possibly the Eliezer of Damascus referred to in Genesis 15:2. For the sake of putting a name to the servant, I will take liberties and call him Eliezer.

Abraham laid out three requirements for Eliezer to follow. He bound him with an oath. First, he was forbidden to take a local Canaanite woman for Isaac. Second, he was instructed to travel some five to six hundred miles to the region from which Abraham had come and find a wife for Isaac from among his own relatives. Third, if no one suitable for Isaac could be found, the servant was released from his obligations. Under no circumstance was Isaac to be taken back to Mesopotamia, because this would negate God's purpose in calling Abraham out of the region in order to establish a separate nation in the Promised Land.

The servant set out on his mission with his entourage and ten camels laden with gifts. After a long arduous journey, he arrived in Nahor in northwestern Mesopotamia. Arriving at the city well, he made his camels kneel in a resting position, while he waited for someone to come. It was evening, around the time when women came to draw water. It was also time for him to pray. The prayer was specific. He prayed God would bless his mission. He asked God for a significant sign. This was his prayer.

Lord, God of my master Abraham, make me successful today, and show kindness to my master Abraham. See, I am standing beside this spring, and the daughters of the towns-people are coming out to draw water. May it be that when I say to a young woman, "Please let down your jar that I may have a drink," and she says, "Drink, and I'll water your camels too"—let her be the one you have chosen for your servant Isaac. By this I will know that you have shown kindness to my master. (Genesis 24:12–14)

It is appropriate to request confirmation of the Lord's leading. Confirmation could be the deep inner peace knowing we have made the right decision. Uneasiness is always a signal not to proceed. Confirmation could come from a friend or friends with whom we have shared the situation, from the Bible itself, or from the amazing way circumstances align with our prayers.

While Eliezer was still praying, a young woman arrived at the well. She was the first to arrive. He finished praying, opened his eyes, and could hardly believe what he saw. Standing in front of him was a stunningly beautiful woman. He watched as she approached the spring, filled her jar, and walked toward him. Eliezer hurried to meet her and asked for a drink. She immediately lowered the jar from her head to her hands and gave him a drink.

What happened next took Eliezer completely by surprise. After she had given him a drink, she voluntarily offered to draw water for the camels until their thirst was completely satisfied. She emptied her jar into the trough, ran back to the well to draw more water, and did this repeatedly until the thirsty camels were satisfied. Drawing water for ten camels required effort, energy, enthusiasm, and endurance. All the time, without saying a word, the servant watched in amazement and thought to himself, "Could this really be happening? Is this actually the woman I prayed for?"

Once the task was completed, the two strangers struck up a conversation, but not before Eliezer gave her a gold nose ring and two golden bracelets for her kindness. He then popped the question "Whose daughter are you? Please tell me, is there room in your father's house for us to spend the night?" Her response floored him. "I am Rebekah."

Was it a coincidence? Or was it divine providence that she happened to be the daughter of Bethuel, the son Milkah bore to Nahor, Abraham's brother, and a great niece of Abraham. Rebekah, continued, "We have plenty of straw and fodder, as well as a room for you to spend the night."

Eliezer's heart pounded as the expectation of answered prayer increased. The very first woman to arrive at the spring was a relative of Abraham. She was a virgin, never having slept with a man.

It couldn't get any better than that. Eliezer had hit a home run, the bull's eye, and the jackpot with one shot.

This amazing answer to prayer called for immediate thanksgiving and praise. Eliezer bowed down and worshiped the Lord, saying, "Praise be to the Lord, the God of my master Abraham, who has not abandoned his kindness and faithfulness to my master. As for me, the Lord has led me on the journey to the house of my master's relatives." (Genesis 24:27)

Let Scripture narrate what Paul Harvey, the famed radio broadcaster for the ABC Radio Networks, used to call "the rest of the story."

Food was eventually set before Eliezer, but he refused to eat until he had told his mission. "Then tell us," Laban said.

So he said, "I am Abraham's servant. The Lord has blessed my master abundantly, and he has become wealthy. He has given him sheep and cattle, silver and gold, male and female servants, and camels and donkeys. My master's wife Sarah has borne him a son in her old age, and he has given him everything he owns. And my master made me swear an oath, and said, 'You must not get a wife for my son from the daughters of the Canaanites, in whose land I live, but go to my father's family and to my own clan, and get a wife for my son.'

Then I asked my master, "What if the woman will not come back with me?" He replied, "The Lord, before whom I have walked faithfully, will send his angel with you and make your journey a success, so that you can get a wife for my son from my own clan and from my father's family. You will be released from my oath if, when you go to my clan, they refuse to give her to you—then you will be released from my oath.'"

When I came to the spring today, I said, "Lord, God of my master Abraham, if you will, please grant success to the journey on which I have come. See, I am standing beside this spring. If a young woman comes out to draw water and I say to her, 'Please let me drink a little water from your jar,' and if she says to me, 'Drink, and I'll draw water for your camels too,' let her be the one the Lord has chosen for my master's son.'

"Before I finished praying in my heart, Rebekah came out, with her jar on her shoulder. She went down to the spring and drew water, and I said to her, 'Please give me a drink.' "She quickly lowered her jar from her shoulder and said, 'Drink, and I'll water your camels too.' So I drank, and she watered the camels also.

"I asked her, 'Whose daughter are you?' "She said, 'The daughter of Bethuel son of Nahor, whom Milkah bore to him.' Then I put the ring in her nose and the bracelets on her arms, and I bowed down and worshiped the Lord. I praised the Lord, the God of my master Abraham, who had led me on the right road to get the granddaughter of my master's brother for his son. Now if you will show kindness and faithfulness to my master, tell me; and if not, tell me, so I may know which way to turn.

Laban and Bethuel answered, "This is from the Lord; we can say nothing to you one way or the other. Here is Rebekah; take her and go, and let her become the wife of your master's son, as the Lord has directed."

When Abraham's servant heard what they said, he bowed down to the ground before the Lord. Then the servant brought out gold and silver jewelry and articles of clothing and gave them to Rebekah; he also gave costly gifts to her brother and to her mother. Then he and the men who were with him ate and drank and spent the night there.

When they got up the next morning, he said, "Send me on my way to my master."

But her brother and her mother replied, "Let the young woman remain with us ten days or so; then you may go." But he said to them, "Do not detain me, now that the Lord has granted success to my journey. Send me on my way so I may go to my master."

Then they said, "Let's call the young woman and ask her about it." So they called Rebekah and asked her, "Will you go with this man?" "I will go," she said.

So they sent their sister Rebekah on her way, along with her nurse and Abraham's servant and his men. And they blessed Rebekah and said to her, "Our sister, may you increase to thousands upon thousands; may your offspring possess the cities of their enemies."

Then Rebekah and her attendants got ready and mounted the camels and went back with the man. So the servant took Rebekah and left.

Now Isaac had come from Beer Lahai Roi, for he was living in the Negev. He went out to the field one evening to meditate, and as he looked up, he saw camels approaching. Rebekah also looked up and saw Isaac. She got down from her camel and asked the servant, "Who is that man in the field coming to meet us?" "He is my master," the servant answered. So she took her veil and covered herself.

Then the servant told Isaac all he had done. Isaac brought her into the tent of his mother Sarah, and he married Rebekah. So she became his wife, and he loved her; and Isaac was comforted after his mother's death. (Genesis 24:33–67)

Imagine the excitement as Eliezer related all that had transpired since Abraham and Sarah left Haran. Imagine the suspense as he related his mission and prayer for God's guidance. Imagine the reservations as Rebekah left her family for a far-away country. Imagine the emotion as Eliezer finally arrived home with his mission accomplished. Imagine the stirring wedding as Isaac and Rebekah were united in marriage. Imagine the worship and praise as God was blessed for His goodness and guidance. It is an exciting story with a happy ending. It is also a story filled with many spiritual lessons that provide insight as to how God guides those who trust in Him and wait for Him to orchestrate events.

God's guidance may be general or specific.

General guidance is the guidance God gives as we encounter Him each day through prayer and His Word, and as we obediently walk in fellowship with Him from day to day. We may not be specifically conscious of His guidance, only of the fact we trust God to order our paths and to lead us in the way we should go. When we finally look in our rearview mirror, we clearly discern God's direction.

Specific guidance is the direction God gives concerning particular needs that arise. We are at a fork in the road or at a crossroad—it could be a five-point intersection. We don't know which road to take. We need to make a decision. What do we do? We pray for specific guidance.

It's like traveling the Pennsylvania Turnpike—the I-76 from Pittsburgh to Philadelphia. Once you are on the turnpike, you don't need specific directions—the highway will take you to Philadelphia. But as you approach the City of Brotherly Love and anticipate your exit, you will need specific directions to your destination. That's when you use your global positioning system. That's special guidance.

Let's see what principles we can glean from this story.

Abraham's Servant Needed Special Guidance

Eliezer set out on the long arduous journey to find the bride for Isaac. It was like looking for a needle in a haystack. He needed special guidance. He needed God's blessing. He could easily have taken the wrong path, made a wrong choice, or said the wrong thing. The overriding concern was to do Abraham's bidding, to follow his directives, and to ultimately please him. He believed he would find the right woman for Isaac. Jeremiah stated it succinctly when he prayed, "Lord, I know that people's lives are not their own; it is not for them to direct their steps" (Jeremiah 10:23). The same principles still apply. We are to follow the directives in God's Word, be obedient, and please Him.

Perhaps you are at a juncture in your life where you need specific guidance. You may be considering one of the following:

- Choosing the college best suited for your chosen major.
- Pursuing a friendship that could become a relationship.
- Committing to a marriage proposal.
- Making a major investment.
- Accepting a job offer or attractive promotion.
- Seeking new employment.
- Making a significant career change necessitating further schooling and training.

- Relocating to another city, state, or country
- Having possible surgery.
- Sending your children to a public or Christian school, or home schooling them.
- Finalizing a contract.
- Entering full-time Christian ministry, attending Bible college or seminary.
- Pulling the plug on a loved one in a coma.

You are at your wit's end, at the fork in the road, or even at what seems to be a dead end. Things can't continue as they are. You need to make a decision. What should you do? The obvious thing is to pray, consult God's Word, confer with reliable friends, look for outward circumstances to align, and wait for the peace of God to quieten your soul.

I was in that predicament one time. I received news my mother had been killed in an auto accident in Durbanville, South Africa. My father was in a coma and in critical condition when I arrived at his bedside two days later. Doctors advised that I "pull the plug" as they reckoned he had little to no chance of surviving. After praying about it, I decided to wait for a few days. Two days later, he came out of the coma and lived for another five years. While seriously impaired, he was nevertheless a great blessing to many.

Abraham's Servant Believed God Would Guide Him

This fact is clearly brought out in the narrative. Eliezer had the assurance God was both able and willing to lead him. He could also rely on Abraham's promise that God would send an angel ahead of him to prepare the way. This raises an interesting dimension. Angels play a greater role in our lives than we can ever imagine.

The writer to the Hebrews asked the rhetorical question, "Are not all angels ministering spirits sent to serve those who will inherit salvation?" God uses angels to prepare the way, to open and close doors, and to protect us along our journey. Read the story of Peter's miraculous escape from a Jerusalem prison and the role an angel played in his release (Acts 12:1–11). There have been at least two memorable occasions when I believe the intervention of angels saved my life. There is no other plausible explanation.

The servant's prayer in the twelfth verse of Genesis 24 was offered with the same assurance. Do you think God would have guided Eliezer had he chosen to look among the Canaanite women in disobedience to Abraham's instructions? No! Eliezer had to follow the instructions.

The same principle applies today; a principle clearly stated in three Old Testament promises. First, "I will instruct you and teach you in the way you should go; I will counsel you with my loving eye on you" (Psalm 32:8). Second, "Commit to the Lord whatever you do, and he will establish your plans" (Proverbs 16:3). Third, "The Lord will guide you always" (Isaiah 58:11).

The Lord is more willing to guide us than we are to be guided. Philip found this to be true when he was ministering in Samaria and an angel told him to go south on the desert road that led from Jerusalem to Gaza. It probably didn't make sense to him as he was in the midst of a successful evangelistic campaign at the time. God had another plan. On the way, he met an Ethiopian official and led him to Christ (Acts 8:26–27). This could well have been the seed for what God is doing in Ethiopia today.

God will lead you as you seek His guidance and trust Him with all your heart.

Abraham's Servant Asked God to Give Him the Special Guidance He Needed

Eliezer's prayer was simple and direct. It revealed he was on speaking terms with God. The prayer lacked a selfish motive and teaches important lessons. First, we need to continually resort to prayer. Second, we need to wait for God's response. Third, we need to accept God's guidance, whether it points down the road we would like to travel or through some tangled path we would rather avoid. The first condition for securing God's guidance in our daily lives is to ask for it; the next is to look for it; the third is to be willing to accept it.

God guides us in the big decisions of life as well as the little things when we humbly bring our needs before Him and ask for His direction and provision. Abraham's servant knew he needed direction from the God of the universe.

Abraham's Servant Asked God for a Special Sign

Eliezer needed confirmation he was in the will of God, so he asked for a sign. It's good to seek confirmation and assurance that we are in the will of God, even though trust is involved. We need to trust God that the decisions we make today will prove the test of time. Today, we have the Word of God, the inner peace wrought by the Holy Spirit, and outward circumstances to verify God's leading. Anything done for God's glory and for His good pleasure must be right.

F. B. Meyer, a pastor in London, England, in the 1800s wrote, "We have no right to ask for signs for the gratification of a morbid curiosity, but we are justified in asking for the concurrence of outward providence indicating the will of God."

God didn't reprimand Gideon when he twice put fleece on the threshing floor and asked Him for a sign (Judges 6:36–40). He does answer prayer and often confirms it with indisputable evidence.

Abraham's Servant Received the Special Guidance He Prayed For

Eliezer was doubtless in a prayerful mood as he traveled the dusty roads to Nahor. God guided him to the very spot where the answer to his prayer would come. What he did on his arrival at Nahor was significant. He could have continued his journey into the city where the people gathered. Instead, he stopped at the well on the outskirts of the town where the younger women came to draw water. He waited at the well. He was willing to wait until God sent the woman He had in mind.

Waiting time should never be wasted time. Eliezer used that time to pour out his heart to God. He took the time to pray. That is where we so often fail. He waited for God to take the initiative. We fail because we impatiently run ahead of God. The servant used the waiting time for a prayer time. What a lesson.

The answer arrived before he had finished praying.

Eliezer experienced the veracity of Isaiah 65:24, "Before they call I will answer; while they are still speaking I will hear." Without realizing it, Rebekah was led by the Lord to be at that exact location at the right time. She was probably wondering what possessed her to be the first woman to arrive at the well that evening. Do you think an angel was guiding her, too? Was God prompting her? Was He orchestrating everything? God put the words of the servant's prayer in her mouth. To Eliezer's utter amazement, Rebekah echoed the very words he had just prayed. She offered to draw water for the camels as well. Talk about a sign.

Rebekah was all Abraham hoped for.

259

God does amaze us. In his second prayer for the Ephesians, Paul assured them "God is able to do immeasurably more than all we ask or imagine" (Ephesians 3:20). Abraham's desires were fully met. God will do the same whenever we seek to do what He desires.

Abraham's Servant Blessed God for the Guidance He Received

When Eliezer realized his prayer had been answered, he immediately burst into praise and thanksgiving. He worshipped God. In his prayer, he acknowledged God's kindness, faithfulness, and leading. This is where we so often fail. We don't pause to acknowledge God's power and give Him the credit and praise He is due. We are to give thanks for everything. God is good—all the time. The tragedy is we don't always show our gratitude. Prayer changes things. Answered prayer deserves all the appreciation we can demonstrate. All too often, we take it for granted.

God will guide us if our motives and prayers are pure and for His glory. If we pray for guidance, it is legitimate to expect God's guidance. Prayer must be accompanied by implicit trust, a genuine belief that God will guide us. We often don't recognize God's guidance when it comes. If we are praying for a particular door to open, and it does, then God expects us to walk through it. God will guide us if we allow Him to.

Lyle was a new believer and wanted to tell someone about Christ. As he got on the bus taking him to his downtown office, he asked God for a sign. A man boarded the bus at the next stop and sat next to him. "Lord, is this the guy?" Lyle prayed. After a while the man turned to Lyle and nervously asked if he could tell him about God. At this Lyle panicked and prayed, "Lord, is this the sign I asked for?"

Luke records how God restrained Paul from taking the gospel into Bithynia in the northern region of western Asia, now Turkey.

Instead, he called Paul and his missionary companions to take the gospel into Macedonia in Europe (Acts 16:6–10). God closes some doors. He also opens others.

The lesson is clear. Never become frustrated, bitter, or angry when God closes a door or when he says "No." We should never attempt to break down doors God closes. We should always walk through the doors God opens.

Lyle's and Paul's stories affirm the fact God will guide us. It assures us He will and does answer prayer offered with the right motives.

Allow me to share two personal stories, the first based on what we have learned about Abraham's servant, the second on how God led me from Africa to America.

It was April 1958—about two months before I celebrated my twenty-first birthday. It was the passing from childhood to adulthood, a significant milestone in one's life. In colonial Africa, this is considered the time a young man or woman is ceremonially given "the key to the door" with the freedom to come and go from their parent's house as they please. It is also the time when one could legally enter into a binding contract without parental approval.

I was teaching a series of Bible studies on the life of Abraham, and the next lesson was from this twenty-fourth chapter of Genesis. I was attempting to teach the importance of seeking God's guidance and blessing in relationships with the opposite sex. The lesson made me think about my future bride. As I had done many times before, I prayed God would lead me to the woman He had chosen for me.

When I was sixteen, I listed the top ten things I was looking for in the girl I hoped to marry. She had to be a committed follower of the Lord Jesus Christ and come from a strong Christian family with several siblings. Her father was to be a leader in their local church. She had to be a sports enthusiast, athletic, and have experience in Christian camping. She had to be serving the Lord in some way. Then for some reason I threw in that she had to be a brunette with brown eyes. After looking intently into many girl's faces growing up, I had come to the conclusion girls with brown eyes were more fun-loving and mischievous—a fact my psychology friends and other experts won't substantiate.

Returning to my lesson preparation, I was deeply struck by Abraham servant's prayer for guidance and the sign he asked God for. Believing God was guiding me, I prayed a prayer I will never forget, "Lord, the woman who says to me that she is right behind me in anything I do for you—let that be an indication she is the one You have chosen for me."

I shared that prayer with my two closest friends. Their spontaneous response took me by surprise, as they in unison said, "We believe that is of the Lord!" I kept that close to my heart. At around the same time, I was planning to start a new Bible study group for high schoolers and young adults. I had the date set for its commencement but lacked a pianist.

In the meanwhile, Nancy Atmore had come to my hometown from the capital city, three hundred miles away, to attend the teacher's college there. I had met her four years earlier when her brother invited me to his home for a meal. I had gotten to know Gerald at a Scripture Union camp two years earlier. Now, I was in Nancy's hometown, playing on my high school cricket team. I admit to not paying much attention to her that day. I was sixteen; she was thirteen. That was early 1954, my senior year in high school.

Almost two years elapsed before I saw Nancy again, this time on Fish Hoek beach in the South African Cape Peninsula. I was a counselor at a Scripture Union camp and had taken the afternoon off. Upon arriving at the beach, I heard guys screaming "Nancy, Libby." Libby was Nancy's best friend in high school. My curiosity was piqued. I had to negotiate an introduction as just about every guy was after them. That was December 1955.

Fifteen months passed before our paths crossed again, this time at a Bible convention in my hometown. Nancy was a high school senior and had come with a group from her church. We met again three months later when I took a group to attend her church's youth camp in July 1957. I laughed off a friend's suggestion Nancy was the one God had for me. My attitude was soon to change.

The next time I saw Nancy was in January 1958, when she walked into my church with her uncle and aunt for a Saturday evening prayer meeting. She was accompanied by her friend, Libby, now her college roommate. Both looked stunning! But my eyes fell on Nancy. She was beautiful. My heart beat rapidly.

I can still picture the long-sleeved dress she wore that night. The bad news, I learned later, was she was dating a guy, named Norman, who had just started a two-year course at a Bible Institute in South Africa. (Norman eventually became Chaplain General of the Rhodesian armed forces, as well as becoming a good friend.) As it has always been my commitment to never break a relationship, I decided to wait on the Lord. In the meanwhile, I treated her as I did every woman—with courtesy, respect, honor, integrity, and dignity.

Fast forward three months to the time I was starting that Bible class and needed a pianist. It was three weeks after I had thrown out the sign to God and felt led to pray "Lord, the woman who says to me that she is right behind me in anything I do for you—let that be an indication she is the one you have chosen for me." After outlining my plans, I asked Nancy if she would be my pianist. Her response stunned me as she echoed my prayer, saying, "I'll be right behind you in anything you do for the Lord." I took a step back and almost proposed on the spot.

Six months passed before I hesitatingly invited her to attend a cricket match I was playing in. It was a "chance" invitation, not one I would normally make to a woman who was dating. Norman was eighteen hundred miles away, finishing his first year at the Bible Institute. However, I knew Nancy enjoyed cricket and would appreciate the break from her college campus. To my surprise, she accepted my invitation.

It was during the drive to the venue, sixty-five miles away, I learned she and Norman had broken off their relationship. The door was wide open. I decided to play it cool and wait to see how God led. Six months passed before I asked Nancy out for our first date. That was April 1959. By that time I was madly in love with her, and she met my top ten criteria. We were engaged two years later, and married the following year.

I don't intend sharing the rest of the story except to say that at the time of writing this chapter, Nancy and I have been married fifty-seven years. She has been wonderfully supportive of my ministry during that time. She has also excelled in her own areas of ministry, primarily to children and women. She proved to be everything I ever looked for in a wife. We have had our disagreements and conflicts, but the vows we made to each other on our wedding day compelled us to remain committed and work through every challenge. We also made the vow to keep the Lord Jesus Christ in the center of our lives. Nancy has been the spiritual partner I longed for and prayed for. She has never obstructed my commitment to do God's will.

I praise God for igniting my heart for her in that prayer meeting, of all places. Our spirits were certainly kindred. For me, there was no better place to fall in love. The best way to be blessed is to be where God is blessing. That's generally within the orbit of a Bible-believing church, a Christian college, mission, or ministry.

Now for a brief overview of my life and how I have experienced God's leading over the years, particularly in directing me from Africa to America—from the savannah grasslands, mud huts, and dirt roads of Central Africa to the concrete jungles, skyscraping buildings, and paved highways of North America.

I was in my senior year in high school when my history teacher asked what I intended doing when I graduated. "I'm thinking of being an accountant," I replied. Before I knew it, he had lined up an appointment with a local partner of a major international accounting firm. In the meanwhile, an uncle and aunt in Scotland had offered to cover my schooling if I moved there. Friends in South Africa made the same offer if I moved to Cape Town. I decided to stay in Rhodesia. There was one problem. There was no university in the country at the time.

I enrolled with the University of South Africa and studied through their correspondence program. At the same time, I was articled, (interned in the United States) to the senior partner who assumed responsibility for my training in the accounting and auditing fields. I also benefitted from periodic classes taught by local accountants, lawyers, and visiting professors. By day, I was engaged in audits, by night in accounting studies.

I welcomed the exposure to diverse industries such as mining, agriculture, manufacturing, commerce, and retail. Unlike many of my peers, I wasn't content with merely following the audit trails; I sought access to the processes involved. This took me down asbestos and tin mines. It took me onto factory floors and into ware-houses. It took me onto cattle ranches and through cattle slaughter-houses. I was not the kind of person to be office-bound. I wanted to see what was behind the numbers. In my spare time, I was also involved in ministering to children and youth. I had no time to pursue my teenage dream to play international cricket for South Africa or England.

In view of the "winds of change"—to quote British Prime Minister Harold McMillan—blowing down the African continent, my studies and career were frequently interrupted by compulsory military training, assignments, and duties. We were automatically drafted at age eighteen. Never realizing how communist terrorist aggression would soon impact the country, I decided against defer-ring boot camp until after graduation. My career was put on hold while I spent four and a half months in boot camp. I was immedi-ately selected for leadership training. This resulted in being com-missioned as an army officer five years later.

Life seems to be upside down in that many major decisions are required to be made when one is young, relatively naïve, and inexperienced. I have often wondered the "what-ifs" had I made alternative decisions. Throughout those years, I constantly cast myself on God for His overruling providence. I trusted Him to guide me, even though the road was often rough and the days sometimes long and dreary.

Among the challenges was the offer of a temporary transfer overseas to broaden my experience. That didn't appeal to me at the time, as I was engaged to be married. Job offers from clients also proved unsettling. However, once married, I began entertaining thoughts of moving into the corporate world where I could be more creative. It drove me to my knees. I remember sharing my struggles with Nancy.

Then one evening, I unexpectedly received an unsolicited phone call offering me the position of chief financial officer in a privately held company involved in milling wheat and corn, the staple diet of the black population. The company was also involved in the baking, animal feed, and grain industries. It later entered the poultry industry. God moved quicker than I ever imagined. I believe God had been preparing me in advance for such a move. Feeling unsettled was one way He did it. In the meanwhile, He was working way ahead of me.

I found myself on the ground floor of a rapidly growing company and soon became involved in general management. The growth necessitated new financial partners. We attracted the personal interest of a Canadian business tycoon and founder of Associated British Foods in England. Garfield Weston later transferred his holding to a major South African public company in which he also held the controlling interest. We became a wholly owned subsidiary of the giant Premier Milling Group. I was seemingly on a fast track to a significant corporate career. But there was one problem. God was calling me into full-time Christian service.

Shortly after graduation from boot camp, I had responded to an altar call to fully surrender my life to Christ, even if it meant full-time ministry. I had been challenged by the powerful preaching of John Cheyne, a Southern Baptist missionary.

I was in a quandary. Should I give more time to business pursuits and reduce my growing ministry and church leadership demands, or quit my job and step out into God's work full-time? I contended with that struggle internally for several years, partly because Nancy was not enthusiastic about me quitting my job. She was an elementary school teacher, and enjoyed teaching scripture in public and private schools, a virtue of the British education system. She also taught Sunday school, wrote Vacation Bible School curriculum, and led dynamic children's outreaches into the community. She did all this in addition to being a wonderful wife and mother to our two daughters.

Nancy was fully aware of my tussles with God, and in the end, I perceived God was using her to accomplish His own timing. As our marriage relationship necessitated us being in one accord, I had no alternative but wait until God released the brake. For that to happen, I figured Nancy needed a personal call into full-time Christian service. That was the sign I prayed for. I committed to waiting it out. In the process, I endeavored to gain as much experience as I could from the corporate world, while also giving more time to Bible preaching and teaching.

Meanwhile, friends were urging me to go into ministry. "That's where you belong," they said. I was receiving more and more invitations to preach and teach. I was even asked by several churches to consider a "pastoral call." While I didn't have a seminary background, correspondence education through the university had taught me the disciplines and benefits of home study. I applied those disciplines to Bible study late into the night, well after Nancy and our girls had gone to bed.

It was during an Easter weekend Bible conference in 1972 that things changed dramatically. The four-day conference began Thursday evening and ended Monday afternoon. One speaker, Noel Flanagan, an Irish preacher and businessman from South Africa, gave a series of four messages on divine guidance. Noel and his wife stayed with us Monday night before returning to their home in Durban. As I had to leave early the next morning for a business trip, I bade our new friends goodbye as we retired for the night.

Upon arriving home Friday evening, Nancy greeted me saying, "When you have the time, there's something I need to share with you." Several days elapsed before I felt ready for what I perceived would be a long and significant session. Other than it being important, I had no idea what was on her mind. I listened intently, almost disbelievingly, as she shared her story.

Unbeknown to me, she too had felt God calling her into full-time Christian ministry. Her personal struggles with God intensified during Noel's preaching and teaching. They finally came to a head during her conversation with him around the breakfast table on the Tuesday morning after I had left. She shared how God had used Noel's messages to speak to her and that his wise counsel had finally brought her to the point of fully surrendering to the will of God. That was the confirmation I needed. Once God took His foot off the brake, we proceeded at top speed.

There's a side story. I first met Noel Flanagan while vacationing in Durban three years earlier. He directed the transit authority for the city. He was also a preacher and, at the time on the eve of a gospel campaign in his local church. His name often was featured prominently in the local newspaper. On one page, he was being slammed for having raised fares, and, on another, his evangelistic campaign was being enthusiastically promoted. Neil Armstrong had just landed Apollo 11 on the moon on July 20, 1969. Noel's campaign theme was, "Man on the moon; God on the earth!"

The "irony" of the Easter weekend was that I was the one who had recommended and invited Noel to be one of the speakers, little realizing the impact his messages would have on our lives. God does indeed work in mysterious ways.

Nancy and I began praying earnestly, "Lord, what do you want us to do."

God laid Bible schools on our hearts. Missionaries with whom we were associated were using the Emmaus Bible correspondence courses as an evangelistic and Bible teaching tool. Our vision was to hold short-term Bible schools around the country to provide more intensive teaching and training, and to help build local churches. Our vision extended into neighboring countries. I even began thinking globally, a vision earlier fostered by Dawson Trotman, founder of the Navigators. He had written a booklet entitled *Born to Reproduce,* which I had read many times on my knees. God had been working in my heart for several years. All the while my motto was, "Don't let waiting time be wasted time."

Life always throws its challenges, as it did us. A business associate for whom I had done some side work was pressing me to join him in an international management consulting firm. On the other hand, without a theology degree, I couldn't imagine myself sitting in a seminary classroom for four years. That wasn't how I had become accustomed to learning. Meanwhile, we continued researching situations where we could become better equipped to fulfil our God-given vision. We finally sounded out Emmaus Bible College in Oak Park, Illinois.

We received a prompt response from the president, John Smart, one of three original founders of the school. Despite my not asking for a job, John Smart offered me the business management position, and opportunity to teach part-time while we equipped ourselves to fulfil our ministry vision for south-central Africa. We committed to a two-year stay. It was only after arriving in Oak Park that we learned my letter containing my "credentials" arrived two days after the administration had decided to combine the two positions offered me. God does work mysteriously.

Planning for the move took several months. As Rhodesians, we were restricted in traveling to most countries—only South Africa and Portugal recognized Rhodesian passports at the time. We needed British passports, visas to the USA, and commissioning by our home and associated churches. Believing God had opened doors to the United States, I gave three months' termination notice to my company. We became concerned as our departure date approached. Everything was in order with the exception of visas for the USA. I visited the American Embassy in Pretoria, South Africa to ascertain the reason for the delay. The news was not good.

In 1965, Rhodesia had declared unilateral independence from Great Britain and, despite a booming economy, was experiencing world-wide economic sanctions as a result. I was told America was not granting visas to Rhodesians, even though I was also a British citizen and we all held British passports. I was told Rhodesians were "undesirable."

I informed the lady in the Embassy with whom I had been speaking that we already had our flights booked and were planning on leaving. Like Nehemiah in the Old Testament, I lifted my eyes to heaven and asked God for help. I told her we would keep our flight dates and asked that our visas be forwarded to the London Embassy where we would await their arrival. Promising to do so, she again emphasized there was no way visas would be granted.

I then shared my testimony of how we believed God had called us to the USA at this time. She responded, "If you ever get your visas, please let me know. I am fascinated by your story." I wrote her once we arrived in Chicago—three weeks later than anticipated.

We arrived in the USA on September 22, 1973, with four suit-cases, one briefcase, and $1,000—the maximum we could take out of Rhodesia because of strict currency restrictions. We arrived without a salary, pledges, or any type of guaranteed support. It was truly a venture of faith.

I immediately immersed myself in the business affairs of the college. Two months after our arrival, John Phillips, the director of the world-wide Bible Correspondence School, a division of the college, suddenly resigned. The president asked if I would serve as interim director. Although I lacked Phillips's credentials, I readily agreed, if only for the exposure to a global ministry.

Three months elapsed without any mention of a permanent director. Upon questioning the president, he said, "Oh, we have one." "Who is he?" I asked innocently. "You," he replied. I was stunned at his response. Directing a global ministry was never on my mind when we landed at JFK Airport. I consented on the understanding we had a commitment to return to Africa within two years. We felt any decision to remain in the USA should be made on African soil.

We returned to Rhodesia in June 1975 for the purpose of assessing the situation and consulting with our church leaders, friends, and missionary partners. To our surprise, they all urged us to stay in the USA, something that conflicted with our own inclinations. We were in a quandary because our hearts were set on accomplishing what we believed God had called us to do.

Conditions in the country had deteriorated during our twenty-one- month absence. Angola and Mozambique, two Portuguese colonies, had been fighting communist-inspired terrorism for two decades. It was a losing battle. Senior military officers were tired of fighting colonial wars. Portugal had also been under a fascist dictatorship for over half a century. It was time for a change. On April 25, 1974, a radical faction within the Portuguese Armed Forces overthrew the government. This led to the restoration of democracy in Portugal and the granting of independence to Angola and Mozambique. The Portuguese communities fled, leaving government in the hands of untrained men under communist influence.

Communist-backed aggression then turned full-scale to Rhodesia. All hell eventually broke loose. This restricted our vision to work the rural areas, making it virtually impossible to fulfill. In addition, I was told I would be reenlisted into the military as the army was running short of officers. At that stage of my life, I did not want to get involved in political wars, even as a chaplain. That was not my calling. We were again in a quandary.

I returned to Chicago via East Africa, the Indian subcontinent, and Southeast Asia in order to visit Emmaus Centers. Nancy and our daughters flew directly home via London. As I hugged and kissed Nancy goodbye, I said, "God will have made it plain by the time we meet again."

The next time we embraced was in Oak Park, Illinois. Nancy and I looked at each other, and in unison said, "I have no idea what God wants us to do." We stood silently for a while until I responded, "Well, we know the rule—stay where you are until God leads you elsewhere." We were in Chicagoland, and that's where we stayed for another nine years until we felt God calling us to Pittsburgh, Pennsylvania.

I embraced the leadership of the international correspondence school (a division of Emmaus Bible College), the largest of its kind in the world. I welcomed the opportunity to teach Bible and missions part-time at the college. I enjoyed the itinerant preaching ministry across North America and the opportunities to share what God was doing world-wide. I traveled six continents and some fifty countries on behalf of the school to help advance the ministry.

Teaching at the college was a different challenge. With one exception, my faculty peers had masters or doctoral degrees in theology or ministry, so I felt like God had dropped me into the ocean depths before learning to swim. However, the disciplines of distant learning stood me in good stead. Once again, I was studying well into the midnight hours to prepare for a heavy teaching and preaching schedule on top of my administrative duties.

It is amazing how God directs our lives without our realizing it. My educational background gave me an immediate affinity for the mission and vision of Emmaus International to reach people where they were. Literally, some students were studying their courses in their mud huts by candlelight. I was also a charter member and an executive officer of the fledging Christian Correspondence School Association (CCSA) which in turn was a member of the secular National Home Study Council. The NHSC, now known as the Distant Education and Training Council (DEAC), is a nonprofit national educational accreditation agency in the United States specializing in the accreditation of distance education programs of study. In the late 1970s, the CCSA endeavored to promote the concept of distant learning to Christian colleges and universities. It was a prelude to the online education available today.

Early into my ministry at Emmaus, God opened doors into penal institutions. This began a prison ministry, which has developed into one of the largest ministries to prisoners and their families in the country.

It was humbling to see the overall correspondence ministry grow over the years as hundreds of global regional directors and their associates shared the vision to reach and teach millions of students the Word of God. Emmaus has certainly made an impact for God, and I praise Him for the unexpected opportunity to participate in one of the great movements over the past seventy-five years.

During my time at Emmaus, I received a number of requests to minister at the local church level. I deferred decisions until God made His will clear. For some reason, I felt attracted to Pittsburgh, Pennsylvania, and began following the Pittsburgh Pirates, Penguins, and Steelers—if only for the fact the Steelers had won four Super Bowls in the 1970s, and the Pirates had just won a World Series. Then in 1983, the college purchased a Catholic seminary in Dubuque, Iowa, and planned to relocate the following year. We did not feel comfortable heading west. We were thinking about heading east. In the meanwhile, I had attended several church-growth semi-nars, and had begun promoting church growth and church planting.

I unexpectedly received a call from a church in Pittsburgh asking if I was interested in ministering there. I felt this was the door God was opening. Uncertain of the duration, we made a three-year commitment and moved to the Steel City in 1984.

God then laid a church plant on my heart. We started that in 1987 and continued with the church for ten years. As I was praying about what God was planning next, one of my daughters told me she had gotten me a job as an independent sales contractor and con-sultant with the company she worked for. I told her I hadn't applied. "No problem," she said, "They have taken my recommendation." Being an independent contractor provided a good revenue stream and afforded me the flexibility of continued ministry as I sensed God's leading. It was the answer to prayer at the time.

I have experienced many twists and turns during my tenure in the USA. For one, I got heavily involved in two murder cases. Rather than being a distraction, I felt these cases were an extension of my ministry at the time. The first involved a student at Emmaus. My first book, *Innocence,* describes his horrifying story of arrest, conviction, sentence, and imprisonment. After a long legal battle, he was eventually exonerated, and his conviction expunged from the records.

The other case involved another believer who received four life sentences for the axe murders of his wife and three children. My involvement in that case was the result of his reading my book *Innocence*. My efforts helped bring about an Illinois Supreme Court reversal, eventual retrial, and acquittal — the first in Illinois for fifty-four years, and only the third time this had occurred in the land of Lincoln during the twentieth century.

The struggle began when I started receiving dozens of requests from around the country to help others who believed they were unjustly convicted and wanted me to write their stories. Through the prison ministry, I learned not every inmate who cried "Innocent" was innocent. For a while I stood at a crossroad of uncertainty, finally concluding God was not calling me to get involved in miscarriages of justice, as appealing as that was.

As I looked in my rearview mirror one day, it struck me that I have never applied for a job. I have declined many offers and overtures. I believe God has always directed my steps as He opened doors of opportunity at the right time. And now here I am writing this book. My burden is to help followers of Christ *know, understand, and do* God's will. It certainly is not elusive.

I have made numerous mistakes, run ahead of God, and often lagged behind. I have experienced severe storms and endured countless struggles. I could have chosen different routes when arriving at forks in the road and have often wondered if I had always made the right choices. My faith has been severely tested. Yet I can say unequivocally in the words of a hymn written by Fanny Crosby (1820–1915) sung at our commissioning service that my Savior has led me all the way. I have also proved the truth of Thomas Chisholm's (1866–1960) hymn "Great is Thy Faithfulness."

Now, I am in the same advanced age category as Abraham when he initiated a search for a bride for Isaac, but a lot younger than him. My goal is to max out for God until the day He calls me home. In football jargon, I need to know the two-minute drill. I was sharing this thought with friends at dinner one evening when one commented, "No, you need to know the overtime drill!"

Yes, I am in the overtime period of life. I often feel like Pittsburgh Steeler Quarterback, Ben Roethlisberger, who, in a recent game against the Jacksonville Jaguars, dove for a game-winning touchdown in the final five seconds of regular time. My longtime desire and prayer is I cross the finishing line running, or diving, across the goal line like Roethlisberger did for the Steelers.

Many of you on this journey have similar stories to share. God has led you in different directions, all the while expecting you live for His honor, praise, and glory. This is why He created you. This is why He saved you. He saved you so you would live for Him and serve Him, and that you bring Him praise and glory in the process.

You may have just started your Christian pilgrimage and are struggling with the concept of God's guidance. God has a wonderful plan for your life. Commit to discovering it.

I trust all who have taken this journey to discover God's will, and experience His guidance and direction, will be willing to fully trust Him and commit their ways to the Lord.

My Prayer

Heavenly Father, I am learning so much of what it means to trust You. Please forgive me for not trusting You the way I should. I confess I have held tightly to everything I possess. Now, I release them to You. Have Your way in my life.

I recommit my life to You and, once again, ask You to direct my steps. This time I really mean it. Take my life and let it be fully consecrated to You—all that I am and have. Please help me use my time wisely to encounter You and to serve You. Please use all my talents, skills, and spiritual giftedness for Your glory and to help further Your kingdom. Help me be a blessing to everyone I meet, including my family, closest friends, and peers. Show me how I can please You in my job, home, and school—wherever I am.

Guide me in my relationships and pursuits in life. Help me use all my resources—emotional, intellectual, physical, financial, and spiritual—for Your praise. Please help me know, understand, and do Your will.

Father, I pray as I look back on my life one day that it will testify to Your great faithfulness, direction, and leading.

I pray all these things in the name of the Lord Jesus, the name above all names. Amen!

Application

Pause for a while and reflect on the occasions you specifically prayed for and waited on God to lead and guide you. Make a list of the times you assuredly knew it was God who was guiding you. What was the result?

Chapter Fourteen

Missing the Will of God

When I began my professional career, I chose a certain men's store in town from which to purchase my clothing needs. It was owned by a Jewish man named Hymie Finkelstein. It wasn't long before I shared my faith and began discussing what I knew of the Old Testament. We were involved in many serious discussions, and at one point, I thought Hymie would accept Christ.

Hymie told me of the time he shared a room at a boarding house with Arthur Knoesen. Arthur was a devout Christian. One night, Hymie had been partying, and when he returned to his room, he found Arthur on his knees motionless and silent. Thinking he had passed out, he filled a bucket with water and poured it over his roommate to revive him. Arthur didn't need reviving, but his prayer time was suddenly squelched.

Another two years elapsed before I personally met Arthur. I had already heard of him because none of the evangelical churches in town welcomed him on account of an earlier divorce. Forlorn and desperate for fellowship, Arthur shared his story. I was awed a man my father's age would pour out his life story to a nineteen-year-old.

Arthur had trusted Christ as a young man, fearlessly proclaiming his faith to everyone he met, including Hymie Finkelstein. He was an evangelist at heart and hoped to preach full time one day. Under a beautiful African star-studded sky, Arthur shared his testimony, one I would never forget. He shared how his life changed after meeting an Australian evangelist by the name of Lionel Fletcher, but not for the best.

Fletcher was a Congregational minister and evangelist who held pastorates in Australia, Wales, and New Zealand. He also led successful evangelistic campaigns across Australia, the British Isles, and South Africa. It was during one of his campaigns that Knoesen and Fletcher first met. His evangelistic fervor, gift, and talent so impressed Fletcher that he invited him to join his evangelistic team. It was an opportunity of a lifetime, a dream come true. Knoesen hesitated to respond. The appeal grew stronger. Again he hesitated. The pressure mounted until he finally declined the invitation.

At the time, Knoesen was dating a young woman whom he hoped to marry, but she resolutely refused to follow him to Australia. On her account, he said "no" to Fletcher's invitation. As it transpired, the friendship soon ended, leaving Arthur frustrated. He had missed a tremendous ministry opportunity to learn from one of the best. Arthur did eventually marry, but the marriage ended in a divorce that resulted in his ostracization by evangelical churches. Divorce was a "dirty" word in that era, and divorcees were treated like lepers. For years, Arthur wondered what might have been had he accepted Fletcher's offer.

I was lost for words on that starry night but finally assured Arthur that God was full of grace and mercy and willing to forgive; that He was the God of the second chance, as Jonah, Peter, and many others discovered. Sadly, Arthur never became the preacher he might have been or recovered the zeal he once had for God.

I have often wondered how different the course of my life would have been had I responded to several opportunities. There's one I often reflect on.

Around the time I met Arthur Knoesen, I attended an Easter camp conducted by the local Baptist church. The Sunday evening speaker was a Brethren in Christ missionary, an ex-marine, by the name of Fred Holland who became a good friend. That night he spoke on four words found in Luke 23:33—"There they crucified Him." Fred spoke passionately, and his message moved me deeply.

Two months later, the elders of my church asked me to preach one Sunday evening. Using Fred's text, I preached my first full sermon in a church. A few months later, I was working with an audit team in a mining town a hundred and twenty miles away. A family there offered to gather a group in their home if I agreed to preach. God laid the same message on my heart. After all, it was the only one in my arsenal.

In the group packing the Kemp home that night was a Southern Baptist missionary by the name of John Cheyne—I mentioned him in chapter twelve. He came up to me afterward and thanked me. His next words stunned me. "I can get you a full-time scholarship to an American Baptist college with all expenses paid. This includes travel and a $200 a month allowance." As attractive as that offer was, I prayerfully turned it down because at the time I had begun the accounting career I believed God wanted me to pursue.

I have often asked myself, "What if I had accepted that offer?" Did I miss the will of God? I will never know the answer to those questions. God led me down different routes and paths to where I am today in the overtime of life.

My testimony is, despite the bumps and bruises, the Savior has led me all the way. I could have done many things differently, but in the end have concluded God was working everything out for my good and His glory. In the process, I believe He has given me a unique perspective. There are zero chances of anyone replicating my life experiences. As a starter, my twin sister and I are the only ones to have the same parents. That in itself makes us unique. Just as no two fingerprints are identical, no two individual sets of circumstances can be matched. Not only was I created unique, the totality of my life's' experiences make me even more unique.

As we approach the end of our journey together, we need to answer, the question, "Can I miss the will of God?" The answer is *yes*! Every believer without exception has missed God's will for the simple reason no one is perfect. You might respond, "Oh, I thought we were all perfect the moment we trusted Christ." That's true in regard to our *standing* in Christ, but we are imperfect when it comes to our *state* in the world.

We can and do miss the will of God. We miss it when we break His commandments, disobey His injunctions, and disregard His imperatives. We miss God's will when we don't confess our sins. We miss God's will when we don't attempt to make things right to whatever extent possible. We miss God's will when we fail to develop an intimate personal relationship with Him. We miss God's will when we dishonor the Lord Jesus Christ and grieve the Holy Spirit. We miss God's will when we rely on our own wisdom. We miss God's will when we fail to assemble and connect with other believers for purposes of worshipping, learning the Scriptures, praying, and serving.

As a result, we need to answer the question, "What if I mess up?" We have all messed up, even as followers of Christ. Some of you on the journey may respond, "You have no idea the things I did before accepting the Lord Jesus as my personal Savior. There's no way God can use me." Wrong!

Others of you might comment, "I have really messed up since placing my trust in Christ. I became an alcoholic or a drug addict. I committed adultery, and my marriage broke up as a result. I have lied, stolen, coveted, borne false witness, and more." Some of you might confess to deliberately ignoring God's will, or never seeking it in the first place. It is never too late to start again. God is loving, gracious, merciful, and forgiving. Jonah and Simon Peter discovered these truths.

Jonah resolutely disobeyed God's instruction to preach to the inhabitants of Nineveh, the capital of the ancient Assyrian

Empire. Instead of traveling northeast to Nineveh, he boarded a ship bound for Tarshish, an unknown city in the western regions of the Mediterranean Sea. His intent was to go as far as possible in the opposite direction—about twenty-seven hundred miles from where God was sending him.

This raises the question, "How far do we have to go to be outside the circle of God's will?" The distance is irrelevant. Don't think in terms of hundreds of miles. One step is all that's needed to cross the forbidden line. Despite his rebellion and stubbornness, God gave Jonah a second chance. God is willing to give you a second, even a third chance, and more.

Simon Peter found himself outside God's will. Seven missteps led to his downfall. Seven steps led to his restoration. They began at the garden tomb when the angel told the women to tell Jesus's disciples that He was risen. Peter got special mention (Mark 16:7). The final step occurred on the shores of the Sea of Galilee when the Lord Jesus, after questioning his love, charged Peter with tending His sheep (John 21:15–17). It took a divine Carpenter to turn a fisherman into a shepherd.

Restoration is possible. I recommend you read Gordon McDonald's book, *Rebuilding Your Broken World*. Writing from personal experience, his book shows how a believer can get back into the will of God.

There is a process to getting back into the will of God.

Respond to the Holy Spirit's Conviction

It is the work of the Holy Spirit to convict us of sin, to strike the conscience, and to make us aware we have fallen short of God's righteous standards, transgressed His laws, and committed iniquity (John 16:8). He gives us a heavy heart in order to prompt confession. Like King David, conviction could last weeks, months, or even years before we respond.

I recall listening to Robert Laidlaw, author of the booklet *The Reason Why* and close friend of the inimitable Oswald Sanders, tell the story of the time he was called to a hospital in Auckland, New Zealand. A Christian woman had called for Laidlaw to visit her. She was not expected to live through the night. For the first time, she confessed to an adulterous relationship, one she had hidden from her husband for many years. Laidlaw carefully explained the words in 1 John 1:9 as she tearfully recounted the sin that now paralyzed her emotionally, spiritually, and physically. As she asked God to forgive her, Laidlaw commented on the sudden joy that lit her face. The next day she was released from the hospital. Unconfessed and unforgiven sin causes unimaginable agony, grief, and sorrow. It is imperative that we respond to the conviction of our sins. Guilt is one prime reason people land in mental health institutions.

Confess Your Sin and Failure

Admit that you sinned, that you missed the mark, and fell short. Admit that you transgressed by committing deliberate acts of disobedience. Admit that you committed iniquity by bending, twisting, and distorting God's laws.

Confession is conditional to experiencing God's forgiveness. Confession is more than just saying sorry. It is agreeing with God that what you did was sinful. It involves heartfelt contrition, genuine sorrow, and remorse. Read the account of David's heartrending confession in Psalm 51. Make it your own, even though you haven't committed David's sins.

Experience God's Forgiveness

God is faithful, just, and willing to forgive our sins, iniquities, and transgressions when we confess them (1 John 1:9). When we do so, He wipes the slate clean and restores us to a right relationship with Himself. An intimate relationship will never become a reality if we don't keep short accounts with God. It's not just the blatant sins we need forgiveness for; the list includes sins of ignorance and omission.

According to Christian tradition, the seven deadly sins are lust, gluttony, greed, sloth, wrath, envy, and pride. Lust is a passion or longing, especially for sexual desires (2 Timothy 2:22). Gluttony includes an excessive ongoing consumption of food or drink (1 Corinthians 10:31). Greed is an aggressive pursuit of material possessions (Hebrews 13:5). Sloth is extreme laziness or failure to act and utilize one's talents and spiritual gift (Proverbs 13:4). Wrath is uncontrollable anger and hate toward another person (Romans 12:19). Envy is the intense desire to have what others possess (Proverbs 14:30). Pride is an excessive view of one's self without regard for others (Jeremiah 9:23–24).

King Solomon listed seven things God detested, "Haughty eyes, a lying tongue, hands that shed innocent blood, a heart that devises wicked schemes, feet that are quick to rush into evil, a false witness who pours out lies, and a person who stirs up conflict in the community" (Proverbs 6:16–19).

Seek God's forgiveness for every sin and failure. Ensure your life stacks up against the plumb line of God's Word.

Relish God's Cleansing

When God forgives, He cleanses. I tell the story of a mother who was preparing for an afternoon tea party. She had dressed her five-year-old son for the occasion and ordered him to stay indoors. As she was preparing the last batch of cookies, he went outside. To his dismay, he slipped and fell into some mud left by a heavy storm. He quietly snuck into the kitchen while her back was turned, knowing he had disobeyed. He stood there crying, "Mommy, I'm sorry, I'm sorry," as she faced the oven. She spun around and said, "Billy, I forgive you!"

The matter didn't rest there, however. She took him to the bathroom, stripped off his dirty clothes, bathed him, and redressed him. The boy who had disobeyed his mother's orders, who was muddied and forgiven, now stood sparkling clean.

When we confess, God not only forgives, He cleanses us. David prayed God would cleanse him of his iniquity. Being clean before a holy God is a tremendous feeling. The psalmist declared only those with clean hands and a pure heart may ascend the mountain of the Lord and stand in His holy place (Psalm 24:3–4).

In another classic psalm, David expressed his relief after confessing his sin and experiencing God's forgiveness. His testimony is worth noting.

Blessed is the one whose transgressions are forgiven, whose sins are covered. Blessed is the one whose sin the Lord does not count against them and in whose spirit is no deceit. When I kept silent, my bones wasted away through my groaning all day long. For day and night your hand was heavy on me; my strength was sapped as in the heat of summer. Then I acknowledged my sin to you and did not cover up my iniquity. I said, "I will confess my transgressions to the Lord. And you forgave the guilt of my sin." (Psalm 32:1–5)

One only has to experience that joy to appreciate how David felt after breaking five of the Ten Commandments God gave to Moses on Mount Sinai.

Welcome the Process of Restoration

Restoration is a necessary process. Disobedience has consequences. I share the story of the young man who had trusted Christ and was growing in his faith and walk with God. One night, he went to a party and became intoxicated. His walk home took him over the railroad tracks, but in his drunken stupor, he slipped and fell with one arm resting on a rail. There he lay, unconscious of an approaching train. His arm was severed. Fortunately help was near, and he was rushed to the closest hospital where his life was saved. Acknowledging his sin, he asked God for forgiveness. While he was forgiven, he nevertheless had to live with a prosthetic arm for the rest of his life. Sin often has irreversible consequences.

Karla Faye Tucker was sentenced to death for the gruesome killing of two people during a robbery in 1983. Later that year, she claimed to become a born-again Christian, a claim backed by a dramatically changed life. She had taken a Bible from the prison ministry program and began reading it in her cell. She later recalled, "I didn't know what I was reading. Before I knew it, I was in the middle of my cell floor on my knees asking God to forgive me." The warden of Huntsville prison in Texas testified she was a model prisoner and that, after fourteen years on death row, she likely had been reformed.

It was January 28, 1998. The nation was in suspense as her appeal for the commutation of her death sentence was being decided. Her plea drew support from abroad and from leaders of American conservatism. Among those who appealed to the state of Texas were Pope John Paul II, Newt Gingrich—Speaker of the US House of Representatives, televangelist Pat Robertson, and Ronald Carlson, the brother of Tucker's murder victim, Debbie Thornton.

With only hours to live, Tucker was waiting to hear if her life would be spared, at least temporarily. Only the possibility of a last-minute stay by the Supreme Court, where an appeal was pending, or intervention by Texas Governor George W. Bush stood between Tucker and the distinction of becoming the first woman executed in Texas since 1863.

In the end, the Texas Board of Pardons and Paroles rejected the plea, a federal judge denied a request for a stay of execution, and George W. Bush refused the final eleventh-hour appeal to block her execution.

Several documentaries, including movies and plays, have been produced on Karla Faye's life story. These include *A Question of Mercy* (1998), a TV documentary directed by Rob Feldman; *The Power of Forgiveness* (2000), a documentary on forgiveness; *Crossed Over* (2002), a film starring Jennifer Jason Leigh and Diane Keaton; and *Forevermore* (2004), a film directed by Helen Gibson.

Even though a person places their faith and trust in Jesus Christ and is forgiven of their sins, no matter their magnitude, there are inevitable consequences—often inescapable.

David painfully enumerates the consequences of his sin, transgressions, and iniquities in Psalm 51. Sin did at least seven things to him. It stained his soul (vv. 2, 5, 7, 10), saturated his mind (v. 3), stilled his conscience (v. 4), saddened his heart (v. 8), sapped his strength (v. 9), soured his spirit (vv. 10–12), and sealed his lips (vv. 14–15). Take time to study this psalm.

What consequences are you facing: church discipline, a court appearance, prison sentence, divorce, broken relationships, job loss, financial ruin, bankruptcy, or temporary suspension from work or ministry? Maybe it's sheer frustration.

Redemption is possible. Accept the consequences, as painful as they are. Then, with God's enablement, determine to discover His will and do it. Obey His commands. Seek the Holy Spirit's enablement. Encounter God each day as you spend time in His Word and in prayer. Develop a personal relationship with the Lord Jesus.

Make these things your top priority—God first, family second, and work last. As you do that, things will fall into a right perspective.

Maybe you made a series of bad decisions, even though you prayed about them. You got involved in a questionable relationship, made unwise financial decisions, acted impatiently and independently, violated a clear command of Scripture, made a wrong move vocationally, all the while believing you were doing the right thing. God will forgive you, despite the difficult road ahead as you recover from what may sometimes be disastrous choices.

Make Restitution to Whatever Extent Is Possible

Restoration also includes the process of restitution. Restitution isn't a popular word and is seldom mentioned in evangelical circles. As much as it depends on you, seek to make things right. If you stole, repay as much as you can over time. Seek to repair broken promises and relationships with your spouse, children, parents, friends, neighbors, and even employers. While your spouse might have remarried and others passed on, seek forgiveness wherever possible for the hurt and damage you caused. Despite every sin being ultimately against God, you need to also confess to those you hurt or wronged.

President Bill Clinton vehemently claims his public apology for his affairs with Monica Lewinsky, a young intern in the White House, was sufficient. After twenty years, he still adamantly refuses to apologize personally to Monica and seek her forgiveness. While Clinton violated his public trust, he nevertheless has an obligation to those he personally violated.

Luke told the graphic story of Zacchaeus's encounter with the Lord Jesus as He passed through Jericho. Zacchaeus, a Jew working for the Roman government, had extorted higher taxes from his Jewish kin than the Romans required. After Christ saved him, he promised to restore fourfold to those he had wronged (Luke 19:1–10).

Craig Rolinger was a first-year student at Emmaus Bible College when I first met him in 1973. He had recently completed military service in Japan, where he lived off-base in a rented apartment owned by an elderly Japanese lady. He returned home without informing her, owing eighteen hundred dollars in back rent. Craig was a young Christian and knew he had wronged her. The conviction grew as he progressed through his Bible curriculum. He knew what he had to do—return to Japan and settle his debt.

Working as many hours as possible, he saved sufficient money to buy a return air ticket and pay the outstanding rent. The landlady couldn't believe her eyes when she responded to the knock on her front door and saw Craig standing there. More than a year had passed since they had faced each other. Stating the reason for his visit, Craig apologized, and begged her forgiveness as he handed her the rental money she thought she would never see. He used the opportunity to share his testimony and the Gospel. It was a defining moment in his spiritual growth.

In the course of conversing with the office manager at a veterinary hospital one day, she asked what I was up to. I told her I was writing this book and, in response to her question, provided a brief overview.

Cindy was a believer, and told me about her son-in-law, also a committed Christian. He had received a significant promotion with a transfer to Toledo, Ohio. He was able to buy that "dream" house in an affluent neighborhood, something way beyond his previous pay scale. All went well until his teenage boys found themselves adversely influenced by the unfamiliar affluence and teenage drug culture in the community. The father made a quick decision as he realized he had stepped out of God's will. He sold the house and moved into a less affluent neighborhood where the pressure to conform was less. It turned out to be both a wise and good decision, as he not only "saved" the lives of his boys but saved money as well.

Two wrongs never make it right. Restitution means making things right.

Some of you may be asking, "How on earth did I do that? How did I step out of God's will? There are several reasons why we miss God's will.

- **Unfamiliarity with God's Word**

  Most American citizens are probably familiar with the legal principle that ignorance of the law is no excuse. In the same way, ignorance of God's Word is a major factor in missing His will. Ignorance leads to frustration, anxiety, and possible ruin. It begs the question: How can God hold us accountable when we haven't had time to read everything in the Bible?

  Even those who have read the Bible many times cannot possibly remember everything they read. That is why it is so important to read the Bible on a regular basis, hopefully daily. Discover what God has commanded, pay attention, and respond to the divine imperatives you come across each day. Live one day at a time. Ensure you are in God's will today.

- **Disobedience**

  God expects obedience. King Saul learned this to his dismay (1 Samuel 15:22). Jesus said if we loved Him, we would keep His commandments. God blesses those who love Him, hear His voice, and obey Him. While we will never lose our salvation, God cannot fully use us if we are not walking in the path He has ordained for us. Obedience is paramount. It is proof we love Him.

• Insufficient Prayer

It takes a heart in tune with God to seek His will. We need to pray earnestly about the decisions we make. Those who walk and talk with God, who read His Word and keep His commandments, will instinctively know what to do and what not to do because their spiritual instincts govern decisions educated and regulated by the Holy Spirit.

Despite our groans (not moans), we should be comforted by the fact that the Holy Spirit also groans on our behalf when we feel weak and helpless. Paul made this clear in his letter to the Romans when he informed them the Spirit helps us in our weakness. When we do not know what to pray for, the Holy Spirit himself intercedes for us through wordless groans. The One who searches our hearts knows the mind of the Spirit because the Spirit intercedes for us in accordance with the will of God (Romans 8:26–27). When we struggle to know God's leading, we have a divine Comforter who prays for us. Like a lawyer, the Holy Spirit is our divine advocate.

What a blessing to discover the Holy Spirit knows what God's will for us is and intercedes accordingly. The problem is that we are so often insensitive to His leading. He is always in step with God.

• Walking out of Step with God

We may feel God is moving too fast and expecting too much of us. He presents opportunities we believe we are not ready for. We lag behind, forgetting God will never expect us to do anything He doesn't equip us to do. Generally, it is us who run ahead of God. We become impatient when our prayers aren't answered within the timeframe we set.

We make our own decisions without sufficient prayer and counsel. We determine to do our own thing regardless of the advice offered. In our fast-paced world, we are reluctant to wait upon the Lord, despite the advice given in Isaiah 40:31. Waiting time should never be wasted time.

- **Attempting to Do Things God Hasn't Equipped Us to Do**

Our God-given abilities and spiritual gifts are given for a purpose. Superimposing our will over God's will never works. Even though David declared God gives us the desires of our heart when we delight ourselves in the Lord (Psalm 37:4), we should never confuse our desires with God's direction.

Our desires can be selfish and sinful. The challenge is allowing God's desires to become our desires. God will never promote us beyond our level of divine competence. That simply means God will never expect us to accomplish something He hasn't called and equipped us to do. Sometimes, we will be amazed at what God accomplishes through us. Often, we will never know this side of eternity the impact our lives have made.

The disciples Jesus called accomplished the unimaginable. Jesus told them they would be empowered by the Holy Spirit (Acts 1:8). That occurred at Pentecost (Acts 2:4). It wasn't long before people took notice of Peter and John. When they saw their courage and realized they were unschooled, ordinary men, they were astonished and realized they had been with Jesus (Acts 4:13).

As D. L. Moody discovered, we have no idea what God can accomplish through men and women who are fully consecrated to Him. Our witness in the marketplace can be just as effective as it could be on a foreign mission field. The marketplace is a mission field. God expects us to be His witness and ambassadors wherever we are.

Failure results from our propensity to go in different directions than those God has chosen. The challenge is ensuring we are in the will of God each day. We have covered several guiding principles to help us know whether or not we are within God's will.

First, obedience to the truth God has revealed in His Word assures us of His guidance—vocationally and geographically. There is a direct correlation between following Scripture and being guided in the unclear choices of life. We can't expect God's guidance if we are deliberately disobeying Him. His divine grace compels Him to act in our best interests for His glory, even though the process may sometimes be painful.

Second, our vertical relationship with the Lord is more important than the daily decisions we face. The Lord Jesus promised if we seek God's kingdom and His righteousness, the necessities of life would be met (Matthew 6:33). God has nowhere promised to give us everything we want, but He has promised to meet our every need according to His riches in glory in Christ (Philippians 4:19).

Third, insufficient prayer, insensitivity to the Holy Spirit, failure to trust God, unresolved issues, permitting questionable practices, and an unwillingness to pay the price of obedience are all factors that cause us to live outside the parameters of God's will. Ensure you are seeking and enjoying God each day and following hard after Christ.

Fourth, if we are disobeying God in one area, why should we expect His guidance in regard to other matters? We become our worst enemy when all the while God is lovingly, graciously, and mercifully reaching out to us. He sends unrecognized help.

Sometimes it's the "earthquakes" and "storms" of life that finally grab our attention. These could take the form of illness, job loss, financial ruin, and more. God generally speaks with a still, small voice, but sometimes His voice sounds like thunder. There are times when we sense God's leading through a gentle breeze. Other times, it takes a hurricane for us to respond.

Some of you on the journey feel you have really messed up. I have friends who were drug and alcohol addicts before trusting Christ, and who are now living vibrantly for the Lord. I have other friends with criminal records whose lives Christ completely turned around.

Steve Thomson, an American GI, was serving time in a Japanese prison for murder. He came to faith in Christ through the ministry of Adrian Presson, an American missionary. Adrian discipled him using Emmaus Bible correspondence courses. Upon his release, Steve enrolled at Emmaus Bible College. For his student ministry, he volunteered for the chaplaincy program in Chicago's Cook County Jail. Upon his college graduation, he became a chaplain. God used him mightily in the Illinois prison system. I included his testimony in a new course we had developed for prisoners—*Born to Win*. His testimony impacted hundreds of thousands of prison inmates over the years. When giving his testimony to prisoners, he always credited God's marvelous grace in turning a convict into a chaplain and a preacher. Only God can do that.

With God's enabling you can turn your life around one hundred and eighty degrees. Once you have been reconciled to God and have done everything you can to put things right with those you hurt, forget the past and live for the future. It was Paul who initially gave this advice to the assembly of Christians in Philippi when he wrote, "One thing I do: Forgetting what is behind and straining toward what is ahead, I press on toward the goal to win the prize for which God has called me heavenward in Christ Jesus" (Philippians 3:13–14). Don't let your past deter you from becoming the person God intends you to be. Determine to live for Him from this moment on.

Others of you have lived an ordinary Christian life but have never really brought God into the equation until you began this journey. You were never serious about *knowing, understanding,* and *doing* God's will because you always found it elusive. The journey has been an eye-opener for you. Now your commitment is to live one hundred and ten percent for God in the home, school, sportsground, or workplace. Determine to be in God's will today.

Clarence Rick McGhee was adopted by an older couple who truly loved God. He trusted Christ as a child and determined to memorize the book of Romans when he was sixteen years of age. But he started taking drugs and became an addict. His brain was fried by age thirty. He was desperate and wanted to die. It was one Christmas Eve that he finally threw himself upon the Lord. God heard his despairing cry and delivered him.

Forty years elapsed before Clarence finally memorized the book of Romans, which he now recites as a one-man play, dressed as the apostle Paul. His recital is titled, *Romans in the Flesh*.

I was present at his inaugural presentation. After hearing his second performance, I wrote a review for Clarence.

Not since Susan Boyle burst onto the world stage in April 2009 when she sang "I Dreamed a Dream" on *Britain's Got Talent* show have I been as excited as when I first heard Clarence McGhee recite the book of Romans at his inaugural performance in December 2016. He was even better when he performed at the Bible Chapel in McMurray, Pennsylvania, two months later.

For fifty-two minutes, after introducing himself as the apostle Paul and dressed like him, Clarence thrilled the audience with his recital of the book of Romans. The book came alive, the message resonated with the largely senior audience, and the impact of God's Word was felt with its convicting power as everyone listened in the quietness. Clarence performed brilliantly, and at the end received a long spontaneous standing ovation from the enthusiastic audience, so powerful was the message delivered with the passion of the apostle Paul himself.

With humility, theatrical poise, and skillful inflection of his voice, Clarence emphasized the great themes of the book of Romans. The truly exciting thing was that we heard, without comment, the pure unadulterated Word of God which is living and active, sharper than any double-edged sword, and penetrating even to the dividing of the soul and spirit, joints and marrow as it judges the thoughts and attitudes of the heart. The message was heard loud and clear. One couldn't escape its power.

Romans in the Flesh should not be limited to senior audiences. It needs to be heard by all ages — particularly fifth and sixth graders, junior high and high schoolers, as well as young adults. It needs to be heard by all! It will inspire Scripture memorization. We as Christians need to hide God's Word in our hearts so as not to sin against Him. More than that, God's Word is a lamp to our feet and a light to our path. God's Word is truth! We need to absorb it. *Romans in the Flesh* will challenge you to do that.

One day, Clarence's son Chase remarked as he was approaching his thirteenth birthday, "Dad, you have changed so much since you memorized the book of Romans." God's Word is transformational!

The children of Israel are a classic example of a nation specially chosen by God that missed His will. We can apply their abject

296

experiences to our own lives. God has made every provision for us to live above the daily grind. But we fail miserably. Like sheep, we go our own way and miss out on his will.

God made a covenantal promise to Abraham, "I will make you into a great nation, and I will bless you; I will make your name great, and you will be a blessing . . . and all peoples on earth will be blessed through you" (Genesis 12:2–3). God's ultimate purpose would be realized through Jesus Christ. Paul was referring to Genesis 22:18 when he declared this in his letter to the Galatian believers (Galatians 3:14, 29). Jesus came through the nation of Israel, and it is through Him alone that salvation is possible.

The covenantal promise God made to Abraham was first extended to Isaac, (Genesis 26:3–5) and then to Jacob, who became known as Israel (Genesis 28:13–15).

The nation of Israel messed up badly. God promised them territory stretching from the River Nile in Egypt to the Euphrates River in Iraq (Genesis 15:15–18). He promised them the land of Canaan for an everlasting possession (Genesis 17:8).

After delivering Israel from slavery in Egypt and miraculously bringing them safely through the Red Sea on dry land, He powerfully led them to Mount Sinai in the Arabian Peninsula where He gave them the Ten Commandments. It was to be their first significant stop on the way to the Promised Land. But they quickly turned from God to idols. They constantly murmured, grumbled, and complained. As a result, they wandered in the wilderness for forty years. An entire generation died in the wilderness when they could have settled in a land "flowing with milk and honey." They never experienced the blessings God had in store for them. They never possessed their possessions.

That has been the case for so many followers of Christ through the centuries, right up to the present day. They are saved by God's grace through faith in Christ alone, but they seldom, if ever, realize God's life purpose in saving them. Like the children of Israel, they wander in a spiritual wilderness. They relive the same experiences year after year, some for their entire lives. Like the believers referred to in the book of Hebrews, they remain in a state of spiritual infancy and their spiritual growth is stunted (Hebrews 5:11–14). All the while God wants them to live like conquerors (Romans 8:37).

Are you "possessing your possessions" in Christ? Are you committed to be all God wants you to be this side of eternity?

Hopefully, while on this journey, you have been challenged to live for God's praise and glory each day, to give the Lord Jesus Christ the pre-eminence He deserves, to love the Lord God with all your heart, mind, soul, and strength, and your neighbors as yourself.

You have been challenged to trust God, to obey His commandments, and to allow the Holy Spirit to enable, equip, energize, and empower you to do God's will. You have been challenged above all else to develop an intimate and personal relationship with Almighty God through His Word and through prayer.

Don't be like the children of Israel who through their disobedience never fully realized God's purpose for their existence. In Psalm 78, Asaph provides a graphic overview of their history to that point. It was dismal, with failure after failure. They constantly disobeyed God's commandments, fell into idolatry, forgot the marvelous and miraculous things God had done for them, were frequently overcome by their enemies, and neglected their spiritual duties. Their worship of God was a farce at times. Yet God constantly loved them, restrained His anger, and delivered them from their yoyo experience. Such is His grace and mercy.

Then God raised up one man, David, to shepherd them with integrity. Despite his failures, God used him to bring hope to the nation. David restored the vision of a temple that would become God's sanctuary, a place where other nations could come to the knowledge of the Almighty, and from where God's fame would spread around the world. Solomon captured that theme in his dedicatory prayer upon construction of the Temple in Jerusalem.

Things didn't change much. God finally delivered them to their enemies and allowed them to be taken into captivity for seventy years.

Today we have a Savior, Jesus Christ, who, through His redemptive work and saving grace, has made it possible for us to be all God wants us to be. We have learned on this journey that God does have a plan for our lives. We need men and women today who are sold out to God. Will you be one of them? Wherever you are, whatever your profession, passion, pursuits, and pleasures in life are, do everything for His honor, praise, and glory. There is no greater calling than this. Commit to bring God glory whether it's in a relationship, in the home, in school, in the workplace, on the battleground, on a sports field, on stage, or in the political arena.

My Prayer

Dear heavenly Father, I thank and praise You for all I have learned about You. You are gracious and merciful, and Your love is everlasting. Thank You! Thank You! Thank You!

I am amazed You are still willing to use me even though I have failed You so often. I haven't always gone through the doors You have opened. I have consistently knocked on doors You have closed. I have even tried breaking down closed doors because of my persistence to force my own will on the outcome. I am broken by my own stupidity and sinfulness. Please forgive me, cleanse me, and empower me to seek your will from this day onward.

Father, I pray You will draw me ever closer to You, that Your Word will constantly cleanse me and guide me. Help me to glorify You, magnify the Lord Jesus Christ, and not grieve the Holy Spirit. Make me a blessing to all I come into contact with.

I pray all this in the precious name of the Lord Jesus. Amen!

Application

This may possibly be the most challenging stage of our journey; one you may have been hoping to avoid. This is a time for personal reflection, conviction, confession, forgiveness, and cleansing. It is a time when you need to prayerfully consider what wrongs you need to put right, what apologies you need to offer, and what restitution you need to make. It is a time to resolutely decide to offer yourself completely to God and say, "Dear God, I want your will to be done in my life." This is the moment to fully surrender your life to God.

Take a time out. Go on a personal retreat and interact with God—just you and God. Tell Him you want to live for Him wholeheartedly, and that you want to do His will.

Chapter Fifteen

God's Perfect and Permissive Will

Many Christians believe all the disappointments, illnesses, distresses, and casualties of life are the result of God's perfect will; that nothing happens to us that God hasn't sovereignly ordained. To think that is to believe God orchestrates murders, rapes, robberies, atrocities, terrorism, or accidents in order to demonstrate His love and mold followers of Christ into the vessels He desires. God is not the architect of evil. He never was and never will be.

Evil happens in the world. A loved one, son or daughter, spouse, or parent is killed in an auto accident caused by a drunken driver. A teenager is killed in a school shooting spree. A cruise ship catches fire, and a good friend is burned to death. Another friend is killed in a diving or skiing accident. Another is left a quadriplegic after being caught in the crossfire of a stray bullet. A woman is attacked and raped by an intruder. A loved one dies of cancer. A spouse unexpectedly leaves on account of a secret illicit relationship. A car breaks down on the expressway, and the driver misses an important appointment. A close relative dies as a result of medical negligence or malpractice. Terrorists storm a village, killing many innocent men, women, and children in the burst of machine gun fire.

Some believe that's all part of God's will. Wrong! To think that is to believe God deliberately endorses insobriety, orchestrates misfortunes, induces mental deficiencies, advocates calamities, causes tragedies and disease, and induces criminality.

A good friend was diagnosed with pancreatic cancer and was given only a few months to live. Many prayed for her. She received the best treatment possible and, in fact, lived for several years, all the while maintaining a strong faith and positive attitude with the assurance she enjoyed eternal life through Christ.

Pat confidently expressed her belief she would be healed one day but didn't know if it would be in this life or the next. She remained cheerful despite the pain, inconvenience, and suffering. The cancer eventually spread throughout her body until she finally slipped quietly into the presence of her Lord and Savior. Some might attribute her cancer to the will of God, in which case we could argue her husband fought against God's will in having the best doctors treat her. Those same people would have called her recovery God's will. We cannot have it both ways. God's will was that she rejoice in adversity, as difficult as that was.

This raises the legitimate question: Why do bad things happen to good people? We live in a sinful world, and the devil is hard at work. He is a deceiver and a destroyer. Don't blame God for the evil in the world. Blame Satan!

I recall an incident during the Congo rebellion in the late 1950s or early '60s. Armed terrorists stormed a village and wreaked havoc. The missionaries sheltered within their walled and gated compound while the sound of gunfire raged outside. They had no idea of the extent of the carnage. Then quietness reigned for several days. Thinking he would take a peek, one missionary climbed a ladder to assess the situation. He was shot as soon as his head appeared above the wall. That began a long and serious discussion among the surviving missionaries as to whether his death was the result of the *perfect* or *permissive* will of God. Had God planned for him to die that way, or did He just allow the tragedy to occur?

The missionaries firmly believed God had called them to serve in the Congo and had led them to this village to establish their base. They believed God was all-knowing and knew in advance that the missionary would die an untimely death. Why didn't He stop it? Was it in fact God's will he be killed with a terrorist's bullet? Where was the man's guardian angel?

Consider this story. The five missionaries slain on the banks of the Curaray River in Ecuador's Amazon jungle believed they were called to that region. They had prayed for God's protection as they set out one fateful morning to land their plane on a beach to make physical contact with the Auca Indians who they felt had made friendly overtures toward them. They knew the dangers. Soldiers and traders who had earlier penetrated the region never returned. This was different, they thought. They were doing God's will in taking the Gospel to this savage people. If they were in the will of God, why weren't they divinely protected? Did their martyrdom fall within the parameters of God's perfect will or permissive will? We will never know the answer to that question this side of eternity.

As is so often the case, tragedy results in triumph. The deaths of those five men galvanized missionary endeavors in the United States and sparked a movement resulting in the outpouring of funding for world evangelization as thousands of young people responded to the call to fill the gap. Two of the missionaries' family members — Jim Elliot's widow, Elizabeth, and Nate Saint's sister, Rachel — returned to Ecuador to work among the Auca tribe where many, including the leader, trusted Christ. I remember being at an Inter-Varsity missionary conference in Urbana, Illinois, when Elizabeth Elliott publicly introduced the man who had killed her husband. He had since become a believer. His testimony was impacting.

What is God's perfect will? God's perfect will is that you live your life for His praise, honor, and glory regardless of your circumstances; that you love Him with your whole heart, mind, soul, and strength; that you obey Him, exalt Him, and enjoy a personal and intimate relationship with Him; and that you know Him and experience Him in your life. His will is that you exalt His Son and allow the Holy Spirit to work unhindered in your life.

God permits adversity and trials to enter our lives. We could be fighting cancer or some other terminal illness, recovering from a serious accident, struggling in the marketplace, grieving from the loss of a loved one, concerned about our financial situation, or worried how we are going to get to the grocery store or doctor's office. What is God's will under those circumstances? God's will is you fully trust Him. He can and will provide the strength to get you through each day, and even help you rejoice in adversity. The correct response to trials builds character.

The apostle James wrote we are to consider it pure joy whenever we face trials, because the testing of our faith produces perseverance which in turn produces maturity and completeness (James 1:2–4). The apostle Paul expressed the same thought. He wrote we should glory in our sufferings because suffering produces perseverance, character, and hope. Hope does not put us to shame because God's love has been poured out into our hearts through the Holy Spirit whom He has given to us (Romans 5:2–5). God gives us the grace we need to get through even the most devastating times of our life. Countless numbers have found this to be true.

The apostle Peter wrote to Jewish believers who had been scattered as a result of persecution and were now facing more serious threats under Nero, the Roman emperor. They were able to rejoice even though they were distressed by various trials. This is a paradox only true believers can understand. It defies the logic of humanistic philosophers who attach various labels on those who trust Christ (1 Peter 1:6–7). Trials are purposeful. God permits trials and adversity. Mark records the occasion when the disciples were caught in a fierce gale on the Sea of Galilee.

One evening the Lord Jesus said to His disciples, "Let us go over to the other side." Leaving the crowd behind, they took Jesus along in the boat. Other boats accompanied them. Suddenly, a furious squall arose, and the waves broke over the boat, almost swamping it. The disciples were terrified. Jesus was in the stern, sleeping peacefully on a cushion.

The disciples woke Him screaming "Teacher, don't you care if we drown?" (Mark 4:35–38). Jesus then commanded the wind and the waves to be still. They obeyed Him, and the sea was calmed. The disciples, whose faith earlier failed, were amazed. The occupants of other boats had no idea what had happened. The Lord of creation demonstrated He was also Lord of the wind and the waves.

The disciples' faith was certainly tested that day. Their testing was both purposeful and meaningful. Jesus was omniscient and knew what lay ahead. It was clearly His purpose to expose them to the elements despite the terrifying experience. Jesus was in control. His purpose was to grow their faith in Him. What He said and didn't say was significant. He said "Let us go *over,* not *under* to the other side." The problem was they didn't believe Him.

This begs the questions, "Why doesn't every situation turn out this way, and why does God allow so many to perish as a result of storms, fires, floods, and landslides? Why doesn't Christ demonstrate His Lordship in such instances and save lives deemed precious?"

The answer is Satan is also active. He is alive and well on Planet Earth. He is a deceiver, a destroyer, and a killer. His intent is to enslave his followers and to keep them bound in chains. One doesn't have to look far before coming face-to-face with the undeniable reality of demonic activity and the terrible and destructive things Satan and his demons attempt to do to those created in the image of God. The apostle John told his readers Jesus came to destroy the works of the devil (1 John 3:8). One glorious day, Jesus will reign over the earth, and righteousness will prevail. In the meanwhile, all of creation groans.

Sometimes God takes us through the fire, floods, and storms. We feel their fury. All the while, He uses those occasions to test us and to mold us. Every silversmith or goldsmith knows the most precious products are forged by fire. In the same way, the finest characters are forged in a furnace, oftentimes a furnace of affliction. Life is full of trials and testings. Sometimes God saves us from the storms that arise. Other times He takes us through the storms.

While God tests us, He will never tempt us. The apostles James makes that clear (James 1:13–15). Neither will God allow us to be tempted beyond what we can bear (1 Corinthians 10:13). Whatever the situation, God's will is that we trust him.

The following is a quotation from my book, *Authentic Christianity*, found on page 82.

A young boy often helped in his father's shoe store. One day, the shelves needed rearranging, and he offered to help. He stood on the carpeted floor with his hands outstretched, while the father stood on a stepladder. Methodically, he took one box after another off the shelf and placed them in his son's arms. The stack grew higher and higher until the boy could no longer see over the boxes. Just as the father was about to place another box on the stack, a stranger walked through the door into the shop and exclaimed, "My, you'll collapse if your father loads any more boxes on you!"

The boy replied, "My father knows just how much I can carry!" God knows how much we can bear.

God allows believers to be tested. Is it He or Satan who tests us? Both do. Satan, however, tests and tempts. His intent is to harm and destroy.

One day God called Abraham to offer his only son Isaac on Mount Moriah (Genesis 22:1–2). On that occasion, God didn't want Isaac's *life* but an expression of Abraham's *love* and *loyalty.*

Sometimes our situation appears to parallel Job's when God allowed Satan to afflict him (Job 1:8–12). Job's story is classic, and one no one would ask for. His testimony was exemplary. He was a godly role model to his family. His wealth was extraordinary. Yet God allowed Satan to take away everything he had, except his faith in Him. The book of Job tells his story. Despite his anguish, it is a story of steadfast faith in God. You have no doubt heard of the "patience of Job."

I thought I was invincible until one day I experienced a severe intestinal bleed. The bleeds reoccurred every two years or so, until finally I was rushed to the emergency room ten times within a five-year period. On one occasion, I lost two thirds of my blood. Despite extensive tests, doctors could never discover the cause or the spots where the bleeding occurred. The incidents certainly turned my life upside down. However, God used those occasions to redirect me and remold me. Over two years have elapsed since my last incident, and today as I write, I am probably more excited about living for Him than any other period of my life. At best, I only have a few years left. I want to max out for God. God can and does use human frailties to magnify His name. Paul discovered it was when he was weak that he was strong in the Lord (2 Corinthians 12:9).

The apostle Paul is an interesting case study regarding God's *perfect* and *permissive* will. He was in Corinth in AD 58 when he wrote his letter to the believers in Rome. In that letter, he expressed his desire to visit them on his way to Spain, something he had longed to do for several years (Romans 15:22–25). He was completing his third missionary journey and had landed at Miletus where he gave

307

his final address and warnings to the elders of the Ephesian church who had come to meet and greet him (Acts 20:15–32). From there he sailed to Caesarea and entered the home of Philip the evangelist where he stayed several days.

In the meanwhile, a prophet named Agabus arrived from Judea and prophesied Paul's arrest upon arriving in Jerusalem. Paul's friends urged him not to go. "It's too dangerous. The Jewish leaders are out to get you," they said. Paul answered, "Why are you weeping and breaking my heart? I am ready not only to be bound, but also to die in Jerusalem for the name of the Lord Jesus." When he would not be dissuaded, they gave up and said, "The Lord's will be done" (Acts 21:8–14).

Why was Paul willing to walk into the lion's den? Should he have played it safe? Was it in fact God's will for him to go to Jerusalem? Was it premature for him to die? Luke's narration of the subsequent events keeps us on the edge of our seats.

When the seven days were nearly over, some Jews from the province of Asia saw Paul at the temple. They stirred up the whole crowd and seized him, shouting, "Fellow Israelites, help us! This is the man who teaches everyone everywhere against our people and our law and this place. And besides, he has brought Greeks into the temple and defiled this holy place." (They had previously seen Trophimus the Ephesian in the city with Paul and assumed that Paul had brought him into the temple.)

The whole city was aroused, and the people came running from all directions. Seizing Paul, they dragged him from the temple, and immediately the gates were shut. While they were trying to kill him, news reached the commander of the Roman troops that the whole city of Jerusalem was in an uproar. He at once took some officers and soldiers and ran down to the crowd. When the rioters saw the commander and his soldiers, they stopped beating Paul.

The commander came up and arrested him and ordered him to be bound with two chains. Then he asked who he was and what he had done. Some in the crowd shouted one thing and some another, and since the commander could not get at the truth because of the uproar, he ordered that Paul be taken into the barracks. When Paul reached the steps, the violence of the mob was so great he had to be carried by the soldiers. The crowd that followed kept shouting, "Get rid of him!" (Acts 21:27–36)

Paul was given opportunity to address the angry crowd. As he shared his Jewish ancestry and told of his persecution of Christians, they quietened down. But when he recounted his testimony about how God had told him to take the Gospel to the Gentiles, the crowd turned against him. Luke narrates the ensuing events.

The crowd listened to Paul until he said this. Then they raised their voices and shouted, "Rid the earth of him! He's not fit to live!"

As they were shouting and throwing off their cloaks and flinging dust into the air, the commander ordered that Paul be taken into the barracks. He directed that he be flogged and interrogated in order to find out why the people were shouting at him like this. As they stretched him out to flog him, Paul said to the centurion standing there, "Is it legal for you to flog a Roman citizen who hasn't even been found guilty?"

When the centurion heard this, he went to the commander and reported it. "What are you going to do?" he asked. "This man is a Roman citizen."

The commander went to Paul and asked, "Tell me, are you a Roman citizen?" "Yes, I am," he answered. Then the commander said, "I had to pay a lot of money for my citizenship." "But I was born a citizen," Paul replied. Those who were about to interrogate him withdrew immediately. The commander himself was alarmed when he realized that he had put Paul, a Roman citizen, in chains.

The commander wanted to find out exactly why Paul was being accused by the Jews. So the next day he released him and ordered the chief priests and all the members of the Sanhedrin to assemble. Then he brought Paul and had him stand before them. Paul looked straight at the Sanhedrin and said, "My brothers, I have fulfilled my duty to God in all good conscience to this day." At this the high priest Ananias ordered those standing near Paul to strike him on the mouth. Then Paul said to him, "God will strike you, you whitewashed wall! You sit there to judge me according to the law, yet you yourself violate the law by commanding that I be struck! Those who were standing near Paul said, "How dare you insult God's high priest!" Paul replied, "Brothers, I did not realize that he was the high priest; for it is written: 'Do not speak evil about the ruler of your people.'"

Then Paul, knowing that some of them were Sadducees and the others Pharisees, called out in the Sanhedrin, "My brothers, I am a Pharisee, descended from Pharisees. I stand on trial because of the hope of the resurrection of the dead." When he said this, a dispute broke out between the

Pharisees and the Sadducees, and the assembly was divided. (The Sadducees say that there is no resurrection, and that there are neither angels nor spirits, but the Pharisees believe all these things.)

There was a great uproar, and some of the teachers of the law who were Pharisees stood up and argued vigorously. "We find nothing wrong with this man," they said. "What if a spirit or an angel has spoken to him?" The dispute became so violent that the commander was afraid Paul would be torn to pieces by them. He ordered the troops to go down and take him away from them by force and bring him into the barracks. The following night the Lord stood near Paul and said, "Take courage! As you have testified about me in Jerusalem, so you must also testify in Rome." (Acts 22:22 to 23:11)

Was Paul in the will of God in the worsening situation as some Jews formed a conspiracy to have him killed? Fortunately, his nephew, hearing of this, warned him. Paul told the commander who then ordered him transferred to Caesarea with instructions that he be accompanied by two hundred soldiers, seventy horsemen, and two hundred spearmen and taken safely to Felix, the Roman governor, to be tried.

Felix was ambivalent, left the case undecided, and had Paul sent to prison where, as a favor to the Jews, he remained for two years. At the end of that time, Felix was succeeded by Porcius Festus who came to Caesarea to hear the case against Paul. It was during this hearing that Paul appealed to Caesar. Festus responded, "You have appealed to Caesar. To Caesar you will go!" That changed the entire course of events. Was Paul in the will of God when he appealed to Caesar?

It so happened that a few days later King Agrippa and his wife Bernice visited Caesarea to pay respects to Festus who took the opportunity to relate the case against Paul. Intrigued by the case, Agrippa told Festus, "I would like to hear this man myself." Festus replied, "Tomorrow you will hear him." Luke describes what happened.

> The next day Agrippa and Bernice came with great pomp and entered the audience room with the high-ranking military officers and the prominent men of the city. At the command of Festus, Paul was brought in. Festus said: "King Agrippa, and all who are present with us, you see this man! The whole Jewish community has petitioned me about him in Jerusalem and here in Caesarea, shouting that he ought not to live any longer. I found he had done nothing deserving of death, but because he made his appeal to the Emperor I decided to send him to Rome. But I have nothing definite to write to His Majesty about him. Therefore I have brought him before all of you, and especially before you, King Agrippa, so that as a result of this investigation I may have something to write. For I think it is unreasonable to send a prisoner on to Rome without specifying the charges against him." (Acts 25:23–27)

Paul delivered his defense before King Agrippa, and in the process shared his testimony. It was a classic. He shared what his life was like before he trusted Christ, how he came to faith in Christ, and finally how his life changed after becoming an ardent follower of Christ—an outline we could all use when sharing our testimony. It was a convincing defense in that Agrippa made two impressive statements.

First, in his response to Paul, he replied, "Do you think that in such a short time you can persuade me to be a Christian?" To which

Paul replied, "Short time or long—I pray to God that not only you but all who are listening to me today may become what I am, except for these chains" (Acts 26:28–29). We don't know whether Agrippa was being sincere or sarcastic, whether he was on the verge of trusting Christ or simply acknowledging Paul's oratory skills. The second statement leaves us guessing and questioning. Once outside the precincts of the courtroom, King Agrippa together with Festus, his wife Bernice, and those sitting with him left the court and conversed with each other saying, "This man is not doing anything that deserves death or imprisonment." In the course of that discussion, Agrippa told Festus, "This man could have been set free had he not appealed to Caesar."

Had Paul made a mistake in trying to reach Jerusalem for the Passover? Should he have heeded the urging of his friends in Philip's house not to go? Was he outside God's will in determining to go, despite the dangers? Did he misread God's will in appealing to Caesar? What do you think?

While still in Macedonia, as he closed out his third missionary journey, Paul restated his desire and intent to see Rome (Acts 19:21), little knowing he would be accompanied by Roman soldiers escorting him to the imperial palace. He could only have imagined that he would experience shipwreck during the voyage. He had no idea he would be placed under house arrest with the palace guard on twenty-four-hour surveillance or that he would be chained to a different guard every four hours. He had no idea he would stay in his own rented house for two years before being released, only to be subsequently rearrested and confined to the Mamertine Prison in Rome where he died a martyr's death. What if he hadn't been so determined to return to Jerusalem in the first instance? Would all this have been avoided?

Was all that transpired the perfect will of God? If so, we would need to accept that God prompted the anger and hatred of the people opposed to Paul and all he stood for, that God inspired their intent to have him killed, and that God intended the preaching of the Gospel he called Paul to deliver be curtailed.

What was God's perfect will for the apostle? Was it God's will or Paul's will that he wanted to see Rome? God's will was that the gospel be proclaimed. God's will included Paul's exhortation to the Corinthian believers to be steadfast, immovable, always abounding in the work of the Lord, knowing that their labors and toil were not in vain. In other words, they were to be *resolute, resilient,* and *resourceful* (1 Corinthians 15:58). That's God's will when we experience adversity and opposition.

What if all this had never happened? Paul would have lost the opportunity to give his testimony to King Agrippa and others who heard it. All those on board the ship taking him to Rome would probably have perished. Members of the Praetorian Guard, to whom he was chained for two years while under house arrest, would probably never have heard the Gospel. All those who visited him while he was in Rome would never have been blessed. He would probably never have written his letters to the Ephesian, Philippian, and Colossian churches. He would never have written to Philemon. He might never have written his letters to Timothy and Titus upon his short release. His circumstances dictated the events.

God was causing everything to work together for His praise and glory. The result is Paul became the greatest Christian in the history of the church as he pioneered a movement that spread and impacted the world. Read Acts chapters 21–28 to gain the full impact of those tumultuous days and events in Paul's life.

Our conclusion is that everything that happened to Paul was within God's permissive will. Regardless of the situation, no matter how severe and strenuous, God gives the grace and divine enablement to persevere and to rise above the daily grind. If that was true of Paul, it can be true of us. God was in sovereign control, something our finite minds have difficulty comprehending.

As I was reworking this manuscript for a final time, I received sad news from Botswana. Jim and Irene Legge were veteran Scottish missionaries. I recall meeting them at their point of entry into Rhodesia (Zimbabwe) after their arrival in Africa and bringing them home for a meal before returning them to the train station for the final leg of their journey to join their missionary colleagues for training. I learned they had just been involved in an auto accident. Irene suffered a fatal heart attack while driving the car. Jim survived with a serious injury.

This was after giving over fifty years to serving God in Africa. Was this God's will? Couldn't Irene have had the heart attack at home and not put her husband's life at risk? Why did it have to be while she was driving? Why didn't God intervene? We will never know the answers to those questions this side of eternity.

The ultimate lesson to learn is whatever circumstance we find ourselves in, whether it's in the perfect or permissive will of God, we are to rejoice and live each moment, each hour, each day, each week, each month, and each year for God's praise and glory. People need to see our fervent love for Christ, even during adversity, pain, and suffering. It's often easier to let our light shine under those circumstances than when we are enjoying the successes of life, which so easily distract from the reason Christ saved us in the first instance—to live for God's glory.

We need to accept the fact God allows us to experience the storms of life, however severe. Sometimes He leads us into the storms in order to increase our faith and teach us amazing lessons. God is too wise to ever make a mistake and too loving to ever be unkind.

We need to dissociate from the phrase "the will of God" everything that is sinful and evil. It is never His will that people treat us harshly or unjustly, or that they injure us emotionally, verbally, psychologically, physically, or financially. When they do, it's God's will that we never retaliate in thought, word, or deed.

You may be groaning (not moaning) under the load you are experiencing at this moment. You may be at your wits' end. Nothing seems to be working for you. You can't find the job you want. You don't have any clear direction despite your frustration, tears, and prayers. You don't really know what to pray for anymore. Your house isn't selling. Your illness seems to be worsening. The planned move in search of a new job isn't panning out. You don't know what to pray for any longer.

Well, Paul provides the answer in his letter to the Romans where he assured them of the Holy Spirit's help when they felt weak, perplexed, and frustrated that their prayers were seemingly being unanswered. It's in those situations that the Holy Spirit intercedes for us (Romans 8:26–27). The passage teaches us that, unbeknown to us, the Holy Spirit takes over and prays for us. He prays in accordance with God's will. He knows God's will for us in every situation. When we reach the point when we throw up our hands in despair and confess we don't know what to pray for anymore, the Holy Spirit takes over and intercedes for us. He is the divine Comforter who comes alongside us to help us.

It's the kind of help we need when we are ill and need a doctor, when we are trapped in a blazing house and need a firefighter, when we are in trouble and need a lawyer, and when our finances are in disarray and need a financial advisor. God knows us through and through. He knows our heart and all we are thinking. He also knows the mind of the Holy Spirit, and the Holy Spirit knows the mind of God. He alone can pray in accordance with God's will when all we can do is pray, "Your will be done."

In earlier chapters, we discovered what God's will is in so many areas. We discovered His sovereign will and aspects of his decretive will. We considered verses where His will is specifically mentioned. We also studied passages that contain divine imperatives calling for our obedient response. You may wish to reread those chapters at this juncture. The point is the Holy Spirit takes all those passages and more and prays in accordance with them. In the process, you may wonder why your thoughts are being redirected, why you are thinking differently about issues, and why you are no longer gung-ho about that move you planned. His prayers on your behalf are effective.

Paul went on to tell the Roman believers a truth we all need to grasp. He told them that in everything God works for the good of those who love Him, who have been called according to His purpose. His purpose is we be conformed to the image of His Son (Romans 8:28–29). Whatever our situation, no matter how hard and unpleasant, God uses those things for our good, to grow us, and to bring us into conformity with His divine purpose. That's why we need to react with joy to every trial we face (James 1:2).

God mysteriously works in the lives of those who love Him. Love for God is the qualifier. Do you love God? Do you really love God? How do you demonstrate your love for God? Is it by obedience and surrender? God loves us with an incredible love and demonstrated it by giving His only Son to die for us on a Roman cross. Our response to that amazing love is to say, "Lord Jesus, You gave your life for me; I now give my life for you."

The hymn-writer, Frances R. Havergal (1836–1879), beautifully expressed this truth in her well-known hymn, *Take My Life*. Make this hymn your closing prayer.

> Take my life and let it be
> Consecrated, Lord, to Thee.
> Take my moments and my days,
> Let them flow in endless praise.
> Take my hands and let them move
> At the impulse of Thy love.
> Take my feet and let them be
> Swift and beautiful for Thee.
> Take my voice and let me sing,
> Always, only for my King.

Take my lips and let them be
Filled with messages from Thee.
Take my silver and my gold,
Not a mite would I withhold.
Take my intellect and use
Every power as Thou shalt choose.
Take my will and make it Thine,
It shall be no longer mine.
Take my heart, it is Thine own,
It shall be Thy royal throne.
Take my love, my Lord, I pour
At Thy feet its treasure store.
Take myself and I will be
Ever, only, all for Thee.
(Public Domain)

Our journey together has ended. However, you are beginning a new journey, a journey that will end when you take your final breath and the Lord calls you home into His glorious presence. What a reward that will be! Until then, with God's enabling, implement all you have learned on this journey. I trust it has been a defining one for you.

Application

Pray about how you can do God's perfect will. You will need to understand what His perfect will for you is. Describe it in your own words.

Then reflect on God's permissive will, and try to understand why He has allowed things to come into your life you decidedly didn't want to experience or happen. List some of the lessons you have learned as a result. Describe how those circumstances have drawn you closer to God.

Conclusion

We have reached our destination. I need to say goodbye. It's been great traveling with you. I trust you have been blessed. Now it's up to you to implement all you have learned. At the outset of our journey, we learned the greatest thing in life is to do the will of God. For that to occur, we need to develop a deep desire for God's will. The desire is to be followed by a determination to discover God's will, to *know* it, to *understand* it, and finally, to *do* it. I trust that has been accomplished.

We have considered the big picture, those things God sovereignly planned in advance for our good and for His glory. We pondered the assertion that 98 percent of God's will has already been revealed in His Word, and all we need do is read the Bible to discover those aspects of His will. We discovered God's will is found in the divine imperatives located in the Holy Scriptures. His Word is true. We learned we need to obey the specific things God has revealed about His will.

We unlocked secrets for experiencing God's daily guidance and direction in our lives. We contemplated how God has uniquely made us, and how we can become His masterpiece. We meditated on the fact that God created us with a divine purpose in view. We discovered how God can order or direct our lives as a shepherd guides his sheep. We identified guiding principles for discovering those circumstantial aspects of God's will not specifically mentioned in Scripture. We reflected on examples of how we can pray for God's specific guidance and direction. We studied what to do when we miss God's will through ignorance, defiance, or disobedience. We poured over the fact that God is loving, gracious, merciful, and kind and readily gives us second chances when we mess up. We discussed the difference between God's perfect and permissive will. Finally, I trust we have answered the question why unpleasant and undesirable things happen to us and to the world around us.

I have done my best to explain and illustrate God's will. I can only pray God's will be done in your life, that seeking it will be your top priority and consuming passion. God's overarching will is everything we do be for His praise and glory and, in the process, we be conformed into the image of Christ, to be more like Him each day.

That pretty much says it all. Is your heart's desire to love God with all your heart, soul, mind, and strength and to do His will?

The time has come for me to thank you for joining me on this journey, to bid you adieu, and to pray God blesses you as you continue your own journey with God. Remember, the greatest thing you can do in life is to know the will of God and do it. Make that your heartfelt goal. It's now over to you.

The writer to the Hebrews expressed it succinctly. "You need to persevere so that when you have done the will of God, you will receive what he has promised" (Hebrews 10:36).

Goodbye and God bless!

Benediction and Final Blessing

Now may the God of peace, who through the blood of the eternal covenant brought back from the dead our Lord Jesus, that great Shepherd of the sheep, *equip you with everything good for doing his will,* and may he work in us what is pleasing to him, through Jesus Christ, to whom be glory for ever and ever. Amen (Hebrews 13:20–21, emphasis added)

Appendix

Use of the Greek words *boule* and *thelema* for "will" in the New Testament

Over fifty verses in the New Testament address God's will, which is referred to in more than one way. Two different Greek words, *boule* and *thelema,* are used to describe God's will, both of which have been translated by the English word *will.*

Boule usually refers to a carefully deliberated plan and is most often used with respect to the counsel of God. It frequently indicates God's providential plan, which is predetermined and inflexible. Peter used it this way in his sermon on the Day of Pentecost: "This man (Jesus), was handed over to you by God's deliberate plan (*boule*) and foreknowledge; and you, with the help of wicked men, put him to death by nailing him to the cross" (Acts 2:23). Here the resolute decree of God is in view, which no human action can set aside. As we noted in chapter four, Gods plan is impregnable. His "will" (*boule*) is unalterable.

The word *thelema* is rich in its diversity of meanings. It refers to what is agreeable, desired, intended, chosen, and commanded. It expresses the notions of consent, desire, purpose, resolution, and command. The force of the various meanings is determined by the context in which *thelema* appears. *Thelema* is used to describe the will of man (Luke 12:47; John 1:13; 1 Corinthians 7:37; 16:12; 2 Peter 1:21), the desires of the flesh (Ephesians 2:3), the will of the Gentiles (1 Peter 4:3), and the will of the devil (2 Timothy 2:26).

When used of God, it describes his intent, desires, pleasure, purposes, and wants.

While this book is a comprehensive, in-depth study of God's will, it is not an exhaustive study. For that reason, I have included all references to the use of the word *thelema* in the New Testament for the sake of the more serious reader who might be interested in further study.

Matthew 6:10   "Your kingdom come, your will (*thelema*) be done, on earth as it is in heaven."

Matthew 7:21   "Not everyone who says to me, 'Lord, Lord,' will enter the kingdom of heaven, but only the one who does the will (*thelema*) of my Father who is in heaven."

Matthew 12:50   "For whoever does the will (*thelema*) of my Father in heaven is my brother and sister and mother."

Matthew 18:14   "In the same way your Father in heaven is not willing (*thelema*) that any of these little ones should perish."

Matthew 21:31   "Which of the two did what his father wanted (*thelema*)?" "The first," they answered. Jesus said to them, "Truly I tell you, the tax collectors and the prostitutes are entering the kingdom of God ahead of you.

Matthew 26:42   "He went away a second time and prayed, "My Father, if it is not possible for this cup to be taken away unless I drink it, may your will (*thelema*) be done."

Mark 3:35	"Whoever does God's will (*thelema*) is my brother and sister and mother."
Luke 12:47	"The servant who knows the master's will (*thelema*) and does not get ready or does not do what the master wants will be beaten with many blow"
Luke 22:42	"Father, if you are willing, take this cup from me; yet not my will, (*thelema*) but yours be done."
Luke 23:25	"He released the man who had been thrown into prison for insurrection and murder, the one they asked for, and surrendered Jesus to their will (*thelemati*)."
John 1:13	"Children born not of natural descent, nor of human decision or a husband's will, (*thelematos*) but born of God."
John 5:30	"By myself I can do nothing; I judge only as I hear, and my judgment is just, for I seek not to please myself but him who sent me." Note, most translations say "do not seek my will (*thelema*), but the will (*thelema*) of Him who sent me."
John 6:38	"For I have come down from heaven not to do my will (*thelema*) but to do the will (*thelema*) of him who sent me."

John 6:39	"And this is the will (*thelema*) of him who sent me, that I shall lose none of all those he has given me, but raise them up at the last day."
John 6:40	"For my Father's will (*thelema*) is that everyone who looks to the Son and believes in him shall have eternal life, and I will raise them up at the last day."
John 7:17	"Anyone who chooses to do the will (*thelema*) of God will find out whether my teaching comes from God or whether I speak on my own."
John 9:31	"We know that God does not listen to sinners. He listens to the godly person who does his will (*thelema*)."
Acts 13:22	"After removing Saul, he made David their king. God testified concerning him: 'I have found David son of Jesse, a man after my own heart; he will do everything I want (*thelema*) him to do.'"
Acts 21:14	"When he would not be dissuaded, we gave up and said, "The Lord's will (*thelema*) be done."
Acts 22:14	"Then he said: 'The God of our ancestors has chosen you to know his will (*thelema*) and to see the Righteous One and to hear words from his mouth."

Romans 1:10   "In my prayers at all times; and I pray that now at last by God's will (*thelema*) the way may be opened for me to come to you."

Romans 2:18   "If you know his will (*thelema*) and approve of what is superior because you are instructed by the law"

Romans 12:2   "Do not conform to the pattern of this world, but be transformed by the renewing of your mind. Then you will be able to test and approve what God's will (*thelema*) is—his good, pleasing and perfect will."

Romans 15:32   "So that I may come to you with joy, by God's will (*thelema*), and in your company be refreshed."

1 Corinthians 1:1   "Paul, called to be an apostle of Christ Jesus by the will (*thelematos*) of God, and our brother Sosthenes,"

1 Corinthians 7:37   "But the man who has settled the matter in his own mind, who is under no compulsion but has control over his own will (*thelematos*), and who has made up his mind not to marry the virgin—this man also does the right thing."

1 Corinthians 16:12   "Now about our brother Apollos: I strongly urged him to go to you with the brothers. He was quite unwilling (*thelema*) to go now, but he will go when he has the opportunity."

2 Corinthians 1:1	"Paul, an apostle of Christ Jesus by the will (*thelematos*) of God, and Timothy our brother,"
2 Corinthians 8:5	"And they exceeded our expectations: They gave themselves first of all to the Lord, and then by the will (*thelematos*) of God also to us."
Galatians 1:4	"Who gave himself for our sins to rescue us from the present evil age, according to the will (*thelema*) of our God and Father,"
Ephesians 1:1	"Paul, an apostle of Christ Jesus by the will (*thelematos*) of God, to God's holy people in Ephesus, the faithful in Christ Jesus:"
Ephesians 1:5	"He predestined us for adoption to sonship through Jesus Christ, in accordance with his pleasure and will (*thelematos*)"
Ephesians 1:9	"He made known to us the mystery of his will (*thelematos*) according to his good pleasure, which he purposed in Christ,"
Ephesians 1:11	"In him we were also chosen, having been predestined according to the plan of him who works out everything in conformity with the purpose of his will (*thelematos*)"
Ephesians 5:17	"Therefore do not be foolish, but understand what the Lord's will (*thelema*) is."

Ephesians 6:6	"Obey them not only to win their favor when their eye is on you, but as slaves of Christ, doing the will (*thelema*) of God from your heart."
Colossians 1:1	"Paul, an apostle of Christ Jesus by the will (*thelematos*) of God, and Timothy our brother"
Colossians 1:9	"For this reason, since the day we heard about you, we have not stopped praying for you. We continually ask God to fill you with the knowledge of his will (*thelematos*) through all the wisdom and understanding that the Spirit gives"
Colossians 4:12	"Epaphras, who is one of you and a servant of Christ Jesus, sends greetings. He is always wrestling in prayer for you, that you may stand firm in all the will (*thelemati*) of God, mature and fully assured."
1 Thessalonians 4:3	"It is God's will (*thelema*) that you should be sanctified: that you should avoid sexual immorality"
1 Thessalonians 5:18	"Give thanks in all circumstances; for this is God's will (*thelema*) for you in Christ Jesus."
2 Timothy 1:1	"Paul, an apostle of Christ Jesus by the will (*thelematos*) of God, in keeping with the promise of life that is in Christ Jesus."

2 Timothy 2:26	"And that they will come to their senses and escape from the trap of the devil, who has taken them captive to do his will (*thelema*)."
Hebrews 10:7	"Then I said, 'Here I am—it is written about me in the scroll—I have come to do your will (*thelema*), my God.'"
Hebrews 10:9	"Then he said, "Here I am, I have come to do your will (*thelema*)."
Hebrews 10:10	"And by that will (*thelemati*), we have been made holy through the sacrifice of the body of Jesus Christ once for all."
Hebrews 10:36	"You need to persevere so that when you have done the will (*thelema*) of God, you will receive what he has promised."
Hebrews 13:21	"Equip you with everything good for doing his will (*thelema*), and may he work in us what is pleasing to him, through Jesus Christ, to whom be glory for ever and ever. Amen"
1 Peter 2:15	"For it is God's will (*thelema*) that by doing good you should silence he ignorant talk of foolish people."
1 Peter 3:17	"For it is better, if it is God's will, (*thelema*) to suffer for doing good than for doing evil."

1 Peter 4:2	"As a result, they do not live the rest of their earthly lives for evil human desires, but rather for the will (*thelemati*) of God."
1 Peter 4:3	"For you have spent enough time in the past doing what pagans choose (*thelema*) to do—living in debauchery, lust, drunkenness, orgies, carousing and detestable idolatry."
1 Peter 4:19	"So then, those who suffer according to God's will (*thelema*) should commit themselves to their faithful Creator and continue to do good."
2 Peter 1:21	"For prophecy never had its origin in the human will (*thelemati*) but prophets, though human, spoke from God as they were carried along by the Holy Spirit.
1 John 2:17	"The world and its desires pass away, but whoever does the will (*thelema*) of God lives forever."
1 John 5:14	"This is the confidence we have in approaching God: that if we ask anything according to his will (*thelema*), he hears us."
Revelation 4:11	"You are worthy, our Lord and God, to receive glory and honor and power, for you created all things, and by your will (*thelema*) they were created and have their being."

Bibliography

Barna Group. *State of the Bible 2018: Seven Top Findings*. Ventura, California

Blackaby, Henry and Richard. *Experiencing God*. Broadman & Holman Publishers

Chambers, Oswald. *My Utmost for His Highest*. Discovery House Publishers

Corexel, *Disc Personality Profiles*. Wilmington, Delaware

Foxe, John. *Foxe's Book of Martyrs*. Whitaker House

Gericke, Paul. *Crucial Experiences in the Life of D. L. Moody*. Insight Press

Laidlaw, Robert. *The Reason Why*. Harper Collins

LaHaye, Tim. *The Spirit-Controlled Temperament*. Tyndale House Publishers

McDonald, Gordon. *Rebuilding Your Broken World*. Thomas Nelson

McMillen, Dr S.I. and Stern, Dr. E. David. *None of These Diseases*. Baker Book House

Packer, *J.I. Knowing God*. Intervarsity Press

Sanders, J. Oswald. *Spiritual Leadership*. Moody Press

Stafford, Tim. *Knowing the Face of God*. Wipt & Stock Publishers

Trotman, Dawson. *Born To Reproduce*. NavPress

Voice of the Martyrs. *Voice of the Martyrs Magazine*. Bartlesville, Oklahoma

Other Books by Gordon Haresign

Innocence

The Steve Linscott Story—the story of a young married Bible college student convicted of a murder he didn't commit.

Published by Zondervan 1986

Authentic Christianity

A radical look at Christianity today, based on Christ's letters to seven churches in Asia Minor toward the close of the first century.

Published by WestBow Press 2014

Pray For The Fire To Fall

A call to prayer based on Elijah's challenge on Mount Carmel.

Published by WestBow Press 2016